The Legends of
BOLLYWOOD

The Legends of
BOLLYWOOD

Tales of madness, mischief & mayhem

RAAJ GROVER

Translated by SUCHITRA IYER

JAICO PUBLISHING HOUSE
Ahmedabad Bangalore Bhopal Bhubaneswar Chennai
Delhi Hyderabad Kolkata Lucknow Mumbai

Published by Jaico Publishing House
A-2 Jash Chambers, 7-A Sir Phirozshah Mehta Road
Fort, Mumbai - 400 001
jaicopub@jaicobooks.com
www.jaicobooks.com

© Raaj Grover

THE LEGENDS OF BOLLYWOOD
ISBN 978-93-86867-99-5

First Jaico Impression: 2018

No part of this book may be reproduced or utilized in
any form or by any means, electronic or
mechanical including photocopying, recording or by any
information storage and retrieval system,
without permission in writing from the publishers.

Page design and layout:
Special Effects Graphics Design Company, Mumbai

To the Nargis Dutt Foundation
My loving father Lala Dina Nath
&
Sunil Dutt, Nargis *bhabhi*, who were no less than my parents

Foreword

It really gives me great pleasure to know that Mr. Raaj Grover has worked very hard at gathering all memories of his close associations with many well-known and respected celebrities of the Indian film fraternity in the form of a book titled *The Legends of Bollywood*, in three languages – English, Urdu and Hindi.

This book will reflect the vision and appreciation of his honest and sincere efforts towards the very interesting anecdotes that he has experienced in almost 50 long years of his association with this industry.

I take this opportunity to congratulate Uncle Grover, who, along with his family, has been emotionally attached to everyone in our family. We appreciate his decision to dedicate this book to the Nargis Dutt Foundation.

My heartfelt thanks for his love towards our family. The Dutt family wishes Uncle Grover grand success for his book *The Legends of Bollywood*.

— Priya Dutt

Author's Note:
A Lifetime of Memories

Just like a mother carries her child in her womb, I have been nurturing some precious memories in my mind for many years, dredging up varied experiences that I have had in my eventful life. *The Legends of Bollywood* is a humble attempt to share the same with you. I feel blessed to know that you will be holding my book with the same hands that hold other knowledgable books written by extraordinary individuals who guide you in one way or another in life.

This book is an assimilation of some pleasant memories from the days gone by, the thought of which is redolent of an enchanting phase of my life. Even today, when I think of those days, like an impatient child, I want to revisit and relive them. It is possible that you have experienced a similar feeling because in this rat race of life, we often leave behind some great memories. *The Legends of Bollywood* peeps into the deep recesses of my soul. Someone has rightly said, "*Waqt ek sood khor baniya hai jo din raat ke hisabon mein zindagi ko kha jata hai.*" (Time is a usurer that engulfs life in the arithmetic of day and night.) I am presenting to you whatever memories I could snatch away from the hands of this unapologetic factor called time and preserve them safely in my mind. It is now no more just my property, but, in fact, everyone's, who wishes to be a part of this journey as I dive into this treasure trove of colourful memories.

Time keeps changing, but the little lamps of memories symbolizing love and complaint that we light on the niche of time keep burning – at times passionately but otherwise with a gentle intensity. Just like the ever-changing seasons, the relationships in our lives also change colours. Life is, after all, a mixed bag of sweet and sour experiences. And this is what makes it so interesting and delectable. From life, I have learnt some invaluable lessons: never be unhappy, never make anyone unhappy and don't let anyone remain unhappy. This is how I made my life a little easier for myself. I asked to be pardoned by some, and pardoned the others.

When Nargis *bhabhi* was in the Sloan Kettering hospital in New York, and Dutt *saheb* was taking care of her day in and day out, she told him, "*Main uparwale ka jitna bhi shukriya karun kam hoga ki aap merey shohar hain. Meri seva mein apna sara kaam-kaaj chhod-chhad kar merey jeetey rehney ki qeemat jo aap chuka rahey hain, uss ka mujhey ehsaas hai. Magar ek khayaal jo aksar mujhey pareshaan karta rehta hai, ye ki merey liye toh aap apna sab kuch qurbaan kar saktey hain, lekin iss tarah ke rog mein phansey kitney hi rogi honge jin ke paas haspatal pahunchney taq ke paise na honge. Ilaaj ka bill chukana toh bahut hi dur aur na-mumkin si baat hai.*"

(How much ever I thank the Lord for bringing you into my life as my husband, it will never be enough. For my well-being, you have left all your work and the price you are paying for that, I appreciate it. But the one thing that keeps bothering me is that so many people suffering from the same disease wouldn't have the money to even travel to a hospital for treatment lest pay the bill for the medicines.)

These words from his wife touched Sunil Dutt's heart and after consulting with a number of his friends and doctors, he founded a trust in India and the USA, and named it the Nargis Dutt Memorial Charitable Trust (now the Nargis Dutt Foundation) with an aim to aid cancer patients who could not afford treatment. Since Sunil Dutt's passing, his daughter Priya Dutt has been taking complete care of the foundation.

I was so touched by this that from the second I started writing this book, I had decided that all the earnings from the sales will be donated to this foundation.

My life is not a simple algebraic equation. It is a compilation of bittersweet experiences. I have also learnt a lot from other people's lives. I don't claim to be someone who can argue about life on an intellectual level, but I have seen enough to know how to tackle problems and differentiate between good and bad. I simply wanted to share these stories with you all and so *The Legends of Bollywood* took shape that you now hold in your hands. I sincerely hope you enjoy it.

Your well-wisher,
— Raaj Grover

Contents

Foreword	vii
Author's Note: A Lifetime of Memories	ix
1. Amitabh Bachchan	1
2. Balraj Sahni	17
3. Dharmendra	25
4. Dilip Kumar	37
5. Dimple Kapadia	49
6. Johnny Walker	55
7. Leena Chandavarkar	61
8. Mahesh Bhatt	65
9. Manoj Kumar	75
10. Nargis	85
11. Prakash Mehra	107
12. Rajendra Kumar	113
13. Rakhee Gulzar	125
14. Sanjay Dutt	139

15. Shabana Azmi	153
16. Shashi Kapoor	157
17. Sunil Dutt	163
18. Tabassum	183
19. The Legend of the Kapoors	189
20. Vinod Khanna	197
21. Zarina Wahab	211
22. Ajanta Arts Welfare Troupe	217
23. The Story of Mohan Studio	229
24. Two Neighbours – The Love-Hate Relationship	237
Epilogue	247
Ackowledgements	257
Testimonials	259
Letter from Suchitra Iyer	267
About the Author	271

Amitabh Bachchan

This saga, which began in the year 1967, belongs to the man who has been blazing a trail ever since he first arrived in Bombay. It all began when *Times of India*, under the aegis of two of its magazines, *Filmfare* and *Madhuri*, launched the *Filmfare Madhuri Film Talent Contest*.

At the same time, a strapping young man from an influential family in Calcutta was harbouring dreams of making it big in the film industry, a fact known by his younger brother, Ajitabh. So as soon as he saw the advertisement, he put in his brother's application, complete with his biodata and a photograph. Ten days later, he got a reply. Rejected. The young man was deeply disappointed to see his dreams destroyed. He slipped into a sad, dejected phase. But his mother, Teji Bachchan, immediately came to her Munna's rescue. And why not? After all, a mother is a mother.

It so happened that two weeks after the rejection, Nargisji received a phone call from Delhi, and from none other than India's then prime minister, Indira Gandhi, a friend of Teji Bachchan. She said, "One of my friends' sons is keen to join the film industry. His efforts have not borne any fruit. Speak to Sunilji (Dutt) to help work something out for him. I will be very happy if he does."

Well, the process had started, but when things would fall into place was still a mystery. Knowing my close relations with Arvind Kumar, the editor of *The Times of India*'s film magazine, *Madhuri*, Nargis bhabhi asked me to meet him and get the photograph of the boy – who had gotten rejected – the very next day. I did so and gave it to her. The following day, both of us were at B.R. Chopra's residence with the photograph. Chopra *saheb* just glimpsed at it for a second and put the photograph back on the table. Even though he didn't say anything, we could see he disapproved of the boy. But then, when I told him that Indira Gandhi had recommended him, he picked it up once more and looked at it for a few more seconds. Then, he said, "*Haan, kuch baat toh hai hut ke isskey chehre mein.*" (Yes, there is definitely something unique about his face.) He ordered some tea and biscuits, picked up the phone and spoke to producer-director Mohan Saigal, informing him that he would like to take a screen test of a new boy during his next shooting schedule, wherever it may be. He said, "Please call me up about the day and time for the test and the boy will definitely be there." He added, "I must tell you that the boy has a unique personality." Once we finished the tea, we thanked Mr. Chopra and bid him adieu.

Meanwhile, as soon as he was informed of Mohan Saigal's schedule, Mr. Chopra informed Nargisji of the same. Immediately, she phoned Prime Minister Indira Gandhi, asking her to inform her friend in Calcutta to send her son to Bombay the very same week. Not to mention, much before the boy's arrival, I was told by *bhabhiji* and Dutt *saheb* to take care of the boy coming from Calcutta and to introduce him to all the big names of the film industry who I knew personally.

Amitabh Bachchan arrived in Bombay after taking four days of leave from his office, Bird & Co., based in Calcutta. He stayed with a friend in Colaba.

This was what we did in those four days:

DAY ONE

Dutt *saheb* had asked me to bring Amitabh to his place, saying that that we would discuss and plan the next steps over dinner. But when we reached, Dutt *saheb* and *bhabhiji* both had gone away to attend a party. However, my tension dissipated within minutes when their cook, Gangaram, came up to me with a note written by *bhabhiji*. It said: Raaj dear, we are close by, attending a party at RK Nayyar and Sadhna's bungalow. There is nothing to worry. You and Amitabh should join us. We will be waiting for you both. That way, he could meet some people too. I will do the introductions myself.

We happily walked across to Bungalow No. 38, Pali Hill. The first person we met there was Dutt *saheb*'s friend Keval Kapoor, who was supposed to be the producer of the film, *Yeh Raaste Hain Pyar Ke*. He was busy chatting with someone in the lawn outside. The party was in full swing. When I approached him for a handshake and to introduce Amitabh, he refused to reciprocate. Keval Kapoor, instead of shaking hands with me, put a hand on my shoulder and said, "What are you doing here? This is Sadhna and RK Nayyar's bungalow. There are people like Shatrughan Sinha, Sanjeev Kumar, Waheeda Rehman, Sunil Dutt, Nargis, Raj Khosla, Prakash Mehra and other biggies here. How come you are here? And who is that? Don't overstep your boundaries. You nobodies walk into parties. Come on now, get going." Seeing the awkward situation, Amitabh, very wisely, moved away to the other end of the lawn.

I let the note from *bhabhiji* remain in my pocket. But the hand that I had initially extended for a handshake now went straight to his collar, and roughed him up nice and good. For Keval Kapoor, perhaps, this was wrong. But when anger takes over you, it doesn't matter who or what is in front of you. There is no reasoning at such a time. As for me, even I forgot at that moment that he was Dutt *saheb*'s friend. On hearing the ruckus, Dutt *saheb* came out. When he got to know the details of the brawl, even before Keval Kapoor could try to justify himself, Dutt *saheb* went inside, brought *bhabhiji* and without so much as glancing at Keval Kapoor, took the three of us back to Bungalow No. 58. Gangaram took good care of four hungry people that night.

DAY TWO

Bhabhiji had already taken an appointment with a producer for 11 in the morning. He had also been informed about the new boy, who was the son of famous writer and poet, Harivansh Rai Bachchan, and was in Bombay to try his luck in films. And also that Raaj Grover would be accompanying him. The two of us reached his office at 11. No sooner did we enter, than the producer looked at Amitabh and thundered, "No heroine would like to work with you! You are very tall. You should follow your father's steps and write poetry like him."

We spent around ten minutes in his office. But the producer

spent more than half of that time chatting about Dutt *saheb* and Nargisji with me. It went somewhat like this: "*Sunil kaisa hai? Kaunsi nayi film bana raha hai? Kitni filmein hain uske paas?* Nargisji *se mera namaste kehna.*"(How is Sunil? What new film is he working on? How many films has he done? Give my regards to Nargisji.) We spent all our time on pleasantries and I couldn't talk to him about that one thing for which I was in his office – Amitabh. The office was of Rajshree Films and the producer was none other than Mr. Tarachand Barjatya.

The end of this inconsequential conversation also marked the end of our second day. Now, the boy only had two more days left.

DAY THREE

It was September 11th, 1967. We took a taxi and arrived at Roop Tara Studio in Dadar where Mohan Sehgal was shooting *Sajan* at 10:30 in the morning. I was happy to find out that the hero of the film was my old pal, Manoj Kumar. When I introduced the young man to Manoj, I could see his face flush. The hero took us to the make-up room where we had tea. Manoj was surprised to know that the boy was his favourite poet, Harivansh Rai Bachchan's son. Manoj said that his calm face and his voice, a mellow whisper, sounded like the murmurs of a thundering cloud. Then, placing his hands on his face, which was very typical of him, Manoj said, "All said and done, this boy has the qualities required to become what he wishes to become."

When the hero was called to the set, he urged us to wait

there. He said he'd inform Sehgal *saheb* that we were already here. Around twenty minutes later, Manoj came into the makeup room with Sehgal *saheb* and without wasting a minute, introduced him to Amitabh. Sehgal *saheb* seemed to have the same reaction towards Amitabh as Manoj. After chatting with us for some time, the director left to shoot for a scene and said he'd do the screen test after lunch. He beckoned me to come to the set. When I reached, I saw Shatrughan Sinha in a police inspector's uniform, rehearsing his lines. Sehgal *saheb* asked me if the boy really thought he could be an actor. "I wonder what Nargisji found in him that she reached Chopra *saheb*'s house with the boy's photo. Anyway, go and eat something. I will call you once I complete two scenes scheduled for after lunch."

It must have been around 1:30 pm when producer Tejnath Zar came and took Manoj Kumar with him, saying he would be back in an hour. Amitabh and I still hadn't eaten and no one had even offered us lunch. So we walked from the studio to Gupta Restaurant, owned by a close friend of mine called Gurpal Singh, or Kaka. It was mostly frequented by taxi drivers and struggling actors from all over India. Other than me, Sunil Dutt, Rajendra Kumar, Manoj Kumar, Dharmendra, Prem Chopra, Anand Bakshi, Jagjeet Singh, Mohan Kumar, Sohanlal Kanwar and Prakash Mehra frequently visited the place.

While we were having lunch, I casually asked Amitabh if he would like to meet Rajesh Khanna. I knew he was shooting at Shree Sound Studio, which was quite close to Gupta Restaurant, for the film *Doli*. Amitabh immediately stopped eating and stood up, and insisted that I take him to meet Rajesh Khanna right away. I didn't budge, and asked him to respect the food in front of him first. He smiled and finished his food. I then took him to the studio and introduced him to Rajesh Khanna, fondly calling the latter 'Kaka'. Amitabh couldn't believe that I had addressed such a big star as Kaka. When I told Kaka that he was the famous poet Harivansh Rai Bachchan's son, the latter immediately extended his hand, like a worshipper waiting for his God's *prasad* (blessings). But, Kaka only said, "Okay, okay." Amitabh seemed quite pleased and thrilled to meet this superstar. It was around three when we walked back to Roop Tara. The shooting was on in full swing. When Sehgal *saheb* saw me, he said, "Just write some dialogues and give them to him. It is only a screen test, not an actual scene." I could not think of anything else so I fished out a very romantic letter from my pocket that I had written for my girlfriend at that time, who lived in Darjeeling. Thanks to this episode, I hadn't been able to post it and had instead come in handy. I wrote the same lines on a piece of paper, but made a few changes such as my girlfriend's name, and showed them to Sehgal *saheb* first. After he gave the go-ahead, I handed it over to Amitabh. The verses that I wrote for the screen test were somewhat like this:

Tum jab bhi mujhe yun dekhti ho, main sab bhool jata hun ki main kaun hun
Kya hun
Kahan hun kuch samajh mein nahi aata.
Nazara chaudhvin ke chand ka ho ya phir Taj Mahal ka...
Khuda jaanta hai tera mere samne hone se badh kar koi aur nazara nahi.

(Whenever you look at me, I forget who I am,
What I am
Where I am, that I don't understand anything.
It's all hazy

Be it a full moon night, or the Taj Mahal
The Lord knows that there isn't a sight more beautiful than you.)

Apart from this, Amitabh also included the famous poem, *Madhushala*, written by his father, extempore in his dialogues. Everyone was thrilled when Sehgal *saheb*, before heading towards his car, said "All the best" to Amitabh. Sehgal *saheb* headed home, but for the two of us, it was: *Dard bhare dil ki zaban... jayen toh jayen kahan*!' (A broken heart's lament, where do we go now?)

Amitabh was staying in Colaba and I in Bandra, so I parted ways with someone who was, though already a close acquaintance, still a stranger.

That was the end of the third day.

DAY FOUR

The next day, the last one, he spent with me, Dutt *saheb* and Nargis *bhabhi* at the 58, Pali Hill, from afternoon till dinner. Years later, whenever Dutt *saheb* would show Amitabh's photograph, the one first shared with the talent contest, to his bigwig producer and director friends or talk about him, they would laugh at how this superstar was bluntly rejected but then went on to become the most desired artist of the directors and producers.

Before Amitabh had left for Calcutta, Dutt *saheb* had

promised Amitabh that he would certainly call him if there was a prominent role in his next film. He fulfilled that promise when Ajanta Arts (Sunil Dutt's production company) started work on *Reshma aur Shera*. Amitabh Bachchan was given a role in this film. He also found a role in another film – famous writer and filmmaker Khwaja Ahmed Abbas' film, *Saat Hindustani*. Though it started after *Reshma aur Shera*, it released earlier.

A lot of effort and money went into making *Reshma aur Shera*. For three months, we camped in the deserts of Rajasthan. But on its release, the film was not a commercial success. When the film's shooting had begun, Amitabh's voice had become more and more famous. Only two people in the entire industry – of all the famous actors and filmmakers – could appreciate and capitalize on Amitabh's unique personality and his booming voice: Sunil Dutt and Manoj Kumar. I would also like to add my name to the list at the risk of being called conceited.

Late writer Ali Raza was as renowned in the world of films as he was in the literary sphere. I consider myself very fortunate that we were always thick as brothers and my wife Shashi and his wife Nimmi had bonded like sisters. During the shooting of *Reshma aur Shera*, Ali Raza *saheb* and Dutt *saheb* decided that in order to evoke sympathy among the audience for Amitabh's character, he should play a mute person. Somehow, (with due respect to Dutt *saheb* and Ali Raza *saheb*) I neither agreed then nor do I agree now.

Meanwhile, *Guddi* by Hrishikesh Mukherjee released and the film saw great success. The heroine of the film, Jaya Bhaduri, had done a brilliant job. There was appreciation from all quarters. Hrishi*da*'s office was like an *adda*. It was in Mohan Studio in Andheri, which was also the office of his guru, Bimal Roy, and my guru, Krishan Chopra. Mohan

Studio was like my second home. Jaya earned a lot of fame and praise after *Guddi* and something similar happened to Amitabh with Hrishi*da*'s other film, *Anand*. The two kept bumping into each other at Mohan Studio and it was there that they signed two films, *Ek Nazar* and *Bansi Birju*, together as hero and heroine.

Both the films did badly and made losses. A couple more of Amitabh's films where he played the hero met with the same fate. I think one was *Parvana*; I can't recollect too clearly now. It is difficult to remember the names of films that don't do well. However, Jaya continued garnering acclaim for her work. Even her role in Hrishi*da*'s *Bavarchi*, opposite Rajesh Khanna, was something special, as was her work in director Narendra Bedi's film *Jawani Diwani*, in which she was paired with Randhir Kapoor.

And then, slowly, although not surprisingly, I witnessed Jaya Bhaduri and Amitabh Bachchan becoming a couple. And it was something! Behind the sound recording room in Mohan Studio, they had a private makeup room. They were spotted there sometimes or in the small theatres used for trial shows. This is where they talked. I have seen their beautiful love story take shape. It was during this period that actor Anwar Ali, who worked with Amitabh in *Saat Hindustani*, introduced him to his elder brother, the famous actor and filmmaker, Mehmood. Their friendship became so strong that soon Amitabh's postal address became C/O Mehmood Bhaijaan. Simultaneously, his film, *Bombay to Goa*, commenced shooting, with Amitabh as the hero and Aruna Irani as the heroine. It turned out to be quite a success. In the meanwhile, I had been talking about Amitabh to my dear friend and director Prakash Mehra regularly. But things didn't really progress there.

Prakash Mehra had heard a story from the writer duo

Salim-Javed that he had liked. This led to a hunt for the hero. Dharmendra was the first one on the list, but he didn't like the story very much. Dev Anand was approached next, but he objected to the fact that while even Pran had a song attributed to him in the film, the hero's character left no scope for a song. So it was a no. When Amitabh's name came up, Prakash Mehra, before talking to him, decided to check with the distributors about the proposition. Just then, the news came in that producer and director Kundan Kumar's half-complete film *Duniya Ka Mela* had been denied the next instalment by the distributors. They had laid down a condition stating that Amitabh be replaced by a hero who was more popular in the market. So it was! Out went Amitabh and in came Sanjay Khan.

Amitabh was shocked beyond words. Disappointed, he decided to leave town and head back to Calcutta. That's when Jaya Bhaduri and Gulzar provided him solace and advised him not to lose hope. Even I met him after this terrible incident. I told him, "Stories for films are written first, but in this case, the journey of your story has already begun. A day will come when you will touch the skies. You will reach so high that I will need binoculars to spot you. The magic of your voice will mesmerize everyone." When I looked at him again, he seemed to have overcome the initial shock. He had given up on the foolish idea of leaving Bombay. By God's grace, the boy, who was born in Allahabad, made Bombay his home. By His grace once more, there was a change in his fortunes.

Things then started falling into place. Like Prakash Mehra had mentioned, Jaya Bhaduri had become the favourite heroine for the producers and distributors. Meanwhile, after Dharmendra and Dev Anand refused that role, word was sent to Raj Kumar. However, his secretary, Mahendra, approached

Prakash Mehra's close buddy Satyen Pal Chaudhari with a strange message about Raj Kumar's rejection of the role. It was that since Prakash Mehra routinely applied mustard oil in his hair, the actor wouldn't be able to work with the *teli* director. He was allergic to mustard oil. This unique and foolish explanation generated a great deal of laughter at first but later led to just as much anger. Considering Jaya was already the heroine of the film, Salim and Javed suggested Amitabh's name. *Bombay to Goa* was almost complete and they decided to analyse his performance in a film before making a decision. A trial show was organised for Jaya Bhaduri and Prakash Mehra. It only took the song with Amitabh and Aruna Irani to convince them that they had found the right person.

The shooting commenced. This was the iconic *Zanjeer*. The film was a gigantic success. The reaction after the premier show in Calcutta attended by Prakash Mehra, Amitabh Bachchan, Jaya Bhaduri and Pran was unparalleled. If you would have seen the road outside the hotel where the actors had stayed, you would have seen a crowd of at least ten thousand people and only one persistent chant: *Amitabh Bachchan!*

According to Prakash Mehra, Amitabh was stunned by the reaction. Speechless and astounded, he shivered with happiness. Tears of joy flowed copiously. Surely, the feeling of elation completely won over the momentary chill. Fate played favourable tricks on his life and bound Amitabh in such a shackle of success that no one could ever break it. Those who tried ended up broken themselves. Following the colossal success of *Zanjeer*, several films made by Prakash Mehra and Manmohan Desai tasted sweet success. And the credit for the same would go to none other than Amitabh Bachchan. The actor could easily credit four people for his successful journey – Hrishikesh Mukherjee, Prakash Mehra, Manmohan Desai and Yash Chopra.

Going back to the famous screen test at Roop Tara Studio, Amitabh returned to Calcutta shortly after completing the test. To find out whether he had passed or not, I went to Sehgal *saheb*'s office after two days. Unfortunately, he wasn't available but I met his assistant director, Sardar Bagga. Before I could even pose my question, he said, "It was a waste of time and a waste of our raw stock," dismissing any scope for acting for Amitabh with a single sentence. While this had transpired, Amitabh had eagerly awaited my response. I did call him but told him it would take a few more days.

Coincidentally, the very next day, Dutt *saheb* had an important meeting to attend in Calcutta. I had already made plans for my Darjeeling trip, which meant breaking journey in Calcutta. So, we took the same flight and while he stayed at the Grand Hotel, I chose to go to my cousin's place. My flight was the next day. But in the evening, Dutt *saheb* called, asking me to come to the hotel as Amitabh's mother was coming over for lunch. He said it was important for me to be there. What could I do? My girlfriend was waiting for me in Darjeeling. I telephoned her and said I'd be there after a couple of days. I could sense her disappointment and sadness.

As planned, I reached Grand Hotel the next morning. At 1 pm, Mrs. Teji Bachchan arrived. The very first thing she said was, "*Mere munne ke liye kuch karna hi hoga aapko.*" (You will have to do something for my Munna.)

Dutt *saheb* looked at me and that mere look said tons about me to Tejiji. She started insisting that I meet her Munna. This insistence was brimming with sincerity and exuded her love and affection for her son. She promptly took my cousin's address and said Munna would be there at 5:30 in the evening the next day.

The next day, as I rushed to buy gifts for my girlfriend and return to my cousin's house on time, I found Amitabh waiting for me there. He had arrived early. When we started talking over tea, we bonded more than before. He too respected me. The next day, on his request, I went to his office at Bird & Company. His enthusiasm was infectious. And I told him to keep at it and that whenever he came to Bombay, I'd do whatever was possible for him. "Don't worry at all. Leave the rest to God. But never leave your job." After this, he saw me out as I proceeded to return to my cousin's place. Something told me that success was just around the corner. And, that's exactly what happened. Even though he turned into Shahenshah (King of kings) from Munna, I am sure that he still has the same respect for me in his heart. When I met Amitabh, he may have been an ordinary person, but there was some sort of fame attached to him. His father was a famous author and poet, and had friendly relations with the prime minister, Pandit Jawaharlal Nehru. His mother was close friends with Indira Gandhi, and both Amitabh and his brother Ajitabh were classmates and friends with Rajiv and Sanjay Gandhi.

Amitabh started off his career as a young boy of twenty-four years. Now, even after being on the wrong side of seventy, his popularity across the world is still intact. I feel the secrets to this longevity of fame are manifold – respect for his parents and the elderly, punctuality, sincerity and hard work.

Unsurprisingly, the situation in the film industry today is such that every actor, actress, producer, director and distributor wants to be associated with a film which has Amitabh Bachchan in it.

The journey of life for Amitabh has been like a caravan – anyone he met on the way became a part of his life. When this journey began, I was in possession of a story titled *Sanskar*. The production bug had bitten me too. I gathered the courage to take the plunge of turning into a producer. I even had a hero in mind. I had already been enamoured by his obsessive dedication and baritone when I met him the first time at Dutt *saheb*'s house. I thought that for my film, I should use an 'available' actor instead of a 'saleable' one to get the best out of him. I left the rest to God. As for Amitabh, on my very first request, he signed the dotted line of the letterhead of my company, Elora Arts. When the advertisement appeared in the papers, there was much discussion on it. I, however, wanted the discussion to take place in the offices of the distributors. Unfortunately, that was not to be for two reasons – firstly, this was my first film as a producer, and secondly, everyone was wondering who this new hero was. As for seasoned distributors, they would only be interested in films that involved well-known producers and directors, like BR Chopra, Bimal Roy, Shakti Samanta, etc. Not to mention, the film should have a big face for a hero, someone like Rajesh Khanna, Manoj Kumar or Dharmendra. I thought a new distributor might take a chance with my project. But somehow, time just went by and things didn't work out as I had expected. In the meantime, while I continued to tread on the same path, Amitabh grew by leaps and bounds, and found himself on an unparalleled success track. He had touched the pinnacle of fame. Now, I can really see him high up in the sky from my binoculars, but I always wonder if he can see Raaj Grover on earth from his high pedestal.

Once I met a movie critic from Lahore in Dubai. While talking to him, I realised he was a big Amitabh Bachchan fan. He told me about an interesting observation that he had made, "Prakash Mehra made superhit films like *Zanjeer,*

Lawaris, Muqadar ka Sikandar, Namak Halal and *Hera Pheri,* and the flag of his banner fluttered proudly. Similarly, Manmohan Desai made *Naseeb, Mard, Coolie, Amar Akbar Anthony* and with their success, the flag of his banner too fluttered high in the sky. But, wasn't there some other underlying reason for this?"

To this, I replied, "*Kamyabi ka jhanda kabhi bhi lehra nahin sakta jab takk usmein danda na laga ho... Aur yeh danda in donon ka koyi aur nahi, sirf aur sirf Amitabh Bachchan hi tha.*" (A flag without its flagstaff is a mere rag. And the upright mast to these flags was none other than Amitabh Bachchan.)

Balraj Sahni

Luck, customers and death – these three things are not bound by the concept of time. They can arrive anytime, unannounced.

Many years ago when our country was divided, fate played its magic on a well-educated boy. Though it didn't give him much grief, it made him wander too much. The boy was born in Rawalpindi, Punjab, on May 1, 1913. As he grew up, he developed a keenness for books. He was so charmed by them that he spent almost every minute in the company of some book or the other. He was fond of writing too. So, books, pen and paper became his permanent companions, much to the chagrin of his father who wanted him to be more social. He would often reproach the young boy, saying, "*Kalam, dawaat aur kitabon ke alawa bhi bahaut kuch hai. Khel, tamashe, dost, yaar. In sab ko bhi apni zindagi mein jagah do, inse milo-julo.*" (There is a lot more to life than just pens, inkpots and books. There lies a whole world full of merriment, frolic and friendship in your reach; make space for these in your life too.)

When his father sent him to Lahore for further studies, his dreams found new wings. He came back from the city with not one, but multiple degrees and met a person named Fielden in Seva Gram. He used to work for BBC in London. He suggested that the boy go to London and his joy knew no bounds. He went and joined the BBC as a radio announcer. He was so proficient in it that it caused the Asians in London to take interest in Urdu. None of this would have been possible without the fate factor. And more twists of fate awaited this boy. In 1943, he landed in Calcutta. He always wanted to see the city because while in London, he had heard a lot about Rabindranath Tagore and his institution, Shanktiniketan. So, he arrived in Calcutta along with his wife, Damyanti.

Tagore too took a liking to the couple and they formed a bond rather soon. So much so that he gave up any ideas of leaving the place. The very next year, his son Parikshit was born, who had the good fortune of being held by Rabindranath Tagore. It was in the order of mother, gurudev and then father, Balraj. With the expansion of the family, Balraj was faced with the burden of earning. And he had to rethink his idea of never leaving Calcutta. However, his ability to think clearly and think ahead held him in good stead. Though he always acknowledged the language of both the heart and the mind, he had decided to only listen to his mind.

So this decision saw him return to Rawalpindi and then proceed to Srinagar in search of a job. Here, by chance, he met his old friend, Chetan Anand. Balraj let him know that he was in search of a job. Chetan Anand was a part of the film industry. He asked Balraj to come to Bombay and said he was making the film *Neecha Nagar*, and that he could get him some work in the same. Balraj recalled his meeting with famous writer Khwaja Ahmad Abbas and felt confident about contacting him. He wrote to him and received a reply within a week, which said, 'Welcome'. That was that! One thing led to the other and Balraj found himself move lock, stock and barrel from Srinagar to Bombay.

Being the creative and artistic visionary that Khwaja Ahmed Abbas was, he had a few writers, actors and directors together under the aegis of a theatrical institution called IPTA – Indian People's Theatre Association. For them, IPTA was no less than a place of worship. Khwaja Ahmed Abbas would help these people dedicatedly in all possible ways. He made Balraj a part of IPTA too. Numerous people from this institute earned a great name for themselves as artistes in various fields through their talent, hard work and perseverance. And among them was Balraj. He understood the value of time, and time, in turn, paid him back bountifully by taking him to the heights of success and earning him immense fame.

Big names like Kaifi Azmi, Abrar Alvi and Chetan Anand, among a few, were associated with IPTA. And thanks to their bonding there, a deep friendship grew between them. Chetan Anand, especially, was impressed by Balraj's personality. After joining IPTA, *Miyan* Balraj turned into an actor, director and writer, and wrote a play titled *Inspector*. Apart from being the writer and director, he even played the main character. It was a huge success and the audience's applause only reinforced his confidence in his capabilities. And then, there was no turning back. Lady luck smiled on Balraj when one day, a filmmaker came to watch *Inspector*. After watching it, he was convinced that Balraj was the right person to play the main role of a police inspector in his film. The very next day, papers were signed and work began. The filmmaker was K Asif and the film was *Hulchal*. The hero of the film was Dilip Kumar. Balraj was so convincing in the role of an inspector that it blurred the line between fiction and reality.

Those were the days when the country was hit by the Communist Party wave. Balraj joined the party too. At one of their awareness programmes, Balraj delivered such a stirring speech that ripples were felt not just in the city, but also throughout the nation. The very next day, he was arrested and jailed with several others. Inside, he ate watery *daal* and shared this story with K Asif. The shooting was still incomplete, but he wasn't concerned. He contacted the police commissioner and made a deal that Sahni would be escorted to the studio in a police van under their scrutiny. So Balraj would change into a police inspector's costume for the film and then back into the prisoner's clothes. This routine continued for ten days. The police commissioner had agreed to this arrangement mainly because his wife was a true-blue Dilip Kumar fan. So how could he turn down K Asif's request? Before the film began, no one knew this prisoner who came in to shoot every day, only to go back to jail at the end of the schedule. But time was on his side. It was as if his pace was in tandem with the hands of the clock. When the film *Hulchal* released, he was released from prison. It was a success and all the actors gained a lot of praise for their work.

Balraj's second film was director Zia Sarhadi's *Hum Log*. This too passed muster with the audience. There was not a single journal that didn't write about Balraj's acting prowess. Then, famous producer/director Bimal Roy signed him for the film *Do Bigha Zameen*. It revolved around a villager who came to Calcutta and became a hand-pulled rickshaw-*wallah* ferrying people around for the entire day as a means of livelihood. For three months before the shooting began, Balraj made friends with a rickshaw-*wallah* who had been running the streets of Calcutta for thirty long years, and stayed with him to get into the head of a rickshaw-puller, and learn his mannerisms, language, etc. He also understood their lifestyle, attire, roads of the city, the art of haggling with the customer, and several other nuances for the role.

He adapted their dressing sense and appearance so well that he eventually looked like one of them. He had even given himself a new name – Deen Bandhu.

Once he was done with his research and homework, the film began with Balraj as the hero and Nirupa Roy as the heroine. The first ever shot of the film was that of him pulling the rickshaw and once he gave the take, all those associated with the film were left awestruck. There was applause all around. The cameraman, Bose, was so touched by the performance he had just witnessed that he first touched Balraj's feet and then embraced him in a warm hug. He then took a photograph with the actor so he could remember it forever. Director Bimal Roy, sitting on his chair, smoking a cigarette, watched the entire episode quietly. He was very pleased too and it was difficult to figure out whether the smoke was from the cigarette or if it was a cloud of contentment and praise. *Do Bigha Zameen* proved to be a change-maker in Sahni's career and placed him amongst the most talented and successful actors of the time. After the film's success, all producers – old and new, big and small – set out to look for stories that could have a lead character revolving around Balraj.

Fate had presented him with success and had arrived unannounced. He was clearly on a winning spree and saw a stream of films, one after the other. The films did such great business that the producers would leave home and go straight to the bank, before reaching their respective offices.

Though the list of Balraj films is rather long, here are a few memorable ones: *Anuradha, Kabuliwala, Kathputli, Pavitra Papi, Waqt, Ghar Sansar, Ek Phool Do Mali, Khazanchi, Heera Moti, Seema, Hanste Zakhm, Haqeeqat* and *Garm Hawa*.

The things I have written above all pertain to the outside

world – information that had been appearing in the press. Matters like his personality, his habits, etc., have been reported with a good dose of *masala* too. But like all of us know, things are pretty different inside the house than outside. Especially in cases of people who have attained a certain status in life. And people are curious to know more and more about them. Balraj had always been a cut above the rest and was a proud man. Few wonder then that his life was so impressive and invoked so much awe.

Khwaja Ahmed Abbas signed Damyanti Sahni as a heroine for the film *Dharti Ke Lal*. The film did well and praise poured in for her performance from various quarters. Now producers began looking for stories that would do her talent justice. Before one could realise, she had become a busy actress. Balraj felt neglected and things had taken a delicate turn for him on the personal front. The couple sat down together to seriously discuss the future course of action. Balraj asked her, "The way your films have been appreciated, under the circumstances, would you want to continue working or would you like to fulfil your responsibilities towards your family?"

Damyanti chose family over profession instantly. The very next year, she gave birth to a daughter who was named Shabnam. The baby was beautiful just like her mother. It was like she found a treasure trove in her father and he too was crazy about her. He began to be known as a great father apart from being just a great actor and writer. He became a paragon of fatherhood. It is said by our elders that when people start talking about someone too often and the person becomes too likeable, he attracts the evil eye. And that is exactly what happened to Balraj's family. Damyanti was rudely and suddenly snatched by death. After her demise, Balraj was a broken man and his situation kept deteriorating. At this crucial juncture, his friends Chetan

Anand and Khwaja Ahmed Abbas stepped in to save him from further decline. They didn't let him break. Thanks to their compassion and love, Balraj's son Parikshit recovered from the tragedy well. Balraj's career took off once again. So much so that he found himself spending over eighteen hours in the studios. The schedule was so punishing that when he left home, the kids would be asleep and when he returned, they would have retired for the day. He was once again face-to-face with the same question he had asked Damyanti. "Work first or family first?" He asked himself, "In the absence of a mother, who will take care of my children's upbringing? How will my home run? If I continue working like this, it is certain that the household will be destroyed." He was drowning in worries. He lost interest in work. Friends and relatives could only show sympathy. What else could they do? All they said were platitudes, asking him to have courage and faith in God. Only the person going through a difficult situation would understand its gravity. Balraj decided to face the situation and find a solution to his problems courageously. After two years of loneliness, when he met his cousin Santosh Chandok, he found a way. Both decided to become life partners and had a daughter, Sanober. The dark clouds of depression cleared out. With the household and the care of the children in the adept hands of the loving Santosh, Balraj found solace in his life and was back on track. Work seemed interesting again!

Balraj has a special place in my life. There are two reasons for this. First, while we lived in Delhi, Balraj's father Harbans Lal Sahni and my father Dina Nath were neighbours and good friends. Second, Balraj had been my main benefactor when I was in Bombay. There is an incident attached to it too. In my youth, one of my stories, School Bus Driver, was published in Khoshtar Grami's popular Urdu magazine

Beesvin Sadi. Balraj's brother Bheeshm Sahni loved the story and mentioned it to his brother. When Balraj read it, he liked it too. He went up to my father and, promising that he'd take care of me, took me to Bombay along with him. In fact, I stayed in his house for about a year. Since I was fluent in Hindi, Urdu and English, he helped me join film director Krishan Chopra as an assistant director. This is not all… he has done me many favours. He and his wife Santosh arranged all the necessities and requirements for my wedding and reception.

Chetan Anand made *Baazi*, based on Balraj's story, with Dev Anand and Geeta Bali in the lead roles. The film was a great success. Balraj's next outing as an actor in the film *Garm Hawa*, in which he played the lead role, is unforgettable. On April 12, 1973, he completed the last session of his dubbing for the film. The lines went like this: *Insan kab tak akela jee sakta hai?* (For how long can a person survive alone?) See the coincidence, the very next day, i.e., April 13, 1973, was Balraj's last day in this world. Without any intimation or indication, death just snatched him away from all of us suddenly.

This may have been his physical departure from the world but mentally he had already given up when his daughter Shabnam married the wrong man and as if to punish herself, said goodbye to life. Balraj simply couldn't get over this grave tragedy. He crumbled beyond repair.

For everyone else, Balraj may be no more, but for me, he will always be alive – in my heart he will always reside.

Dharmendra

Punjab enjoys prominence in India's books of history, mainly because it has been an integral part of the country's narrative. Lala Lajpat Rai was an influential freedom fighter. Dhyan Chand brought India on the hockey map of the world. Milkha Singh came to be known as a world-class athlete and Lala Amarnath was a name to reckon with in the field of cricket.

A young man from the village Sahanewal near Ludhiana in Punjab, who used to drive a tractor at a farm, was particularly lucky. He came to Bombay and won over the hearts of everyone, especially the ladies – oh, how he made them swoon! His name is Dharmendra. This 75-year-'young' actor has been the sweetheart of the film industry for the past fifty years. His attitude towards everyone – right from the director, producer, and the heroine, to the spot boy, the light man and other colleagues – has always been that of love and humility.

How this man became an actor is an interesting story. The thought crossed his mind when he saw an announcement for an actors' contest in *The Times of India's Filmfare* magazine. Just like a lot of other aspiring actors, he sent his application along with his photographs too. To begin with, ten names were shortlisted from all the applications, which were then brought down to two. As far as I can remember, these two names were that of Suresh Puri and Dharmendra. When they arrived in Bombay, many newspapers and magazines wrote about them. This went on for months. Suresh Puri started getting film offers, but the farmer from Punjab was yet to realise his dream. But, later, as we all know, it was Dharmendra who shone like pure gold.

Like any struggling person in Bombay, he faced food and shelter problems. Dharmendra's only contact in Bombay was a Punjabi fellow who used to live in the railway quarters right next to the railway lines between Dadar and Matunga. He made a small room under the staircase his abode.

It was Gurpal Singh's nature to help those in need. Plenty of struggling actors and taxi drivers would frequent Gupta Restaurant to avail of the credit that was on offer. Another person who has taken his help is me. He would treat most of his regular customers like his own brothers and convey his love for them with the line, "Eat well, and the bill – payable when 'able'". Apart from me, Sunil Dutt, Rajendra Kumar, Manoj Kumar, Anand Bakshi, Sahir Ludhianvi, Prakash Mehra and *ghazal* singer Jagjit Singh have been the recipients of Kaka's generosity. Dharmendra found succour in the *daal roti* served at the *dhaba*. Dharmendra's relationship with him remains unchanged till this day. When I saw this future actor at the *dhaba* for the first time, I didn't know him, but a thought that crossed my mind was: "Had I been a girl, my heart would have definitely fluttered on seeing him." Kaka is quite close to Dharmendra in age. He may be old today, but in mind, spirit and body, he is fit and kicking, just like Dharmendra.

In those days, I was working on producer-director

Ramesh Sehgal's film, *Phir Subah Hogi*, as Chief Assistant Director. Our office was in Ranjit Studio in Dadar. Producer Kuldip Sehgal and Director Lekhraj Bhakri's offices were next to ours. Lekhraj Bhakri happened to be a close relative of Manoj Kumar and he would often drop by to meet him. That way, I would get to meet Manoj Kumar too. One day, I was just leaving office to get back to my house in Kurla when Manoj Kumar stopped me. He asked me to introduce and recommend the guy he was with to Ramesh Sehgal. The guy was Dharmendra. Manoj left thereafter, leaving the boy with me and I started talking to him. He took out some photographs from the bag that hung on his shoulder. When he was removing pictures from his bag, I could see two *pavs* in his bag. When I saw the pictures, I was stunned and muttered, "You look like the Hollywood actor, James Dean!" He replied, "Everyone says this, but no one wants to give me work." "Don't worry," I said, "I will not only introduce you to Ramesh Sehgal, but also put in a strong recommendation." Disappointment reflected on his face. I told him to leave some photographs with me to be shown to Ramesh Sehgal. I asked him to return in a couple of days to find out the result of my meeting with the producer-director. After saying this, I left, but he continued to remain there, dreaming with wide open eyes. It was a Friday. The next day, I went to Sehgal *saheb*'s bungalow with the photographs and spoke exaggeratedly about Dharmendra's talents. He said, "Send him to me tomorrow morning. Let me see if he is really everything that you have said." Now, I was in a dilemma because I didn't know the boy's whereabouts. How was I supposed to give him the message? Finally, the meeting got pushed to next Sunday.

Keeping Ramesh Sehgal's nature in mind, I gave Dharmendra some tips like, "Give precise answers. Don't initiate the conversation. Listen to his question first and give well-thought-out answers." The next day, when Dharmendra reached Sehgal *saheb*'s house, he was in a good mood. After a short chat over tea and snacks, though he didn't commit to anything, he introduced Dharmendra to his relatives – younger brother Naresh Sehgal, his cousin Kewal and nephew Santosh. Dharmendra was so comfortable around them that every time he spoke to them, he felt that his dreams were about to be fulfilled.

A month after the meeting, Sehgal *saheb* got busy with his next film and he assigned quite a lot of responsibility to Kewal and Santosh. The film *Shola Aur Shabnam* began with Gujarati heroine Tarla and the newcomer Dharmendra.

When the film released, it became an example of what success really meant and this ordinary farmer's career took off. The space under the staircase that was his home became just a forgettable memory as he moved on to a much better place, even though a rented one. As time went on, he moved from one bungalow to the other – each more lavish than the other, and became the owner of several bungalows. As for cars, he possessed many of those too. For many heroines, Dharmendra became their most preferred hero. The film *Izzat* with a Tamil heroine, Jayalalitha, became a hit and this led to some spicy gossip about them too. This dynamic lady went on to become the chief minister of Tamil Nadu, ruled the state successfully for many years, and very recently, succumbed to ill health.

Meanwhile, Dharmendra's friendship with Santosh grew deeper. They began trusting each other on every matter. However, with time, this friendship diluted and differences between them cropped up. While Dharmendra, who was a lost soul some time ago, became a stable person, it was the exact opposite for Santosh. From being a steady and mature individual, he began to stumble a bit. The reason was, he had fallen in love with his neighbour, actress Vijayalakshmi. His love for her reached obsessive proportions. Being a friend, Dharmendra tried his best to dissuade him, but it didn't work. Finally, the actress found someone else whom she liked. She fell for him. This marked the beginning of a new chapter. When their affair reached dizzying heights, Santosh was relegated to the background like old news. This was too much for him to bear because he still loved the woman. Dejected and forlorn, he ended the misery by taking his own life.

Ulti ho gayeen sab tedbeerein
Kuch na dawa ne kaam kiya
Dekha iss beemari-e-dil ne aakhir
Kaam tamaam kiya.

(The tables turned
The medicines didn't work
See how the loverlorn heart destroyed everything.)

Santosh's death led to an unbearable melancholy in the Sehgal household. As for Dharmendra, he couldn't get over the tragedy for a very long time.

Meanwhile, Dharmendra's rise to stardom continued unabated. When a person becomes so busy that he can't spare enough time to take care of himself and his official affairs, he starts looking for someone to share the burden with – a secretary. While Dharmendra's younger brother, Ajit Deol, was always by his side and could have easily taken on the responsibility, it wasn't his cup of tea. A hero's secretary not only has to be cunning and shrewd, but also capable and efficient. Dharmendra found such a person in Dina Nath Shastri, whom he very much trusted. Trust was important because his hectic schedule and the meteoric success he was experiencing left no time for Dharmendra to look into anything himself.

Many years ago, when Dharmendra went to Dilip Kumar's house on his birthday, as a fan, he told Dilip Kumar, *"Aap ke saamne duniya ka koi bhi actor bhala kaise act karega. Iss sawal ka jawaab dhundhne se bhi na milega kisi ko. You are a great actor, sir."* (How can any actor in this world act in front of you? No one will ever be able to find an answer to this question.)

Dilip Kumar replied, *"Khuda ko kya koi rishwat di thi tumne, ki usne tumhe itna achha chehera, itni achhi chodhi chhati, aur dil par hamlawar muskarahat se baksha. Mein tab na jaane kahan tha. Aur phir mein jaanta hun, teri personality ke aage, bhala kaun khada ho kar mukabala kar sakta hai, mein bhi nahi."* (Did you bribe God that he blessed you with such a handsome face, a broad chest and a killer smile? I wonder where I was then. And, I know that no one's personality can be compared to yours, not even mine).

All of us display a certain element of greed at times, but there are those who resort to tools like sycophancy and flattery to fulfil their selfish interests. Such people began to use Dharmendra's secretary for their own gain. They poisoned his mind by telling him Dharmendra was successful only because of his efforts. Such stories are enough to plant a seed of doubt in people's minds. And, it so happened that the secretary began spending more time with hotel and *botal* (bottle). The producers were using the secretary so that they would get Dharmendra's dates for their films easily because once the hero is finalised, the remaining cast, music director, and other crew members, can be taken care of easily. Even in success, Dharmendra maintained his sense of equanimity and simplicity, but when he realised that his secretary was crossing the line, he began to lose trust in him. This caused a rift between them. When the relationship finally ended, Shastri*ji* must have only had these words on his lips:

Yun hi beech gale mein atka hai dum,
Na idhar ke rahe na udhar ke.

(Stuck between a rock and a difficult place,
I belong neither here nor there.)

Arjun Hingorani was perhaps the only Indian film producer who made every single film with Dharmendra as the hero. Soon after winning the *Filmfare* contest, the first film Dharmendra did was Arjun Hingorani's *Dil Bhi Tera Hum Bhi Tere*. Before the film could start, the hero was called for a song recording. And in those days, just to reach Famous Laboratory, Dharmendra had to borrow money from Kaka for the taxi fare. Arjun Hingorani was hard of hearing and it was interesting to watch people moving closer to his ears and 'raising their voices' at him. For many years, the actor and the producer remained each other's support system.

During the same time, producer-director OP Ralhan made the film *Phool aur Pathhar* with Dharmendra and Meena Kumari, which was a major hit. The pair became an even bigger hit. Following this, producer-director Madan Mohla made two films with Dharmendra and Hema Malini, *Raja Jaani* and *Sharafat*, which were successful too. There were times when Dharmendra used to be busy for eighteen hours every day. He was doing three films at once and ended up shuttling between studios, only to return home exhausted. This continued for years.

It is a fact that God has been generous to Dharmendra when it comes to looks and intelligence. There was a time when every girl was besotted by his looks. Many girls came into his life and both he and his family were troubled by this development. But who could blame the hero? His broad chest and toned body were reasons enough to attract the opposite sex.

Though Bombay is full of residential and commercial areas, Bandra and Juhu are considered prime. They are also very expensive. Most film personalities live in these areas. Anyone who gets into the film industry harbours a dream of living there. There were many who came to Bombay penniless, stayed in cramped, rented houses, and later succeeded in building plush bungalows in these areas. Some of them are Dharmendra, Manoj Kumar, Shatrughan Sinha and Ranjit. I am personally aware of how arduous their journeys were.

Dharmendra even built a farmhouse in Khandala that lies between Pune and Bombay. He would go and stay there whenever he had free time from his hectic schedule. Exercise, a game of badminton and a drink in the evening – this was his routine there. This son of a school teacher also remained an ideal son to his parents. He has managed to keep his family together. His brother Ajit Deol, along with his two sons and their families, continue to stay together under one roof. There may be several cooks in the household, but the kitchen is one.

In life, there are often instances, the memories of which bring a smile to your face. Let me tell you one such occurrence from Dharmendra's life. It happened years ago when Dharmendra was extremely busy with work. One fine day, a Sardarji, along with his wife and daughter, reached Dharmendra's house in a truck all the way from Ludhiana. He parked the truck and asked the *chowkidar* to inform those inside that he had come from Dharmendra's town, Ludhiana. This was enough for the family members to let them in. Once inside the house, the first person he met was Dharmendra's father, Kewal Kishan Singh Deol, lovingly called Bauji. When he was told the guest was from Ludhiana, he thought his son's old friend was visiting. So he spoke to him about Punjab for a while and then retired to his room. In the ground floor of the bungalow was a special air-conditioned room, which was used as the guest room. It is still there. The guests were put up there. When Dharmendra returned late at night, and the guard told him about Bauji's special guest from Ludhiana, he told the guard only this: "*Jab tak yahan rahenge, unki achchi tarah dekhbhal karna.*" (Take good care of them for as long as they are here.) He then went straight to his room. For a week, the guest was indulged with *parathas* of different kinds – *aloo, gobhi*, and *lassi*, and of course, Black Label in the evening. Dharmendra even took them along to the set thinking they were his father's special guests. After enjoying a week's hospitality, when the guests finally bade farewell to the guard at the gate, Dharmendra was busy shooting and his father had left for the Arya Samaj temple. When the father and son met at night, they found out that both, the guests and the truck, were missing. It was only then that they realised that both had mistaken the guests to be each other's when in reality, neither of them knew who they were! Whenever Dharmendra remembers this incident, a smile appears on his face.

In fact, anyone belonging to Ludhiana, or even Phagwara for that matter, had a special place in Dharmendra's heart. Whether he knew them or not, they automatically became family. There was an instant feeling of informality, as if he had known the person forever. Once, a close relation of mine had come to India from the USA. She belonged to Ludhiana, so a visit to fellow Ludhianvi, Dharmendra's house, was imperative. When he met Sarla Thapar, within minutes, they bonded like long lost friends, and talked and laughed for hours reminiscing about every street, corner and shop of Ludhiana and the wonderful times they spent there. They would even get emotional. I must add here that the lady in question is my daughter Jalpa's mother-in-law.

God has been kind to Dharmendra when it comes to wealth, fame, respect and love. Not to forget, a successful career. When he reached the epitome of success and paused, he realised that his children had grown up. Now, he worried about their future. When his older son Ajay stood in front of his dad, he looked a lot like his younger brother. One fine day, the father decided to make a film to launch his son. From Ajay Deol, he became Sunny. Then, with his Delhi friend Madam Rukhsana's daughter Amrita Singh, he launched *Betaab*. It was a roaring success. The producers of this *mayanagri* even made another thing possible – many heroines who worked with Dharmendra were now being paired with his son, Sunny!

Hema Malini had done a dozen films with Dharmendra and they were a super hit *jodi*. This was the talk of the town. Gossip about the two was being written about widely. Slowly, it emerged that what was brewing between them was not mere gossip. They were really serious about each other. As was destined, both came together and tied the knot. Now, Dharmendra's new routine was to have a breakfast of *idli, dosa, sambar* and coffee in his new South Indian house and return to his North Indian home for a drink or two, followed by a typical Punjabi dinner with family before finally retiring to bed. This routine that was established years ago continues. Along with Sunny and Bobby, even their sisters are married and well-settled. The same is the case with Hema and Dharmendra's daughters.

Dharmendra may enjoy the status of a celebrity because

of his achievements, but to his friends, he is the same simple man even today. He is blessed with a simplicity that is rare to find. One day, at the end of a busy day of shooting, when he got off at around 11 pm, he remembered it was actress Mumtaz's birthday. He picked up a bouquet on the way and drove straight to her house. He knocked on the door thinking even though it was late, at least he'd be able to wish her. When the guard opened the door to find Dharmendra in front of him, he was flummoxed. When he asked about the birthday, the guard replied that it was the day before and had already been celebrated with great pomp. He cursed his memory and asked the guard if he had anything to eat as he was starving. The guard immediately went into his quarters and came back with some *daal*, pickle and bread on a plate. Dharmendra ate the food along with him and handed over the bouquet to him saying it was for his family. Then, he got into his car and returned home.

When Dharmendra's sons Ajay and Bobby were still young, they all used to live in a building called Woodland in Bandra on rent. In those days, in order to take care of household work and his children plus as his own masseur, he had hired a Bengali guy called Bikram Chowdhury. He served Dharmendra and his family well. When Dharmendra shifted to another bungalow, Bikram was never to be seen again. Time is so transient and things seem unbelievable at times. Once, I went to a yoga centre in Los Angeles, and ran into none other than Bikram Chowdhury. He would travel by buses or local trains while in Bombay. And here in the Los Angeles, he had a huge bungalow and a massive building as his yoga centre, plus more than twenty luxury limos and cars including a Mercedes, BMW, Lexus and a couple of Rolls Royces. He didn't know I was there. When we were stopped at the gate, we had to meet his secretary.

When he was informed about us, he came and stood in front of us. He knew I was Dharmendra's friend. When he saw me, he touched my feet and embraced me. While chatting with him, I got to know that he had several such centres all over America. What an irony that the person who used to give Dharmendra massages had famous Hollywood actors coming to his yoga centre now to learn from him! Even Richard Nixon learnt yoga from Bikram Chowdhury. This is what I'd like to say for this change in circumstances:

Din beetey badle halaat
Badli kal aur aaj ki baat

(Days passed, circumstances changed
With them changed the matters of yesterday and today.)

Dilip Kumar

The cities of Kabul and Peshawar are not far from each other. As neighbouring cities, there is a similarity in the people's lifestyles, occupations, etc. Peshawar has been known for its fruits and dry fruits since ages. The credit for the flourishing businesses would easily go to the experience, hard work and honesty shown by the Pathans and the Sikhs of the region. The only difference is that while earlier the deals were made in Farsi, Urdu or Pashto, it isn't so anymore. The Queen's tongue has made inroads there too and now dominates business proceedings. Anyone speaking even a single sentence in English there is accorded extra respect and a special status.

A particular Pathan family in Peshawar had been in this business since generations. This successful and well-known family had a boy, known as Yusuf Khan then, who not only studied *Alif Be Pe*, but also took a keen interest in English. This skill of his immediately made him popular among his family and friends. His proud father was the happiest of all. And why not? The boy was special after all, and his dad's favourite. He showered his son with a lot of love, but at the same time, always carried a cane with him. His simple logic was that if the boy made an ignorant mistake, he could be taught with love. However, if the mistake was deliberate, the cane would come in handy.

Now, most of us know that the Pathans are known for their extravagant hospitality. They also welcomed the English language with the same warmth. Khan's family was ecstatic about Yusuf speaking English. The elders may not have known a single word of the language, but hearing it from the mouths of their children gave them boundless joy and a sense of pride. Yusuf Khan even went for further studies. While all his degrees and certificates carried the name Yusuf Khan on them, it was soon going to change to Dilip Kumar, the popularity and weight of which is impossible to measure even today. The new name became such an integral part of his identity that except for a few people, he was only known as Dilip Kumar. The name lodged itself into every cinemagoer's heart and has remained irreplaceable till date.

He became famous not only for his acting prowess and his on-screen persona, but also for his off-screen personality. He has fans and admirers in almost every part of the world. Apart from being a talented actor, he was also an extremely well-read man. Be it Hindi, English, or Urdu, he had read numerous books in those languages. It was for this reason perhaps that when the famous poet from Pakistan, Faiz Ahmad Faiz, came to India, he made it a point to meet Dilip Kumar. Their admiration for each other was mutual.

The lord seems to have always bestowed on the Peshawari Pathan, Yusuf Khan, special blessings and continues to do so even today. Perhaps that is how he could carry the burden that his new name brought upon him with such panache. A close friend of mine, Bunny Reuben, also a good friend of Dilip Kumar, had interviewed him long ago. The following is a gist of the same. "I was never interested in becoming an actor. For a shy person with a rueful face, it was impossible to even think about it. My father was a businessman. Thanks to his efforts, honesty, experience and goodness, the business was flourishing and we (me and the elders of the family) were happy and content. Today, some of them are no more and others aren't as happy. When I was studying, my father and his friends would coax me to speak in English that I had recently learned. I had to speak. And though they didn't understand a word, I could see the pride in their stance when they heard me. In those moments, I was far from worried. But when the family fell into troubled times, I understood what that word meant. This situation motivated me to contribute monetarily.

"The aftershocks of Partition saw us moving lock, stock and barrel to Bombay. My father opened a dry fruit shop in the famous Crawford Market in the city. His experience helped. Initially, even I would help out in the shop, but when I saw that things had settled down, I went searching for another job. All my brothers, however, continued to be a part of the family business.

"The first job I landed was that of an assistant manager in the army canteen in Pune, then Poona. The salary was ₹75 per month. I had also set up a small fruit stall. Between 11 am to 2 pm, I would sell the fruits. Because this ran successfully, I was encouraged to open a seekh kebab stall. Our financial situation started improving because of these ventures. The day I gave my mother my hard-earned ₹5,000 was the happiest day of my life. She was elated. However, when my father realised that I was rejoicing for an amount of ₹5,000, he was livid. I could see it on his face. He said, 'Is this some great earning that you are feeling so proud about? I want my son to earn in lakhs and deal in lakhs.'

"These words from my father changed my thinking and

my career. When I stood in front of the mirror and took a good look at myself, I realised that the 'Yusuf Khan' in the mirror was a changed man. Now, I had a new career and along with it, a new name. Yusuf Khan made way for Dilip Kumar. It was a new beginning."

Devika Rani was not only a popular actress and a well-known figure, but also the head of the Bombay Talkies Film Company in Malad. One fine day, she bumped into Yusuf Khan, who had been lurking around to try and find some work. At this meeting, he transformed from a fruit-wala to a film-wala! Even though Yusuf Khan was a good enough name, Devika Rani felt a name should be attractive and ooze sweetness, like Ashok Kumar, this Kumar and that Kumar, and so... Dilip Kumar. The moment she uttered this name, Yusuf Khan adopted it. And the first film with Devika Rani and Dilip Kumar in lead roles was *Jawar Bhata*. It was a big hit; Dilip Kumar was a hero now! He was earning fame and fortune rather rapidly, so much so that his acting set a benchmark of sorts. Soon, Dilip Kumar earned the much-deserved suffix of *saheb*, marking the pinnacle of his success in a way. He amassed success, money, fame and love in good measure and continues to receive the same love and respect, if not more.

I wonder if all this was God's will or his direct orders. There was one other question that Bunny Reuben had asked Dilip Kumar during that interview – whether his choice of career in acting was approved by his father, he took it up to earn money or was it really his passion?

Dilip Kumar said he was a hundred percent sure that his father looked down upon the film business and, in fact, felt that Bombay wasn't fit for Pathans from Peshawar. "He was sad that I didn't care about his disapproval, but we came from different schools of thought. I always respected him from my heart, and nothing could change that. As for him, despite his anger, he always loved me. It was immeasurable. Ironically, back in Peshawar, Raj Kapoor's grandfather, Dewan Bashishar Nath, and my father knew each other rather well. And thanks to this connection, Prithviraj Kapoor and my father became friends in Bombay. Both were Pathans – in Peshawar, everyone is a Pathan, Hindu or Muslim. This is the mark of Peshawar. It was a mixed community and being Pathan was their religion. Every citizen proudly flaunted his moustache – be it a Hindu, Sikh or Muslim – all of them were Peshori Pathans!

"I was brought up in this kind of environment. When my father and Prithviraj Kapoor would meet, there would be a lot of laughter. My father would ask him about Raj Kapoor, 'Why is your talented son going around acting like a joker in films?' Prithiviraj Kapoor would reply, 'He is doing what he is destined to do.' It was difficult for my father to understand. Can you gauge his state of mind when he came to know that his own son had landed in the same circus as the joker he was referring to? After realising his discontentment towards films, I got worried and started avoiding him, but when he fell sick, I felt guilty and so immediately catered to his every need. Since that day, I have never been able to forget his love, his unhappiness or his cane, and I don't think I will ever be able to.

"When my films were successful, newspapers and magazines were filled with my photographs and articles. My father read the paper every morning as a rule. One day, he read articles that were praising me. It made him so happy. Though he was aging, at that moment, he looked young. He bought eight to ten copies of the paper and took it to Crawford Market to show his friends. He told them, 'Turn down your moustaches or shave them off.' He was happy about my success, after all. It's true when they say, '*Wahi hota hai jo manzoor-e-khuda hota hai.*'" (Only what God wills, happens.)

Well, these were Dilip Kumar's reflections on his personal life which I added for your benefit.

Coming back to him becoming Dilip Kumar, I don't know what to write. Since the last seventy years, there has not been a single newspaper or film magazine that hasn't reported an update about the star's personal or professional life. So much so that even if he had a common cold, the news would reach his doctor through the media and he would land up at the star's doorstep to treat him. The Pali Hill and Bandstand areas of Bandra are filled with film stars. Dr. GS Gokhale, a renowned and proficient doctor of the area, is well-respected by the film folk here. He has been Dilip Kumar's family doctor for years. He has even treated Dilip *saheb*'s siblings. Let me tell you a story about the doctor's popularity and the trust people bestowed on him.

Once, Dilip *saheb* was the chief guest at a programme organised by the Assam government. When in Assam, he got so ill that he had to be admitted to the hospital. The entire medical team of the state, along with the chief minister, rallied around the actor, but he only wanted to be treated by Dr. Gokhale. On the request of the chief minister, Dr. Gokhale was flown to Assam, and the minute Dilip *saheb* looked at him, he started to feel better. This was the magic that Dr. Gokhale's personality exuded. Dilip *saheb* was treated, and in the next few days, both of them returned to Bombay.

No newspaper garners good readership unless it contains news about the government, the city, some sensational stuff, or something about Pakistan. *Masaledar* news about the reigning superstars of the day such as Dilip Kumar, Raj Kapoor, Meena Kumari or Lata Mangeshkar was like icing on the cake. If they usually sold a hundred copies, it would easily go up by another fifty in such cases. We have all read such articles, while some generate much laughter, others can make one cry. The people written about are not regular people; they are stars who have entertained audiences on the big screen. Dev Anand, who had played a romantic hero for almost forty years, was given the title of 'Evergreen Hero'. Manoj Kumar, whether in the capacity of an actor, writer, producer or director, was always referred to as 'Bharat' (India), in all his films. Be it Bharat's people or its gold-spewing earth (*desh ki dharti sona ugle*), his stories were generally based on the country. And it was because of all these successful films that he earned the title of 'Bharat'.

In his younger days, Amitabh Bachchan was referred to as the 'Angry Young Man' and then later, he became the 'Shahenshah'. Shah Rukh Khan is called the 'King', but Dilip Kumar was known as the 'Tragedy King' not due to just one, but several reasons. When a person gives it his best to achieve something in life, he undergoes several life-altering experiences. And, these are what change the course of his life. This experience separates his existence from the others. Dilip Kumar would immerse himself in the roles he was playing with such intensity that even the filmmaker would wonder whether he was looking at the actor or the character he had created. People would often walk into the theatre to watch a Dilip Kumar movie with smiles on their lips but would leave the theatre dewy-eyed. Films like *Jogan*, *Babul*, *Deedar* and *Devdas* had this effect on people, they made them feel one with the character. The effect wore out only after they got back to the real world. It was only then they would realise that it was in fact not Devdas, but Dilip Kumar, who had had that effect on them.

Just like Bombay is the film hub of Bollywood, the cities

of Madras and Coimbatore are regional hubs for south Indian film industries. While the studios there make mainly south Indian films, some filmmakers have ventured into Hindi films too. They have a very professional approach. A famous producer from Coimbatore, SMS Naidu, was the owner of a huge studio in Coimbatore; it was like an entire city in itself. Apart from all the services required for film production, it also houses a hospital, petrol pump, cinema hall, a five-star hotel, and various shops! The entire crew would stay in the studio till the film's completion. No one was allowed to go out of the studio during that period. This particular clause, in fact, used to be included in their contracts. SMS Naidu made the film *Azad* with Dilip Kumar and Meena Kumari who used to charge exorbitant fees for their time. Dilip Kumar was given whatever he demanded on time, perhaps even before time. The actor and producer were both happy and became rather friendly. During the shooting, Dilip *saheb* encountered a thrilling experience. He wanted to go to Bombay for a few days. But Naidu *saheb* flatly said no. People were stunned at Naidu *saheb*'s audacity for having refused such a big actor's demand. This matter somehow made its way to the press. When he heard about this, Naidu *saheb* told Dilip Kumar, "Sir, I know you are the finest and a priceless actor. Nobody can deny it. I just cannot think of buying anything from you, sir... I have only bought your costly time at your demand price. Your signed contract is with me, complete the shooting, sir, and then go. I am thankful for your time."

Dilip *saheb* heard him quietly and realised that the producer was right – work should always precede rest.

Manoj Kumar, Rajendra Kumar, Dharmendra and Shah Rukh Khan – all of them have made a name for themselves, and they learned by watching Dilip Kumar's films several times over. They eventually reached such heights that they themselves could teach a few things to others.

Dilip Kumar, being the big star that he was, always remained a soft target for the press, which is always looking for sensational news about film stars. So, his romantic liaisons were always in the news. Whether Vyjayanthimala, Waheeda Rehman or Madhubala, there was news about his relationships with the leading ladies of the time. When he signed a new film with a lady other than these, he would dramatically say, "*Lo, ab ek naya chakkar shuru hoga.*" (Well, now there will be a new affair!)

While he continued to maintain warm and cordial relationships with all his co-stars, it was only Madhubala with whom he was really romantically involved. They were both interested in each other. In the film *Mughal-e-Azam*, the director, K Asif, had incorporated many romantic scenes between the two. He would be pretty amused when upon filming the scenes, he would realise that both were rather well-rehearsed! While the couple was ecstatic at the prospect of marriage, Madhubala's father refused to accept the proposal. Madhubala was always scared of her father and between her fear and her father's stubbornness, their love story died a natural death.

After several years, another story took seed. It was about a nine-year-old beautiful child who was studying in London but was holidaying in Bombay. Even at that age, she was besotted by Dilip Kumar. When she went to the set of *Mughal-e-Azam* to see the shooting, her favourite hero even introduced her to Madhubala. Dilip Kumar seated the little girl on his lap and showered her with affection. Madhubala did the same. This little girl was Saira Banu, daughter of famous heroine Naseem Bano, also known as Fairy Face. Both the families knew each other well. When Saira turned sixteen, she pestered her mother about wanting to join the film industry. Naseem Bano asked Dilip Kumar to discourage her. Everyone tried their best to dissuade her, but her mind was set. To get work wasn't difficult for Saira. Not only was she Naseem Bano's daughter, her beauty was unparalleled. Eventually her career took off. Once, Dilip Kumar signed a film, but the minute he realised Saira was the lead heroine, he refused saying that there was a huge age difference between them. The producer was heartbroken, but this was not the end. When Saira heard the news, she was unhappy too. Her mother had already suspected her of having an affair as she had been acting cranky since a few days. She requested Dilip Kumar to talk sense into her daughter again. When he met Saira, she was calm and composed, and told him, "Okay, don't act with me. But… marry me." Dilip Kumar was caught off-guard but he did not waste a moment and said yes, and soon, they were married. The news of the wedding was something to rejoice for Dilip Kumar's fans the world over, who, apart from his professional success, also wished him a happy personal life. And that is how it worked out. His marriage was as successful as his career and continues to be so.

Saira Banu, who had met Dilip Kumar on the sets of *Mughal-e-Azam* as a little girl, has been showering him with love as a wife ever since. Today, she plays the doting role of a mother to her husband.

The Pakistani government accorded great honour to the city where Yusuf Khan was born and later became famous as Dilip Kumar to the world. The house where Dilip Kumar was born has been made a landmark by the Pakistani government. A board on the door reads: "Dilip Kumar *ki yaad mein zinda hai*" (It lives in the memory of Dilip Kumar). I really wish that whenever I go to the land of my ancestors in Multan and visit my grandmother's old house, I also go to Peshawar to venerate Dilip Kumar's ancestors through their house.

For all those born in Peshawar, it is painful to talk about the city, given the current situation there. Only time will tell when the city, once known for its love and bonhomie, will return to its former glory.

Sometimes, I wonder why this perturbs me so much. Perhaps it is because a lot of people I know, like Dilip Kumar and another friend, Jitendra Billu, belong to Peshawar. There was a time when this place was heaven and its people angels.

December 16, 2014. This is a black letter day in history. I still cannot understand why it happened. I leave the rest to God. I would like you to read one poem, which I came across in an Urdu newspaper in New York, dedicated to the innocent school children, who were shot dead in Peshawar, and their families.

Ma, kaash main aaj school na jaata
Shayad tumhe phir se dekh paata
Teri aavaz sunne ko kaan taras rahe hain
Dekho na ma! Barood ke gole baras rahe hain
Saare bache apni apni ma ko pukaar rahe hain
Tiffin me tumhari di hui roti bhi nahi khaayi hai
Ma aaj goliyon ne meri bhukh mita di hai
Papa se kehna mujhe ab school lene na aayein
Dekh nahi paunga unhe mera janaza uthaye
Mere jaane se apna hosla mat khona
Ma mujh se bichhad ke tum mat rona
Mere khilone, meri kitabein, mera basta
Jaanta hun teri aankhein dekhti ranhegi mera rasta
Bhaiya se kehna uska saath ruth gaya hai
Ammi se kehna mere liye aasun na bahaye
Roz meri tasweer pe chhota sa phool chadhaye

Teri yaadon mein, khwabon mein, zikr mein reh jaunga
Ma mein ab kabhi wapis nahin aaunga!
Ma mein ab kabhi wapis nahin aaunga!

Ma, I wish I hadn't gone to school today
Maybe I would have seen you again
My ears are longing to hear your voice
Look, ma! Bullets are flying everywhere
All the children are calling out to their mothers
I have not eaten the roti you had packed in my tiffin
The bullets have killed my appetite
Tell Papa not to pick me up from school
I will not be able to see him carry my coffin
Don't lose courage just because I am gone
Don't cry because we have been separated
My toys, my books, my bag
I know your eyes will be looking for me
Tell Brother that his companion is brooding
Tell Ammi not to cry for me
Put a small flower on my picture every day
I will remain alive in your memories, in your dreams, in your words
I will never come back!
I will never come back!

Dimple Kapadia

Bobby was a successful film of its time. The first thing that one associates with it is Raj Kapoor. But no one can forget Raj Kapoor's discovery – the beautiful, intelligent and talented 16-year-old girl from Gujarat – Dimple Kapadia – who played the titular role brilliantly. Rishi Kapoor, Raj Kapoor's son, who played the hero, was so good that Raj Kapoor had this to say, "*Yeh toh Kapoor parivar mein apne baap ka bhi baap nikla.*" (He is his father's father in the Kapoor family.)

Having just begun their journey, the film's success instantly catapulted the young Rishi and Dimple to unimaginable heights.

When I joined the film industry, I was eighteen and now I am over seventy. Over the course of several decades, I have been a witness to innumerable incidents – sweet and sour. Most of them have been forgotten, ringing the popular Hindi saying, '*Samay bada balwan*' (Time is most powerful), rather true. I have also learnt and observed that any young and beautiful girl who becomes an overnight sensation in the film industry should necessarily have the complete support of her parents. Or else she will be prone to becoming a victim of opportunists in no time. While there are many small and harmless birds around in this world, there is no shortage of cunning vultures either. And Dimple's beauty was of the kind that attracted everyone. And fortunately, always there to protect and save Dimple from such devious elements was her father, Chunnibhai.

Chunnibhai was friends with the well-known writer, KK Shukla, a friend of mine too. So when KK married Daisy Irani, the friendship between the three of us only deepened.

Even before the release of *Bobby,* one saw Dimple being written about in almost all the prominent magazines – whether English or Urdu. Her photographs were everywhere, and she had become not only the talk of the town, but also of the entire country. Thanks to the pre-emptive hullabaloo, the day the film released, the view outside the theatres was no less than that of Kumbh Mela! It was of course a great hit, and the praise wasn't limited to just Raj and Rishi Kapoor; a lot of appreciation came Dimple's way too.

Raj Kapoor had invited Idris Dehlvi, the editor of *Shama*, an Urdu magazine very popular in Delhi, to Mumbai. This was before *Bobby*'s release. He accepted the invitation and arrived in Bombay within two days. I had known Idris since the exodus from Pakistan to India during the Partition. We were on very friendly terms with each other and whenever we were together, my mother would say, "*Mere Ram Lakhan aa gaye.*" (There come my Ram and Lakhan.)

Since Idris Dehlvi was Raj Kapoor's guest, he would spend the entire day at RK Studio with his host, and in the evenings, we would spend time at a hotel or at my place. I introduced Dehlvi to KK Shukla, and he, in turn, introduced me to Chunnibhai. This meeting developed into a great friendship between the four of us. Chunnibhai and I became fast friends pretty soon. One day, he called me to his place in Juhu and asked me to take over Dimple's publicity and other work-related responsibilities. I was happy to comply. While dining at a Chinese restaurant in Bandra, when I told Dimple about this proposal, she was elated too. She told me about how she and Chintu (Rishi Kapoor) had gone to the coffee shop at Oberoi the previous evening and he had bought her silver bangles and even helped her put them on. Before we parted, I told her that considering all the popularity she had already garnered, she didn't require any publicity. Besides, even though I didn't have much experience of being a secretary, I told her I'd use all the goodwill I had earned to help her out.

I used to live near Bandstand in Bandra. One evening, my wife and I were surprised to see Dimple Kapadia and her sister, Simple, at our doorstep. After spending an hour or so with us, they bid us goodbye. But I was shocked to see that there was no car or driver to take them back. I was even more shocked when I saw the girls ride off on their bicycles, giggling. This was about two months before the release of *Bobby*. Even though everyone was talking about the film and Dimple, no one had seen her on screen yet. Not only was she beautiful, but she was also *bindaas*, as they say in Bombay. And she is so, even today.

Bobby created ripples from the day it released. The very first screening made Dimple Kapadia and Rishi Kapoor stars overnight. A few days later, news of superstar Rajesh Khanna breaking up with his girlfriend and marrying Dimple shocked the nation. But Dimple had only been a fan of Rajesh Khanna's, and had not been involved with him as people had speculated. However, when she met the superstar was she was so smitten that they ended up marrying each other.

I had got the news even before I received the wedding invitation from Chunnibhai. When I arrived at the venue, I saw that there was a long queue of people waiting to greet the bride and groom. It looked as if the entire film industry had congregated there. So I went and stood in the queue too. I had kept some money in the pockets of my shirt and trousers. But someone picked my back pocket. Chunnibhai noticed the consternation on my face and asked if everything was okay. When I told him the reason, he asked me if I remembered who was standing behind me in the line. But I didn't know. Someone who was eavesdropping said Waheeda Rahman was standing behind me. On hearing this, Chunnibhai burst into laughter, but he started looking tense shortly after. I realised that he was looking for the person who had taken Waheeda*ji*'s name. He suspected the man to be the pickpocket, but unfortunately, we never spotted him again.

The Times of India used to bring out a Hindi film magazine called *Madhuri* and its editor was Arvind Kumar. I had, and still have, friendly relations with him. At a meeting with him, he informed me that they were putting Dimple on the cover of their next issue and that I had to do the cover story. I couldn't say no. As promised, within a week, I reached his office with the article. The headline was, *Bharpoor qismat ki tokri, ghazab ki chokri* (A basket full of luck: an incredible woman). There were three reasons why the *tokri* had gotten rather heavy:

1. For being blessed with not only good looks, but equal amounts of intelligence.

2. For being able to work with a filmmaker like Raj Kapoor.

3. For being the daughter of a fine gentleman called Chunnibhai.

People loved the article, and Arvind Kumar and Dimple were flooded with congratulatory messages. But along with the bouquets came the brickbats. All three of us – Arvind Kumar, Rajesh Khanna and I – received notices from a court in Ujjain. A reader, after reading the article, had decided to sue us. He was objecting to the line, "*Desh ki har jawaan ladki Rajesh Khanna par marti hai.*" (Every girl in India is crazy about Rajesh Khanna.) The man who sued us had a *jawaan beti,* and said, "*Woh bhi desh ki jawaan ladki hai. Woh toh iss actor par nahin marti.*" (My daughter is also a young Indian. But she is not crazy about this actor.) While the magazine and Khanna didn't take cognisance of the notice and it saw its way to the dustbin, I was worried and took the piece of paper to Arvind Kumar's office. He wasn't available then, so I met Khushwant Singh instead, the editor of *The Illustrated Weekly*, another Times publication. Thanks to Sunil Dutt, he knew me well. We had tea, and while leaving, he assured me, "Don't worry about the notice. I will call this guy and ask for an apology in person." I then proceeded to take the local to Bandra and he walked to his place in Colaba.

The next day, when I narrated this incident to Chunnibhai, he laughed and told me I had done a foolish thing. Before I could respond, the phone rang. Chunnibhai was smiling widely. It was Dimple on the other line, telling her father that he was to become a grandfather in seven months' time. I celebrated the good news with him and his wife Betty. Rajesh Khanna and Dimple Kapadia had two daughters soon after their marriage – Twinkle and Rinkie Khanna.

Unfortunately, with time, the magic in the couple's relationship began to wilt. When I looked deeper, I could understand the reason. In reality, Kaka would have drinking sessions with his close friends from evening till late in the night. The inebriated friends would heap praises on Rajesh Khanna, and Dimple would just spend the night waiting for her husband to come back to her. She would go to sleep and wake up, only to find Kaka fast asleep next to her. She would never know when he got back. This became a regular event, and led to many fights until one day, Dimple decided she had enough. She picked up both the daughters and went to her father's place. Thanks to her sensibility, she started working again. Time went by and the children grew up to be two beautiful young girls.

I feel a sense of relief and pleasure when I think of Dimple's life. From a young heroine to a wife, from a mother to a mother-in-law, and now finally a grandmother, Dimple's life has been tumultuous but a rewarding one. Despite a few wrinkles, she looks younger than ever!

Johnny Walker

Mumbai is a city where money rules. It dictates almost everything and the solution to most problems is also money. People from all over the country come here with big dreams, leaving behind their friends and family. Once here, they wait ravenously to find fame and fortune, no matter how long it may take. And until that time, they live on sheer hope.

Badruddin Jamaluddin Kazi from Indore made his way to this city too, to make a name for himself. But his dreams didn't materialise as he had expected, and he kept waiting for that one crucial turn of fate, in spite of how dejected he constantly felt. But the truth is that you can never be happy when you are hungry for one of the most basic necessities – food. However, Badruddin's struggle for a job ended when he was hired as a bus conductor. He could then afford two square meals. His dreams of becoming an actor were infused with a new lease of life.

The bus route he was assigned was route no. 231 that started from Santacruz station, passed through Juhu beach and ended at Juhu Church. Apart from Balraj Sahni, many other prominent people also travelled this route, including Abrar Alwi, Shauqat Azmi, and Usha Anand. A prime locality in Bombay with a vast and imposing view of the Arabian Sea, several prominent eateries and frolicking people, it is such a place that one can easily lose oneself in the vivacious environment. Even today, from time to time, one can spot filmstars there.

Badruddin's bus route had a regular to whom life had been very generous. He had tasted success, including many cars and a big house. But he still chose to ride on that bus. Perhaps, that was his favourite journey. Badruddin would see him every day and could glean from his conversations that he was a Punjabi. One day, when Badruddin finished his duty, this gentleman, who had piqued Badruddin's curiosity, took him to a tea shop. And it was during this tea session that their friendship blossomed. As they grew closer, Badruddin realised the person was highly educated, with several degrees under his belt. Badruddin, on the other hand, didn't even come close in terms of education. But the profundity of his knowledge on various topics made up for the lack of higher education. This special passenger was none other than Balraj Sahni. Apart from Badruddin, all of Balraj Sahni's friends were highly educated. One of them was the famous director Chetan Anand. They bonded like brothers. Chetan Anand wouldn't proceed with anything in life until he had consulted Sahni. Even if it was a brainstorming session about a minor aspect of an upcoming film, Balraj had to be a part of it.

One day, Balraj found out that Badruddin was passionate about working in films but hadn't gotten the opportunity. After giving it a lot of thought, Balraj told Badruddin that he was going to introduce him to a very famous producer and director. He further added, "But, when you meet him, only say and do what I tell you to." Two days later, Balraj, along with the producer-director, reached Chetan Anand's office. He made Badruddin wait outside, reminding him to only say what he had been told to, and went into the office. This made Badruddin nervous.

Inside the office, Balraj and Chetan *saheb* were busy talking about a script written by the former. They were engaged in a serious conversation when out of the blue, a fully sozzled drunkard entered the room and fell on Balraj Sahni. Then he asked for forgiveness with folded hands. But Chetan Anand was livid. Face red with anger, he screamed for the peon. Even before he arrived, the drunk man jumped on Chetan Anand's desk saying "*Main manta hun ki Dev Anand aap ka chhota bhai hai, magar meri baat dhyan se suniye. Main bhi kam nahi hun uss actor se... kya naam hai... haan yaad aya... Dev Anand se.*' (I understand that Dev Anand is your younger brother, but I assure you, I am no less than that actor... What was his name again? Ah yes, Dev Anand.)

All this sudden activity created a stir in the office. The peon came and threw the drunkard out. Balraj *saheb* had been watching the drama quietly. Then, he burst out laughing. Chetan Anand couldn't understand what was happening. Then Balraj Sahni said, "All the drama that happened just now has been written and directed by me, and the person thrown out is my bus conductor, Badruddin. I am so happy to see how well he played the part, including the climax. It was exactly how I wanted it to be."

What lay at the helm of this entire charade was Balraj Sahni's next film, *Aandhiyan*, which was also written by him. The film required someone to play the role of a drunkard, who was crucial to the plot. Balraj Sahni had envisioned Badruddin in that role while writing the script itself, which explained the whole act. When Chetan Anand heard all this, he told Balraj Sahni, "The way this guy acted atop the table, I can never imagine Dev Anand doing the part with the same intensity."

That evening, Chetan Anand and Balraj Sahni met at the former's place for drinks. The bottle of whisky they opened to raise a toast was a Johnnie Walker. And that was it! Badruddin was immediately rechristened as Johnny Walker. Interestingly and ironically, the person who went through his entire film career being called Johnny Walker had never tasted a drop of alcohol in his entire life.

Life changed for the better and Johnny Walker's career took off. Big-time producers realized his talent. A prominent one among them was Guru Dutt. Every film he made had Walker playing a significant part in it. Apart from this, he was associated with many other great films as well.

Once, it so happened that a filmmaker, who also owned a studio, called Walker for a very vital role in his film. Fatefully, he turned out to be the same person Walker had approached when he was looking to get into the industry. At that time, the director had shunned him saying, "*Shakl dekhi hai apni aine mein? Bevakoof! Chalo niklo yahan se abhi.*" (Have you seen your face in the mirror? Idiot! Get out of here right now.) Even though Johnny Walker was a successful actor by then, he went to the studio. He immediately said yes to the role but when money matters were being discussed, he demanded one lakh rupees. The producer was shocked. He said, "But you work with Guru Dutt and Raj Khosla for ₹25,000 and ₹50,000. Why are you asking me for a lakh? Look, we are both Muslims. I consider you my younger brother. Why are you behaving this way? Okay, I will give you ₹60,000, now just sign the papers." To this, Johnny Walker's reply was this:

"*Janab, bahut bahut shukriya aapka mujhe apna chhota bhai samajhne ke liye aur bula bhejne ke liye. Mujhe bhi dekhiye ki aapke bulane par main fauran hazir ho gaya. Rahi baat Guru Dutt aur Raaj Khosla ke saath kaam karne ki aur paise lene ki, toh woh mujhe jab bulate hain toh main*

Badruddin hota hun aur aapne aaj 'Johnny Walker' ko bulaya hai. Panch saal pehle wale Badruddin ko nahi."

(Sir, thank you for calling me your younger brother and summoning me here. Look at me! I came here as soon as you called me. But as far as working with Guru Dutt and Raaj Khosla, and matters of money are concerned, when they call me, I am Badruddin for them. You have called Johnny Walker, not the Badruddin I was five years ago.)

This was the perfect response to the insult he had received during his struggling days. The producer was none other than Mr. Kardar Miyan and the film was the Dilip Kumar and Waheeda Rehman starrer *Dil Diya Dard Liya*.

Leena Chandavarkar

Sunil Dutt had made the film *Man ka Meet* under the banner of Ajanta Arts for his brother, Som Dutt. It launched three new faces and was a successful one. However, Som Dutt, the hero of the film, didn't make it as big as its heroine Leena Chandavarkar and the man who had played the villain, Vinod Khanna.

Leena Chandavarkar considered work to be her religion, and was dedicated and industrious. She could settle into and could relate to any character she was asked to play. She would become one with it. Leena also scored high in the looks department and had a certain innocence about her that charmed the audience. These are some of the numerous reasons for her success. She even worked with the top heroes of the time – Rajesh Khanna, Jeetendra, Sanjeev Kumar, Dharmendra and Dilip Kumar, and did justice to all her roles.

In her initial days, when she moved to Bombay from Dharwad, she lived with her parents and brother in Jogeshwari. When she signed *Man ka Meet*, Dutt *saheb* wanted her to shift to a rented place in Bandra, Khar or Santa Cruz, since Jogeshwari was too far from his office. Fortunately, we found a place rather soon – a ground-floor apartment in a building in Bandra. Leena shifted into the new flat with her family, but left within a week. I remember that day. I was in Dutt *saheb*'s office sitting in front of him when Leena's father entered the room. When Dutt *saheb* asked him the reason for their decision to shift, he hesitated at first and then said, "Last night, around midnight, three drunk men came over and rang the doorbell. When my son opened the door, they said, '*Suna hai bade kamaal ka maal hai andar, zara dekhen toh… ek baar dekh lein toh phir paison ki baat kar lenge.*' (We hear there is a prostitute inside. Let us see her first, and then we'll talk about money.) On hearing this, my son took out his pistol and they ran for their lives."

We supported their decision to move but were surprised that prostitution houses were prevalent in a posh area like Bandra.

Anyway, they shifted houses again. Leena had begun to receive numerous roles by then and she went on to buy not one but two flats. However, she was always embroiled in problems when it came to her family. She was married to a prominent politician but sadly, he passed away too soon. Within a year, she lost her parents too and soon after that, in a tragic incident, her brother shot himself with a pistol and died. The strong lady that she was, Leena faced all these difficulties bravely. When she married the famous actor-singer Kishore Kumar, there was an end to her loneliness. Perhaps, she was destined to be his wife and bear his son.

Leena and I recently got back in touch through Facebook. And because of her loving messages, I reminisced the old days. She told me how she missed me and the good old days, and demanded that we catch up whenever I came to Bombay. "*Aaj Raksha Bandhan hai, Raaj bhaiyya. Subah se aap ki bahut yaad aa rahi hai, jab se aap ko FB pe paaya hai bahut khush hoon… Happy Raksha Bandhan!*"

(It is Raksha Bandhan today, Raaj *bhaiya*. I have been missing you a lot since morning. I'm extremely happy to have found you on Facebook. Happy Raksha Bandhan!)
On Bhai Dooj, we spoke again. "*Aaj Bhai Dooj hai... Raksha Bandhan nahi... phir bhi kitna achha hota main aap ki aarti utarti, maathe par teeka lagati...mithhai khilaati... khair, koi baat nahi. Ab toh aap se milne ki ummeeden hain... aur Bhagwan ye ichha zaroor poori karenge... aap ko bahut bahut pyaar aur Bhai Dooj ki shubhkamnayein.*"
(It is Bhai Dooj today, not Raksha Bandhan. But it would have been so good to do *aarti*, put vermillion on your forehead, feed you sweets, but alas... I genuinely hope to meet you soon, and surely God will fulfil this wish of mine. Lots of love and Bhai Dooj greetings.)
In another conversation, she was emotional and said, "*Raaj bhaiyya, aap mujhe apna number denge toh main phone karungi aur bahut saari baatein karenge. Aapse baat karne ko mera bahut dil karta hai. Aapke India aane ka intezar kar rahi hun. Thank you, Raaj bhaiyya, Love you.*"
(Raaj *bhaiya*, if only you would give me your number, we could talk all day. My heart longs to talk to you. I await your return to India. Thank you, Raaj *bhaiya*. Love you.)
Floodgates of old memories open whenever I read our chat. How could I say no to such a heartfelt appeal?

Mahesh Bhatt

The film industry in India is over a hundred years old, but it continues to grow and produce fresh talent every year. Behind this phenomenon are the talented and dedicated people who have contributed to the industry's growth and have nurtured it with extreme love and care, refusing to let it age. Even when these people leave their mortal bodies, the industry is infused with fresh vigour that melts into the rich experience and legacy left behind by the stalwarts.

The Indian film industry has seen a lot of great names in its journey, but the people whom I have known closely and who have a special place in my heart are Hrishikesh Mukherjee, Gulzar and Mahesh Bhatt. In this industry, the Bhatt family is just as prominent and well-known as the Khannas, the Kapoors, the Khans and the Kumars. There was a time when Nana Bhai Bhatt was a big name in the film industry. To direct three different films in a day, complete them on time, and achieve success on their release was no less than a miracle. And, he was no less than a superhero.

But his son Mahesh Bhatt turned out to be steps ahead of him in matters of intelligence and wisdom. Some of these blessings from God passed on to Mahesh's younger brother

Mukesh Bhatt too. It doesn't end there. There is also Vishesh Bhatt, Pooja Bhatt, Robin Bhatt, Vikram Bhatt, Pravin Bhatt, and now Alia Bhatt from the same family, who are shining like stars in the film fraternity.

Mukesh Bhatt, along with his son, Vishesh Bhatt, started a film company that has produced and distributed several hit films. If I had to draw parallels between the Bhatt family and a church, I would say that Mahesh Bhatt would enjoy the status of the Pope in it. But before he reached this stage, he struggled for twenty years. However, his daughter Alia, who is relatively new to films, is already ruling the industry. The situation now is such that while earlier, she was known as Mahesh Bhatt's daughter, he is now known as Alia Bhatt's father. And he couldn't be prouder! Another father in the same situation was Raj Kapoor. His son Randhir Kapoor (Dabbu) once advised his dad to buy a luxury car, a BMW or a Mercedes, instead of the outdated Oldsmobile, for his personal use. After all, his dad was a star. But the father replied, "*Beta*, you have a career in films, but people still address you as Raj Kapoor's son. A proud day for me will be when people look at me and say, 'Look at that old man in the car; he's the father of the hero – Randhir Kapoor.'"

Filmmakers like Mahesh Bhatt, Hrishikesh Mukherjee, Gulzar and Rajkumar Hirani are institutions in themselves. Films like Mahesh Bhatt's *Arth*, *Saransh* and *Naam* are a learning ground for all the new filmmakers.

Mahesh is a fine director and Mukesh has played a great part in Mahesh's success. Mukesh is a very well-informed and forthright person. All the trade-related matters are handled by him. And right from the start of the film up to its release, it is he who coordinates with the writers, directors, music directors, cameramen and other technicians. Though both the brothers are younger than me, in terms of experience and success, they are way ahead. Perhaps it is because of the talent and ability they inherited from their father, Nana Bhai Bhatt.

Meanwhile, despite all his achievements, Mahesh Bhatt was also destined to take the less-trodden path. For when he was being flooded with success, money and fame from all sides, he unexpectedly decided to leave everything and join Acharya Rajneesh's ashram. At times, he even took recourse to the bottle and found himself tottering on the path of life. Because Mahesh Bhatt is a kind-hearted soul with a tender heart, when he found actress Parveen Babi caught in a web of problems, he was distraught. He got so involved in her complicated life, trying to give her solace, that she mistook it for love. And eventually, he fell for her too. When this news, sprinkled with a lot of spice, made its way to the media, both of them passed it off as plain rumour. But I will tell you what I saw.

During the course of my film, *Taaqat*, Parveen Babi's secretary Ved Sharma suddenly changed her dates. When the director Narendra Bedi and hero Vinod Khanna got to know this, they were upset and argued about it. It was a difficult situation for me. So, instead of contacting Ved Sharma, I landed straight at Parveen Babi's house in Juhu. When I rang the doorbell, the maid opened the door, and before I could speak, she said, "Madam is not at home." I heard her, but suddenly my attention was diverted to the footwear in the house. I had seen the same pair being worn by Mahesh Bhatt on several occasions. I was upset with the maid for lying but what could I do? I just reminded myself that I was no saint. It was the case of, '*Iss hamaam mein sab nange hain.*' (Everyone is naked in this bathroom.)

When Mahesh Bhatt came to know about my predicament, his sympathetic heart fluttered. Ignoring Ved Sharma, he directly convinced Parveen Babi. When she reached the set, director Narendra Bedi, along with all the others working on the film, welcomed her. Parveen Babi got emotional and tears welled up in her eyes. Instantly, my eyes became watery too.

Guru Dutt and Mahesh Bhatt have one thing in common – their perspective on various things. And you see this similarity reflected in the characters of their respective films. Music is one of the best mediums to symbolise emotions. For example, while Guru Dutt's films had a hero and heroine, the story and the music were also its protagonists. I personally feel that Guru Dutt's assistant Raj Khosla learned this from him, which was later passed on to his assistant Mahesh Bhatt. If you really paid attention, you'd be convinced with my reasoning. In case of all the three, music and story are at the centre of the film, so they never compromise on these two factors. In fact, to match the voice of his actors, Mahesh Bhatt even invited Pakistani singers. For instance, the songs in *Paap* were sung by Rahat Fateh Ali Khan, *Zehar* had Atif Aslam, and *Jism* had Amir Jamal.

Another one of his unique qualities is that he only works with people who are not just talented but also worship their work. It is probably for this reason that there is always a sense of newness in his films.

Now coming to my *zara zara si yadein*, there is one memory that keeps haunting me and the person in the memory is Ved Sharma, the name I mentioned earlier. He was in charge of handling Parveen Babi's affairs – both personal and professional. I would like to quote a popular saying of our elders, '*Main toh iss kambal* (blanket) *ko chhodna chahta hun par yeh kambal saala mujhe nahin chhodhta.*'

Let me explain. As bad luck would have it, after having signed Anil Kapoor as the hero, Mahesh Bhatt as the director and Amrita Singh as the heroine for my next project *Thikana*, I realised that the same *kambal* was handling this heroine's business also. He was a gain to the heroine but a pain to her producer. But my friend Mahesh Bhatt came to my rescue like a soothing balm to get this pain off my head. This man was a junior group dancer in the industry, but being clever and wise, he climbed the ranks high enough to have the producers dancing to his tunes. I really want to thank Mahesh Bhatt for having relieved me of the same pain that I went through during my first project. Thanks to him, my second project was a smooth sail.

So bad was my experience with Ved Sharma that when I found out he was handling Amrita Singh, I actually thought of changing the heroine rather than having to deal with him. But a worldly-wise good old friend, Mukesh Bhatt, proved to be an angel in disguise and saw to it that the dirty *kambal* was sent for some much-needed dry cleaning. And it worked. In fact, during the shoot of *Thikana*, I started seeing a good friend in Ved. Not just me, several other producers too were thankful to Mukesh Bhatt, who later turned into a filmmaker of repute, producing one hit film after another. I would address him as Mukesh Bhatt, PhD (Films).

Let me tell you a little about how Anil Kapoor became the hero of *Thikana*. One evening, just by chance, I met Shukla *bhabhi* (Mrs. Rajendra Kumar) at her bungalow. She took me to their private preview theatre located in the bungalow itself for the trial show of *Woh Saat Din*, starring a new hero, Anil Kapoor. It was his first film as the hero. I urged his brother Boney Kapoor to convince him to accept my offer of the lead role in my next project, *Thikana*. I got his go-ahead in just fifteen minutes after the end of the trial show of *Woh Saat Din*. And on the eighth day was *Thikana*'s next meeting at my residence where the director Mahesh Bhatt, hero Anil Kapoor and story writer Sujit Sen were also present.

I was in possession of two stories – one was a single-hero

story and the other one had two. Though I preferred the latter, the former was good too. I took the suggestion of my hero Anil Kapoor, chose the former and decided to make a film based on it. It was called *Thikana*. The *mahurat* and the first day of the shoot was March 21, 1984, at Mehboob Studios and the title song was recorded the very next day.

The second story with two heroes was acquired by my close friend Jubilee Kumar, or Rajendra Kumar, who made the film with his son Kumar Gaurav and Sanjay Dutt. The film was *Naam*, directed by Mahesh Bhatt.

Before I started *Thikana*, I had arranged for the entire finance and I was not stressed about completing the film. But don't they say greed is a bad thing? Well, I became a victim of greed. When a friend in New York – we had studied together in school – got to know about my film, he called me and expressed his wish to be a co-producer of the film. He said he'd give all the money without charging interest. As an emotional person, I felt happy about the proposal. I said yes, believing it to be a generous offer from my friend.

Since I had great goodwill in the industry and had already made a film named *Taaqat* earlier, I was wise enough to begin *Thikana* with my own money. After I accepted my friend's offer, his money started flowing into the project. Around the same time, Anil Kapoor's brother Boney Kapoor got engaged. Since their father Surendra Kapoor was a good friend, it was like a family member's wedding. After the wedding, when Boney wanted to go to the USA with his wife Mona for their honeymoon, I called up my friend there and told him to take good care of them.

A week after the couple returned from their honeymoon in the USA, my friend from New York landed up in Bombay with his brother. What could have been a better place for lodging and boarding than my house? My driver Salim was at his beck and call. Now that we were partners and his money was already being used in the film, I began to trust him and his brother. And in a foolhardy move, I signed papers declaring them as signing authorities.

Both Mahesh and Mukesh Bhatt weren't happy about it. But the deed was already done. First, the brothers took hold of my accountant and then started using my office and my vehicle like they owned them. Though I knew my friends, I failed to truly understand them. Besides, I am not a crooked person, so I missed their ploy. When the Bhatt brothers gave me an earful for my stupidity, I could do nothing but accept my foolishness.

When the two of them, after fleecing me, moved to Marriott Hotel in Juhu, we were left with about eight days of shooting. The next evening, as per their phone call, I reached Marriott to try and sort out the problem. To my total shock, I found my accountant, all smiles, holding a glass of Black Label whisky and chatting happily with the brothers. And within just ten minutes of my being in the room, I realised I couldn't continue staying there. I left the next minute. But the problems only multiplied after this incident. It was decided that the situation would be sorted out through an arbitrator, who was Prakash Mehra. When the decision was being taken in Prakash Mehra's office, apart from the brothers, Mahesh Bhatt and Boney Kapoor were also present. Prakash Mehra said that since the brothers' money had been used in the film, they will be called the producers instead of Raaj Grover. And that since Raaj Grover had worked hard to complete the film, he will be compensated akin to a director. Everyone was quiet when Mahesh Bhatt spoke up. He said since it was Raaj Grover who had signed him and paid him the advance amount, he would complete the remaining shoot only on his instructions.

The brothers were livid when they heard this. Boney Kapoor was silent, but I could see on his face traces of a smile that I couldn't understand. Maybe it was because of the way the brothers took care of the honeymooning couple's needs in the US.

Meanwhile, Prakash Mehra appealed to Mahesh Bhatt to complete the film and decided that till the time Raaj Grover's cheque was not cleared, the exposed negative of the day's shoot would be sent to Prakash Mehra's house instead of the laboratory. I knew that the exposed negative was supposed to be put under a certain degree of cool temperature, but the temperature of my bedroom also happened to be the same as that of the lab. It would be given to the brothers only after the clearance of the cheque.

When I was returning from Prakash Mehra's office, I was cursing myself for my imprudence. I also felt like I had sold out *Thikana*, which was like my baby. Ultimately, business took over emotions. Boney Kapoor's silent smile kept haunting me.

I respect Mahesh Bhatt as much as his brother Mukesh. Though they are friends, I feel they are much wiser than me when it comes to worldly dealings. They too are emotional, but not fools like me.

When I was ousted from my own film, the media latched on to the news. Senior journalists contacted Mahesh Bhatt first. When questioned about this, he told them in his typical straightforward manner, "Raaj Grover is hard-working, honest and a good human being, but he is emotional. And as a producer, instead of displaying emotions, he should be strong, which he is not. Even I am not cunning, and one can see my sensitive nature in my films. So, in a way, we belong to the same clan."

But now, filmmaking is more about technology and science

than feelings and sentiments. Overly dramatic endings are more popular than relatable ones. There are films where a couple emerges out of a car released by a parachute, which, in turn, has just come out of a plane. The hero and heroine emerge from the said car smiling, leading to the end. How do films with sensitive stories and melodious songs stand a chance against that?

Manoj Kumar

The name Hari Krishna Goswami conjures up the image of a *tilak-smeared* pujari in a temple. However, if this person turns out to be a good man with great intelligence, integrity and good looks, one can overlook the confusion the name might otherwise cause. In the Rajendra Nagar area of Delhi, two young boys, both schoolmates, were destined to come to Bombay to make a name for themselves. One of them was Jitendra Billu, who was from Peshawar, and the other one, associated with Abbottabad, was Hari Krishna Goswami. With such a holy name, an innocent face and gentle nature, he was a cut above the rest. Bombay, the city of dreams, sees so many people struggling for success in the fields of their choice. When Jitendra Billu, who was my cricket-mate and a great bowler, introduced me to his friend Hari Krishna Goswami, I felt joyous. They were very close friends. Just like me, he too made several friends along the way who helped him realise his dreams. This help was like a loan that was later repaid.

There was a successful film director by the name of Lekhraj Bhakdi, who was also Goswami's close relative. He taught the boy production work and at the same time, cast him as an old beggar roaming the streets singing in his film. The film starred Pradeep Kumar and Mala Sinha. Though Goswami did a decent job, it wasn't enough to bring to life the dreams with which he had come to Bombay. He was not financially lucky either, with his pockets running dry quickly. I was acquainted with Goswami in Delhi. I had a very good friend, director-producer Homi Sethna, and I introduced him to Goswami. He was signed for Sethna's documentary, *Gangu Teli*, in which he was to play the main role. He was paid a lump sum of ₹1,000, before leaving for Dehradun for the shooting. Finally, his pockets saw some money flowing in. Along with the change in the work front came the change in his name. Hari Krishna Goswami became Manoj Kumar.

Once work picked up, it showed no signs of slowing down. Manoj found himself spending more and more time in the studio than at home. He did many films in the lead role, such as *Do Badan, Hariyali Aur Rasta, Neel Kamal, Woh Kaun Thi* and *Pathar Ke Sanam*. These films brought him great success and unimaginable fame, besides getting him closer to his destiny – making films written and produced by him. The films he made as an actor, writer, director or producer were hits too, such as *Upkar, Purab Aur Pashchim, Shor, Shaheed, Roti Kapda aur Makan* and *Kranti*. Not just in India, I witnessed his popularity in London, New York and Dubai too. When I heard his praises on foreign shores, I felt a great of sense of pride. His success catapulted him into the league of stalwarts of the time like Raj Kapoor, Guru Dutt and Bimal Roy, whose filmmaking abilities are quoted as examples.

Just like anywhere else in the world, Bollywood too is full of good and bad people. There are those who take pride in others' success and then there are those who suffer the pangs of envy. Those who are envious are rather self-destructive because:

Muddayi lakh bura chahe toh kya hota hai
Wahi hota hai jo manzoor-e-khuda hota hai.

(Man can think of the worst
But only what God wills, happens.)

There can't be anything closer to the truth than these lines. When I meet my friends, in the course of our conversations, we often veer towards people like Sunil Dutt, Dilip Kumar or Manoj Kumar; it is easy to ascertain their opinions about each one of them, like my friend in New York, Tirlok Malik, an NRI filmmaker, whose film *Lonely in America* was highly successful and critically acclaimed. I should mention here, though a little out of context, that Tirlok was my true anchor when I first shifted to America from Bombay. Coming back to Manoj, Tirlok has always profusely praised Manoj Kumar and supported him rather enthusiastically. He confesses that whatever he has learnt about filmmaking has been after repeatedly watching films made by Manoj Kumar. He has watched *Purab Aur Pashchim* several times because he can relate to it – a story about a student whose journey starts in the East and continues in the West.

Once, Dev Anand came to New York for the shooting of *Love at Times Square*. Unfortunately, his cameraman fell sick. Dev Anand asked me if I could arrange for an alternate. I asked Tirlok Malik, who had a production set-up there, and he found someone immediately.

I have not, and I am sure neither has my friend Manoj

Kumar, forgotten the days when I lived in a room in Kurla in Bombay, as a paying guest, for which I paid ₹50 per month. Close to my house was a *dhaba* owned by an elderly Punjabi man named Ganda Ram. He was good-hearted but quite short-tempered. When he started abusing in his native language, everyone, including his customers, would be blown away by the barrage that ensued. He was a staunch devotee of Lord Shiva. The *dhaba* walls were covered with photographs of the god and he even wore a Shiva pendant around his neck. He would continuously chant Lord Shiva's name too. I was one customer who he considered as his son. I was allowed to eat anything anytime and pay for it whenever convenient.

Every morning, I had to stand in a queue, with a *lota* of *paani* in hand, to use the toilet. Hari Krishna Goswami had become Manoj Kumar, but wasn't so famous that he would be recognised on the streets. He used to stay with me in my room every weekend. Our long conversations would include his ideas for new stories. He would make tea as I didn't know how to, and after that, both of us would take our *lotas* and join the toilet queue. After finishing our jobs, we would be at Ganda Ram's *dhaba* for breakfast. Often, even Jitendra Billu and Sohan Lal Kunwar would join us in my room. Sohan Lal went on to become a successful producer and director, and made *Sanyasi* and *Dus Nambari* with Manoj Kumar.

One morning, while at the *dhaba,* when the four of us had just ordered our toast and tea, Ganda Ram, who was busy smoking his hookah, lounging on a charpoy, gestured me to approach him. When I was close enough, he roared in Punjabi, "Your coming here and eating without paying for it can be tolerated. But now that you are bringing your chums (*chamchas*) along with you, I will not take it." Loud as he was, my friends heard him clearly. When he saw them get up from their seats, Ganda Ram's heart melted and he served them breakfast personally. Satisfied, we went our own way. At night, when I was returning to Kurla alone, I found Ganda Ram asleep outdoors on his charpoy, snoring merrily and disturbing the surrounding's peace. I shook his leg and told him to move inside as the dew may make him sick. He ignored my offer to take the charpoy inside and instead, said, "You go away from here and don't worry about me. Shiv*ji* will take care of me." On hearing this, I couldn't control myself and said jokingly, "How can Shiva and Parvati take care of you when they are peacefully asleep in heaven?" He got up with a sudden start, pushed me away and drowned me in a deluge of cuss words. This left me stunned. Next day onwards, I was barred from entering his eatery. I was so broke that I had to go without food for three days. I just didn't know who to approach for help. Neither I, nor my three friends had a telephone. On the third night, when I reached home, I found Ganda Ram sitting on my doorstep. I don't know what came over him, but he got up, gave me a tight hug and started sobbing. I cried too. Then he stuffed ₹200 into my pocket, thereby lifting the ban on my entry from his restaurant. The next morning, when he saw me in the toilet queue, he told me to come and have breakfast soon.

When I narrated the incident to Manoj Kumar, he said, "You have to be lucky to get to know such good-hearted people. Another such person is Homi Sethna, whom you introduced me to. And look at me today, Hari Krishna Goswami has gone from being Gangu Teli to Manoj Kumar." Interestingly, Manoj Kumar's pet name is Ghulu. Jitendra is Billu and I am Ranjhu. We address each other by these names till date.

Manoj Kumar was on the express train to success. His

life changed, and along with it, his lifestyle and status did too. Manoj has a unique quality. Anyone going to him for a favour will never hear a no, as if the word doesn't even exist in his vocabulary. He also doesn't believe in making excuses. I know how perceptive and sensitive he is. Apart from me, Jitendra Billu, Kewal P Kashyap and Sita Ram have been his close friends. They may have never gone to him for anything, but it would only be a matter of time before Manoj Kumar sensed their need and fulfilled it. There is this one thing that he always said, which was very typical of him, "*Dosti ho ya mohabbat, yeh ki nahi jaati, bas ho jaati hai. Isliye jo dil ko achcha lagey us se dosti yeh jaan ke karo ke woh kaun aur kya hai, na ki us ke paas kya hai aur kitna hai.*" (Be it in friendship or love, you don't have to do anything, it just happens. So before becoming friends with someone, think about who and what that person is like, instead of what and how much he possesses.) I have learnt a lot from him in life. He too agrees that his other friends and I have influenced him positively and that he has benefitted from our association. It fills me with immense pride to see his photographs in magazines and newspapers.

Besides Manoj, I have had friends in this city who continue to have the same place in my heart as they did many years ago. Like Rakhee Gulzar, Amitabh and Ajitabh Bachchan, Ranjit, BB Bhalla, Tabassum, Zahida Sahay, Vinod Khanna's brother Pramod Khanna, Nimmi*ji* and Kumar Gaurav. As for those who are no more, I can never forget them – Balraj Sahni, Krishen Chopra, Sunil Dutt, Nargis *bhabhi*, Rajendra Kumar, Naresh Kumar, Ali Raza, Pran *saheb*, Vinod Khanna, Prakash Mehra and Idris Dehlvi. It has never been a one-way relationship with these people. I have constantly been showered with their love and have never found any bank where I could go and deposit all that love and keep it safe forever. I want to dedicate Javed Akhtar's song to these wonderful people:

'*Chithhi na koi sandes, jane hai woh
kaunsa des jahan tum chale gaye.*'

(No letter or a message, I wonder where
it is that you have gone.)

When I lived in Kurla, there was a single charpoy in my room. Whenever Manoj Kumar would come, we would take turns sleeping on it and on a mattress on the floor. At times, while waiting to fall asleep, we would spend hours talking, which was mostly Manoj. I remember he told me two beautiful stories at that time. I thought they would be very difficult to make into movies and that they would take years to complete. But Manoj's fervour for them was unshakeable and so I kept my thoughts to myself. The stories eventually took the form of two super-hit movies – *Upkar* and *Purab Aur Pashchim*. Even Raj Kapoor admired Manoj's filmmaking, and, in fact, once told Manoj, in my presence, that people could learn a lot from his films.

Manoj is always striving to do something new and innovative and often says, "One shouldn't do things that everyone does." He had made this his overriding principle as an actor, writer, director and producer. Even his style of script- and screenplay-writing was unique. Most writers would go to quiet places like a hill station to write in peace, without any interferences. But not him. What he did was totally exceptional. He would book a bogey in the Rajdhani Express, which would leave from Bombay at around 4:30 pm and reach Delhi the next morning, only to take the train back to Bombay the same evening. He would repeat this twice or thrice a week. He would write copiously once in the train and would finish the script during the journey. He would take his assistant director along with him, and his cook to take care of his food.

Pran *saheb* and Prem Chopra have been the greatest villains that the Indian film industry has seen. Their portrayal of their roles was so authentic that they would often invoke the feeling of hatred in people. However, according to these two stalwarts, it was Manoj Kumar who managed to change this perception about them through his films, much to their happiness.

Everyone knows that Manoj Kumar is a capable and successful actor, writer, director and producer, and a recipient of the Dada Saheb Phalke Award for his talent, but very few people know that he is also a good homeopathy practitioner. Only those who go from one doctor to another for a cure to their maladies would know this. After all the running around, if they get free medication from Manoj Kumar that will cure their ailment, why won't they be pleased? Even Ashok Kumar, the doyen of the film industry, dabbled in homeopathy, but Manoj Kumar treated him too with his expertise in homeopathy.

Once I took my wife to Manoj Kumar for a problem she was facing. A homeopath normally starts by asking the patient details about his/her life and lifestyle, before deciding on the course of treatment. Like a good doctor, Manoj too understood the entire history of my wife's ailment. He then wrote a prescription and asked her to update him in a couple of days. She took the medicine and felt better, but forgot to call him. After a week, he called her himself. As soon as I said hello, he sternly asked me to pass on the phone to my wife. When Shashi spoke into the phone, he asked her, sounding surprised, "Oh, so you are still alive? My medicines did work!" And, my wife couldn't stop laughing and neither could Manoj.

The name of both our respective wives is Shashi, which means full moon. While the full moon in the sky offers a sense of calmness, the same does not necessarily hold true for the Shashis on earth. One can never know when, along with all the love they shower, one might be at the receiving end of their fury! Let me end the chapter on this note.

Nargis

It is said that when a person's good fortunes take a bad turn, it embitters them, and to use a Hindi phrase, '*Nani yaad aa jati hai*'. (To be at one's wit's end.) This is particularly true for Nargis. She has had to quite literally 'remember her *nani*' (maternal grandmother) numerous times in her life!

Dilipa Devi was Nargis' *nani*. She belonged to Balia in Uttar Pradesh. She was married at the age of twelve and widowed at thirteen. As per the archaic traditions followed back then, her head was shaved off, was given a drab piece of white cloth, which was a sorry excuse for a sari, had to walk barefoot, sit on the floor and eat her meals, and sleep on the floor on a durrie. She would have to walk quite a distance to the well to fetch water. Even talking to anyone at home or outside was prohibited.

Ironically, however, it seemed that it wasn't a crime to be exploited sexually by her own relatives. It was apparently not a big deal. In my opinion, it is these orthodox and rather unacceptable beliefs and practices created foolishly by some self-professed agents of their community that forced several lower caste Hindus to denounce their religion and convert to other religions. What choice did they have?

Anyway, what has to happen, happens. Despite what Dilipa Devi had to go through, God had already decided his plan of action for her. The time finally came which rid Dilipa Devi of her predicament. Good times seemed to be in the offing. On one fateful hot afternoon, when, like every other day, she set out to the well to fetch water barefoot, she heard a stranger's voice, asking her for water to quench his thirst. Dilipa Devi froze in shock. It had been ages since anyone had spoken to her. Meanwhile, on seeing Dilipa's get-up, her shaved head and her struggle in walking on the burning sandy path, the stranger immediately understood her pathetic situation. As soon as he drank the water, he told her, "I have understood your pain. I have read the story that your face tells. Now, just forget about all your worries and come with me. Just think that Allah has sent me only to get you."

On hearing him, without uttering a word, Dilipa Devi held his hand, and without any fear, left with the stranger. His name was Miya Jaan. He was a Muslim, and an expert and popular Sarangi player who accompanied the *tawaifs of kothas* in Banaras. They started living as man and wife, and the very next year, a daughter was born to them. Their joy knew no bounds. Dilipa said to her husband, "*Aaj door hua andhera; ab jab main teri aur tu mera, toh bas savera hi savera.*" (Today, the darkness has come to an end; now that I am yours and you are mine, there is only sunshine and more sunshine.)

The baby was named Jaddan Begum. Even before she entered adolescence, her magical voice had created ripples. She was not only put under the tutelage of Bade Ghulam Ali Khan and his brother, Barkat Ali Khan, but even the queen of music of those days, Begum Akhtar, trained the young girl. The result, of course, was phenomenal. This is how Dilipa Devi's daughter Jaddan Begum transformed into Jaddan Bai and remained so for the rest of her life. The magic of her voice spread from Banaras, Agra and Allahabad to Lucknow, Kanpur and Calcutta. She drowned in the applause that her singing generated. She travelled through the big cities, while earning a big name and making big money. She had her mother Dilipa Devi's support throughout her journey. After the demise of Miya Jaan, the mother and daughter stood by each other and travelled from one city to another. That became their destiny. But when they came to Lucknow, their lives took a dramatic turn.

The people of Lucknow are known for their innate sense of etiquette, and the love and respect they harbour for one another. Nature too has supported this quality of the city abundantly, making it culturally rich. It barely comes as a surprise then that Jaddan Bai's voice found avid admirers there. While catering to the demands of her listeners, Jaddan Bai went on tirelessly, until her health couldn't take it anymore. She was admitted to a big hospital in Lucknow for treatment. The student doctor who was assigned to Jaddan Bai had come there from Rawalpindi for his training period, before heading off abroad. This boy, who belonged to a respected Punjabi family, while treating the patient, became a patient himself. He was afflicted by love, which, as Manoj Kumar says, just happens. The fire of love in his patient was equally intense.

It was a classic case of, '*Rog badhta gaya jyun jyun dawa ki.*' (The illness only got graver with every dose of medicine.) While the boy forgot all about his foreign trip, the girl too lost track of her destination. She, who had lit the lamp of love in thousands of hearts with her music, found herself afflicted by the same obsession. And what to say about the boy's insane love! Irrespective of whether she performed in Calcutta, Kanpur or anywhere else, he found himself there. The story of their love was unending. In this story, the heroine was Jaddan Bai, a patient at a Lucknow hospital, and the hero, the doctor from Rawalpindi, was Mohan Babu. Then came the proposal for marriage. She didn't answer immediately, but in her silence one could clearly hear the sound of the *shehnai* playing, which lasted a long time. Jaddan Bai was thirty at the time and a mother of two. Mohan Babu, twenty-six. In 1928, both of them were married. In 1929, in the first week of June, they became parents to a beautiful baby girl. Since the father was Hindu and mother Muslim, the child's name became a dilemma for her parents. While the mother named her daughter Fatima, her father called her Tejaswari. While introducing his wife, Mohan Babu would call her Jaya Devi and Jaddan Bai, in turn, would introduce her husband as Abdur Rashid. So after much deliberation, it was decided that they would register two names for the child: Fatima Abdur Rashid and Tejaswari Mohan.

However, the child, a product of mixed-faith love, found it difficult to deal with two different names as she grew up. Life started again and this time the journey had Jaddan, Mohan and their daughter in it, but there was still no destination in sight. They say that when God bestows his blessings on you, the road to the future makes itself visible. Fate brought the three of them to Bombay and they found their elusive port of call here. The home they found here became their final stop and their own. It exists even today. Located on Marine Drive, it was, and is still, called Chateau Marine. They saw life on the streets of Bombay running, stopping, falling, getting up and running again. The mesmerising view of the sun rising and setting remains even today, but unfortunately, those who witnessed it from that house are no more. Life is a caravan… some people leave it, only for new people to join. And life simply goes on. In Chateau Marine too, people kept joining in. Adding Jaddan Bai, Mohan Babu, Fatima, Akhtar Hussain, Anwar Hussain, Iqbal (Akhtar's wife), Rashida (Anwar's wife) and their children, the total came up to nineteen! The twentieth member to join them and exercise control over all of them was the lady with the powerful voice, Fatima's grandmother (*Nani*), Dilipa Devi.

She could often be spotted outside the house, sitting on a charpoy, smoking from the hookah. She would invariably be wearing a *ghaghra* and a *jhabba*. Love, respect, service and prayer were her anchors, but if she lost her temper, she would turn highly abusive.

Jaddan Bai ruled the household. She made sure her home reverberated with the sounds of laughter and music. She organised musical evenings in her house which, at times, continued till late at night. Some guests who were always a part of this *mehfil* were Dilip Kumar, Allah Rakha, Bade Ghulam Ali Khan, K Asif, Ramanand Sagar, Naushad and Majrooh Sultanpuri, among many others. They would enjoy the evenings on the ground floor hall of Chateau Marine, comfortably sitting on mattresses laid down on the floor. The evening would see someone reciting their poems, while someone else would regale the guests with funny stories. On one hand, you had the guests, their laughter and their applause, and on the other was Fatima's *nani*, sitting on the charpoy, smoking her hookah. Her abuses would compete with the sounds of the clapping. Hookah in hand, she would start hurling abuses in her native Bhojpuri language. Then she wouldn't care whether she was standing in front of Dilip Kumar or Mehboob. Her monologue went somewhat like this: "*Abe, jao ab tum log, nahi toh yeh hookah tumhari %&*$$ mein daal dungi, muh se hookeh ka dhuan nikalta nazar ayega ghar pahunche tak.*" (Now get lost all of you! Or else, I will shove this hookah in your backside and you will be able to see the smoke from your mouth until you reach home.)

The guests, however, thinking this was a part of the entertainment, would tell Anwar and Akhtar how much they enjoyed themselves and ask them about the next session. One fine day, out of the blue, a gentleman from Baliya's neighbouring town, Amroha, turned up with a story to tell Jaddan Bai. He came to Chateau Marine straight from the station. It was a strange sight. His clothes were dishevelled, and he didn't have a paisa in his pocket. On seeing him, Jaddan Bai, handing him her son Akhtar's *kurta pyjama*, said, "Freshen up first. Then we can listen to the story you have written." After freshening up, the man started narrating the story in a muffled, nervous voice. However, just a short while into the narration, Jaddan Bai said she would listen to the rest the next morning. She asked him to go and rest and return the next morning.

The man in question was Kamaal Amrohi. Though he reached Jaddan Bai's house straight from the station, his condition was far from straight. It was so twisted that no one could have straightened it. Not to forget that he was broke. The person who brought him out of this heart-rending situation was Jaddan Bai. Not only did she help him out, her widespread fame in the big city of Bombay too helped Kamaal Amrohi solve many of his unresolved issues. Jaddan Bai's influence helped him emerge as a producer and director. Besides, she was impressed by the way Kamaal spoke, his keen interest in the Urdu language and his skill. All his qualities truly justified his name, Kamaal! His films *Mahal* and *Pakeezah* vindicate the God's gift he possessed.

The truth is that only a seasoned goldsmith (*sunar*) can be the true judge of the authenticity of gold. Jaddan Bai had a close relationship with Mehboob Khan. She would often refer to him as a goldsmith. For a mother, all her children are pure gold, but eventually, it is for the goldsmith to determine its value. Besides, how many can know what fate has in store for them? *Na jane qismat mein kya likha hai.* (No one knows their fate.) One requires an acute vision to fathom that too. Mehboob Khan used to often joke about fate. He would ask, "Is it written in Hindi or Urdu?" The maker of films like *Najma*, *Ek Hi Raasta* and *Aurat*, Mehboob Khan not only remained a *sunar* (goldsmith) in Jaddan Bai's life, but was also her permanent guru.

When he was ready with the idea for his next film, everything was set except for the right heroine. The vision of the heroine he had in his mind didn't match with any of the actresses working in the industry. But like they say, '*Wahi hota hai jo manzoor-e-khuda hota hai*'. (Everything that happens is God's will.)

Now Mehboob Khan was a frequent visitor to Jaddan Bai's house – be it for some discussion, or as a guest at her *mehfil*. One day, he reached Jaddan Bai's house with the writer Agha Jani Kashmiri for some discussion and told her about his problem of finding the right heroine for his film. Just then, Jaddan Bai's young daughter Fatima burst into the room and started jumping up and down on the sofa, only to collapse on it, panting, once she was tired. The minute the two gentlemen saw the little bundle of energy, they found their solution to the heroine problem. That very moment, Fatima was rechristened Nargis. The film was *Taqdeer* – with a fourteen-year-old Nargis as the heroine and a thirty-three-year-old Moti Lal as the hero. The film was a super hit and Nargis' career took off instantly, changing her destiny forever.

Destiny, like the weather, changes with time. While we all have to face the vagaries of the weather, when it comes to fate, only those who brave its quirks with full faith emerge as winners. This was the case with Nargis. She continued to keep complete faith in herself and never gave up. This is not to say that there weren't any obstacles on the way or that she didn't err. After all, she was only human, not God. The love and respect she earned as an actress far exceeded the money she earned. Money is evanescent, but love and respect are the intangible wealth that cannot be measured. You can only share them and that is what Nargis did. She continued to climb the ladder of success with each film. Producers, directors and heroes craved for her to be the heroine of their films. This went on for years and she became a part of some beautiful films of the time. She left us all too soon because perhaps that was her destiny and beyond our control. But her memories have been etched in the sands of time indelibly.

Nargis's success can be compared to the heights that actors like Dilip Kumar, Raaj Kumar, Dev Anand and Balraj Sahni reached. The reason for her success can be attributed to her mother Jaddan Bai, then Mehboob Khan and then Raj Kapoor. She acknowledged that there were several people in her life whom she owed her success to.

She shot to fame with Raj Kapoor's *Aag* and continued for a long time. Mehboob Khan, who gave the young fourteen-year-old a new name and a break with *Taqdeer*, cast Nargis as Radha in *Mother India* fourteen years later. The film's success touched epic proportions. It also saw the end of the bad period that producer and director Mehboob Khan was going through at that time. Fame and wealth multiplied tremendously. Mehboob Khan was bestowed with great respect. While it's true that the entire cast contributed to the film's success, there is no doubt that Nargis did an exemplary job.

Nargis' popularity soared with the film *Aag*, and this *aag* (fire) wasn't ready to let go of the actress any time soon. So, what was this *aag*? The answer to this came after the success of *Mother India*, which saw Nargis perambulate the holy fire with her soulmate, her lifelong partner, Sunil Dutt. Their beautiful relationship can be best described in this song – *Tu mera chand main teri chandni.* (You are my moon and I your moonlight.)

They faced several roadblocks together, many allegations, but they continued their life's journey unfazed. Together, they only believed love and humanity to be their religion. Their love story became an example for others to follow. They may not be with us today, but their love for each other still serves as a reference point for those in love. Today, when I try to recollect all the memories I have of them, there are so many that it tires me out. But they keep gushing into my mind endlessly, and the pen finds itself unable to stop writing their beautiful stories. It is as if this simple story will turn into a saga. I had known Nargisji for long, but only by name. I was somewhat acquainted with her brothers and their children too. I used to love playing football and Nargisji's elder brother Akhtar Hussain was a big football fan too. It was this game that brought me closer to not only her, but the rest of their family, so much that I became a part of it.

When Nargisji married the love of her life and moved from Chateau Marine to Bandra, our bond only strengthened. I lived close to Sunil Dutt's Pali Hill house. When Nargisji came to Bandra, I started addressing her as *bhabhiji*. This relationship would never end. While initially our interaction was limited to casual chats, it eventually became intense. And since her death on May 3rd, 1981, I even became a part of the lives of her children, Sanju, Anju and Priya. They are still an integral part of my life.

When Nargis lived on Marine Drive, her brothers lived there with their families too. Though she used to spend most of her days shooting outdoors, after coming home, it used to be a tradition to interact with the excited children. It was as if Akhtar Hussain's three daughters, Rehana, Zahida and Shahida, and Nargisji were friends from birth. They were inseparable.

Though the three sisters were all rather outspoken, they were different from each other. Rehana was so homely that all responsibilities of the household lay on her shoulders, but she was as authoritative as her grandmother, Jaddan Bai. Zahida had taken after her aunt Pappu (Nargisji) when it came to looks. Meanwhile, Shahida was quite tomboyish. To use a Bombay slang, she was *bindaas*. She was a staunch devotee of Sai Baba of Shirdi. So much so that she had a temple built in his honour on the ground floor of Chateau Marine. It used to attract hordes of devotees. The three sisters were an important part of Nargisji's life because not only was she their only aunt, but also because she was crazy about the girls. They shared a unique bond. In the same house, there were two other members who started off as outsiders but became a part of the family – Amina Bai and Kasim Bhai.

When Nargis started school, her mother hired an *ayah* to take care of her needs. Her name was Amina Bai. When she came into the household to work, she brought her husband Kasim bhai along with her. He became Jaddan Bai's driver. Nargis remained under Amina Bai's care even after she became a heroine. And after her wedding, when she left her father's house as a bride, it was Kasim bhai who drove her to Bandra to her husband's home. When Kasim bhai loaded her dowry into the car, he made an addition – Amina Bai. Sunil Dutt used to say that they were a part of the dowry. They continued doing the same work in their new abode. They took care of Nargis's children in the same way that they had taken care of her. The kids, in turn, loved them equally. They would address Amina Bai as *nani* and Kasim bhai as *mamu*. Whenever Nargis and Sunil Dutt travelled, all the keys of the household used to be entrusted to Amina Bai.

Nargisji loved her husband a lot. Maybe that explains her suspicious nature, which is a common feature of many of our loved ones. I have noticed it in my wife and mother too. If Sunil Dutt had to shoot, she would immediately find out its whereabouts and who the heroine was. It was Sunil Dutt's practice that every evening after returning from the day's shoot, he would stand in front of the mirror and rehearse the lines for the next day's scene. Sunil Dutt preferred home food on the sets. And interestingly, if the scene was a romantic one, Nargis would make sure she added enough garlic and onion to the dishes. Apart from Amina Bai, Nargis was also fond of two other women. One was actress Shammi, and the other was her neighbour's daughter Asha, who was a group dancer in films, who later married famous film director Nasir Hussain. Both Nargis and Sunil Dutt loved them a lot.

Rehana married Dev Anand's friend, producer Amarjit Singh Thind. He was a happy-go-lucky man and we soon became friends. An exciting incident related to their wedding comes to mind whenever I think of them. After the rituals, when he set off to his home in Bandra with his new bride, he knew I lived nearby too. He forced me into the car in order to drop me off. When I got off, out of formality, I asked if they'd like to have anything warm or cold to drink at my place. Surprisingly, they got off and the first threshold they stepped into as husband and wife was of my house. Amarjit had studied abroad, so I knew his choice of beverage. As both of us clinked glasses, my wife and Rehana were stunned and I remember they just kept laughing at what was going on. After the first drink was finished, Rehana gestured me not to offer another one and I obliged. When I went to see them off to their car, I told Rehana that apart from Chateau Marine, she could consider this house as her *naihar* or *maika* too. Tears welled up in her eyes and I turned away to hide mine. The car departed towards her groom's place. When Nargis got to know about the incident the next day, she laughed and said, "Amarjit *aur* Raaj Grover *dono pagal hain saaley!*" (Both Amarjit and Raaj Grover are bloody mad.) On hearing Nargis' comment, Amarjit told Rehana that though her aunt wasn't mad, he could spot glimpses of madness in her. Amarjit was strange, but a colourful personality and to top it all, was a No. 1 host. No, this is not the title of a David Dhawan film, but a reality. For whatever he was, Amarjit was a wonderful person. I met him once when I was going home from Mehboob Studio. He gave me a ride saying he would drop me home, but instead drove straight to his house on Mount Mary Road and asked the driver to stop there. His face turned mischievous as soon as he saw the questioning look on my face. After that, I just listened to whatever he said. He said, "Come on, let's go up and wet our throats. The Johnny Walker and Black Label whiskies are imported; the painting on the wall is imported, as is everything in the kitchen and the living room. Only the soda and the ice are Indian. Of course, there is one more thing which is Indian, my wife and your sister, Rehana."

I thought to myself that Nargis was right about calling us both insane.

Just as we were about to open the bottles, the phone rang. It was my wife. Amarjit said right after picking up the phone, "Raaj is here with me at home. *Uska kehna hai ke tum khana kha ke so jao, main khake zara late aunga.'* (He is saying you have your food and go to sleep; he will eat here and come home late.')

When Rehana was narrating the entire scene to Nargis on the telephone, I was with Dutt *saheb* discussing Ajanta Arts' next film. On my way out, I heard Nargis say, on the phone, "*Main theek hi toh kehti hun ki pagal hain yeh dono saaley.*" (I was right to say that both of them are bloody mad.)

When Dutt *saheb* asked Nargis who she was on the phone with, she said it was just a wrong number. When I heard her reply, I was reminded of Amarjit's observation about Nargis having a mad streak in her! I strongly feel there is no successful person in this world who doesn't possess an iota of madness. Is there?

If I understood anything about Nargisji, it was that in worldly matters, she was very smart and would respect others' talents. While interacting with anyone at a function or the studio, her tone would always be soft, and she'd always wear a smile on her lips. However, I never found warmth in it. Even then, this outwardly gesture was worth appreciating. This is not to say that she was selfish. In fact, she was filled with love and compassion. She had very warm relationships with many people. Indira Gandhi was a close friend. And this was not all. When American President Jimmy Carter's mother Lillian Carter came to India, she met Nargisji. She knew how to present herself and respect the guests, and this quality of hers was commendable. Whether anyone else understood Nargisji or not, her three nieces did very well. I also feel that her three children – Sanju, Anju and Priya – are the luckiest children to have such loving parents.

I have so much to say about Nargisji that if I tried, I think I will run out of paper and ink. Our relationship was that of a mother and son. Being away from my parents, I once again understood what a mother's love meant in a person's life.

Everyone knows that at any function or gathering, Nargisji used to maintain an air of formality. But if anyone had a special place in her heart, she would become one with them, shedding all that formality. Typically, she would start addressing them with a curse word, although endearingly. Like, '*woh saala*', '*harami hai*', or '*woh pagal hai*'. This meant that the said person had found a permanent place in her heart. If she didn't speak like this, it seemed like a dessert without sugar. I can count myself among those fortunate people who were subjected to her affectionate expletives.

When she found out about my girlfriend Rosy in Darjeeling, she angrily said, "*Woh saala Raaj kahan ghayab hai itne dinon se? Ullu ka pattha phone tak nahi uthata. Gaya hoga saala Darjeeling apni chhammak chhallo Rosy se milne. Mujhe dar hai ke agar us uchakki saali se shadi kar dali toh Rosy rahegi na roti, na ghar ka rahega na ghat ka. Mere ghar woh us ko sath lekar aya toh pehle iske ki woh andar paaon rakhe, main darvaze par hi uski tange tod doongi.*" (Where is that idiot Raaj? Bugger doesn't even pick up the phone. He must've gone to Darjeeling, to meet that girl of his, Rosy. I'm worried that he'll marry her, and then things won't be as 'rosy' anymore. If he brings her to my home, I'll break his legs at the gate itself.)

I got to know of this episode the next day from my close friend Sarvar Hussain, who was Nargisji's nephew. He also told me that he felt the same way as Pappu *bua*. I was so hurt on hearing this that I took recourse to alcohol and don't even remember when Sarvar Hussain left my house.

I got to go to Darjeeling just before the shooting of the film *Man ka Meet* was about to start. Any shooting at a different location requires a lot of preparation – government permissions, hotel reservations and *dak* bungalow bookings, and even meals for the entire unit. Dutt *saheb* had entrusted me with all the arrangements. Everything was accomplished wonderfully and the film's director, Subba Rao, was very happy with my work. After he reached Calcutta, he sang praises of me to Dutt *saheb* on the phone.

When I reached Darjeeling, Subba Rao from Madras was with me for location hunting for the various scenes of the film. Both of us got busy with our respective duties. During this time, we met a beautiful girl from Darjeeling named Rosy. Her beauty was captivating, to say the least. Though much older than me, Subba Rao felt the same way about the girl. She was related to the owner of the hotel where the director was put up. The owner was British and had departed from the world a couple of years ago. Subba Rao told me that though there was still time for the shooting of Som Dutt's *Man ka Meet*, it looked like Rosalyn had already found her *Man ka Meet* in Raaj Grover. I hadn't even found the time to interact with her properly yet, but Subba Rao had already passed on the information to the producer who, in turn, relayed it to the person who used to call me '*Ullu ka pattha*'!

In two months, the shooting began and within two weeks of that, Subba Rao, actor Om Prakash and Achla Sachdev met Rosy's Nepalese mother and fixed a date for our engagement. On the set date, apart from the above-mentioned three people, Som Dutt, Leena Chandavarkar, Vinod Khanna and my friend, Sarvar Hussain, were also present. It was also decided that I would wed Rosy in Mumbai on February 14, 1968. Two days before the wedding, Rosy, along with her mother and uncle, reached Mumbai. The next day, her sister arrived from London with her husband. After the demise of their father, it was the brother-in-law who had taken care of the family, so he held an important place in the family. The day he arrived, he set a condition for the wedding – that I would have to convert to Christianity early next morning at the church. I was devastated. I was caught off-guard by my own inner conflict. First and foremost, I had to deal with Nargis *bhabhi*'s anger. When Dutt *saheb* told her about the entire episode, she was so cross that she said I couldn't enter their house anymore. Another problem was that for my wedding the next day at the Arya Samaj, my parents were to reach Mumbai by the afternoon flight. The third was, of course, the conversion part. I couldn't think straight and was at a loss. After giving it a lot of thought, I decided to say no. This time, the bomb exploded on Rosy. Two years of our courtship and love tragically ended simply because of one reason.

My parents arrived on the scheduled date and when they saw me looking like a fused bulb, they immediately inferred that something was wrong. After hearing the entire story, all my mother wanted to do was to meet Nargis *bhabhi*. The next day, when we went to meet her, Nargisji looked ecstatic but my mother looked upset. Nargisji asked me to leave them alone. When I returned, I saw my mother smiling from ear to ear and Nargisji laughing. I couldn't understand what had transpired between the two. They had met each other a couple of times earlier, but it seemed like with this meeting, the two had understood each other completely. Nargisji said, "Your mother is a very simple person. Knowing that you were to marry an English girl, she had been taking English tuitions. And now that the wedding is not taking place, she is regretful that she spent so much of Lala*ji*'s money on learning English."

"*Saare paise waste ho gaye.* (All the money is wasted.) What to do now?"

The next day, when I reached my office, I saw Dutt *saheb* was lost in his thoughts. As soon as he saw me, he burst out laughing and when he could stop, he said, "So what if your mother's money got wasted. I too wasted money at your party in Kalimpong." He kept laughing over this for a long time after that.

One fine day, I told Nargisji and my parents, "I will get whatever I am destined to. I don't have anyone who would wish anything ill for me. So, *wahi hoga jo manzoor-e-khuda hoga*." (Only what God wills, happens.)

Nargisji, Dutt *saheb* and Balraj Sahni's efforts bore fruit and soon I was getting good proposals. It went on for some time in a casual manner. One day, my mother complained to Nargisji saying, "He is as much your son as he is mine. I know that this Darjeeling one wasn't his first affair. He has had a few more before that. His father and my other two sons are not like this. Then why has he turned out this way?" Nargisji blamed my mother for this when she replied, "*Jab yeh bachcha tha toh isey nehlati toh aap hi thi. Sabun lagane ke baad, nehlate samay shayad dil ke neeche laga hua sabun aap ne theek se poncha nahin tha. Issi karan se sabun ki yeh fislan ban gayi hai.*" (You used to bathe him as a kid, didn't you? Perhaps you weren't careful in washing all the soap off, especially near his heart, and that's what causes it to slip so often.)

Now, the search for the right girl for me began – the one who was made for me and for whom I was made. The search was taking place in Delhi, Mumbai and Kolkata by the people I knew in these places. I may have lost out on one girl from the mountains, but it seemed that I was ultimately fated to get a girl from there. My family found the girl who was meant for me in the hills of Srinagar. In the lines of my palm, I can read her name now – Shashi Vasant.

August 18, 1968, was the day our lives became one. A few days before the wedding, I confided in her about all my flings. I even showed her my photograph with Rosy, which my wife has still preserved in her album. When I asked her the reason for this, she said she'd show it to our kids saying, "Such a beautiful girl could have been their mother, but unfortunately that was not to be." I consider my wife a gift from God for changing my life for the better. We have two beautiful children – a girl and a boy.

A couple of days before the wedding, when I took Shashi to meet Nargisji, I told her, "I hope you won't break my legs now." Laughingly, she muttered '*Ullu*', but put a brake on saying *ka pattha*. With a sheepish grin, she put her hand on Shashi's head and said, "*Yeh hone wali nahi, balki ab meri bahu ho chuki hai*." (She is not a daughter-in-law to-be, but is already one to me.)

From this story, you can very well gauge that my wedding was quite dramatic. My parents and family were happy, but the happiest person was indeed Nargisji. It was as if she were at her brother's or son's wedding. I will forever remain in debt for the love she showered on me. Many of my friends, including Shashi Kapoor, Prem Chopra and Prakash Mehra, were present at my wedding. However, the love that Balraj Sahni and Yash Chopra showered on me and my wife is something I will never forget in my entire life. That memory is my life's most precious treasure.

When Shashi met Nargisji the second time, she started telling my wife stories about my past. The daughter-in-law told her 'mother-in-law', "I have reached here after passing an exam. I needed new books to get here, but will make do with second-hand ones." Nargisji liked her response so much that every year, both the ladies would observe *Karva Chauth* together, praying, thirsty and on an empty stomach, for the long lives of their respective husbands. This became a ritual of sorts.

The very next year after our wedding, when our daughter Jalpa was born, Nargisji couldn't contain her happiness. On her first birthday, we invited around hundred guests. On the occasion, from afternoon till evening, Nargisji was present with Shashi, helping her out in every possible way. Just before the cake-cutting ceremony, Dutt *saheb* too arrived with their daughter Priya. After the party, only when all the guests had left did Nargisji and Dutt *saheb* bid us adieu. I can't even imagine doing justice to what both of them mean to me in my life. Even to imagine it would be a travesty.

Nargisji was quite popular in political circles. After the 1971 war, the then President, VV Giri's daughter, Mohini Giri, set up the War Widows Association for the widows of war heroes. Mohini Giri certainly has to be saluted for this commendable effort. The association's headquarters were in Delhi, but Nargisji was made in charge of its Bombay operations. The wife of the Governor of Maharashtra at that time, Ali Yavar Jung, contributed a lot towards this cause and was a big help to Nargisji. Meanwhile, in Bombay, Nargisji put the responsibility of organising a show, under the association's aegis, on my shoulders. My job was to convince some stars to devote their time to the show, *Ek Sham Kaum Ke Shahidon Ki Bewaon Ke Naam*. The proceeds of the show were to go to the widows.

After two weeks of running around, I got Sanjeev Kumar, Shashi Kapoor, Shankar Jai Kishan, Shailendra, Asha Bhosle, Talat Mahmood and Mukesh on board for the programme. The show took place in the Birla Matoshree Hall and was a grand success. In the same week, Mrs. Jung organised a meeting in Raj Bhawan to discuss the ways and means of generating funds for the association. Nargis immediately handed over a cheque of two lakh rupees which we had earned through the show. She praised me so much regarding the success of the programme that instead of being flattered, I felt embarrassed. About fifteen war widows were also present at the meeting. In the meeting, there also was an innocent child no more than two or three years old. He was accompanying his beautiful widowed mother. There was something unique in that child. I went to him, took permission from his mother and took him towards the Raj Bhavan kitchen. There, he was treated to ice cream. He said his mother called him Sajid. When I returned to the hall, I saw that Mrs. Jung had organised a sort of high tea for those present. Both she and Nargis were busy playing the perfect hostesses. Sajid, meanwhile, just wouldn't leave my side. When I gestured to his mother to take him, I don't know why but she simply turned her face, her eyes welling with tears. It was only later that I came to know that the child was still in his mother's womb when his father sacrificed his life for the country. He had seen his father's photograph and had heard his name, but wasn't fortunate enough to have known him. I got extremely emotional on hearing this.

Nargisji, meanwhile, had watched the entire scene rather attentively and became cautious. Apparently, even Mrs. Jung found out about the episode. She was on the verge of getting me and the lady in question together when Nargisji stepped in, in the nick of time to tell her that I was a married man with a kid. That ended matters, but Nargis was ready to bury me alive that very moment. She asked me the same question she had asked my mother, "*Kya woh sabun ki fislan abhi bhi tere dil ke paas vaise hi hai jaise pehle thi?*" (Does the soap still cause your heart to slip?)

What could I say? I was both embarrassed and ashamed. I heard her say in clear and strict words, "*Sudhar ja, ullu ke patthe.* You have such a nice wife, by God's grace. *Teri Ma toh bholi hai jo yeh sabun ki fislan na mita saki, ab mujhe Shashi se hi kehna padega ki woh aisa kare jo uski saas na kar payi.*" (It's high time you mended your ways, idiot... I'll have to ask Shashi to do something her mother-in-law was too innocent to do.)

Nargisji' life story may be one, but it is replete with chapters that reflect the various aspects of her personality. One of these aspects came to light from a black-and-white photo taken in Delhi's Safdarjung Hospital. It shows her humane and noble nature. The person, a patient in the hospital, was, in fact, a Pakistani soldier and had connections through past generations with the town of Baliya. He had been brought to Delhi from Dhaka as a POW. And Nargisji was in Delhi on Indira Gandhi's request. So the two friends just decided to visit the hospital to check whether the injured soldiers were being given proper care or not. When Nargisji reached the patient in question, even before the photographer from Ajanta Arts, Panchal, could click a few pictures, small talk led to the realisation that he was Nargisji's *nani*'s (grandmother) neighbour's grandson. The lady at the back in the picture was the soldier's late sister's daughter, whom Nargisji had arranged for to come to Delhi to see her *Mamu*. This picture by Panchal really tugged at Nargis' heartstrings, so much so that '*Nani toh na thee par yaad uski aati chali gayi.*' (Though there was no nani, she couldn't stop thinking of her.)

Till the time Nargisji lived, her name shone like a star in the sky, but never once did ego creep into her being. She was always rooted to the ground. It was like her heart was a magnificent palace that housed all her family members, and after her wedding, it belonged to someone who loved her more than anyone else, Sunil Dutt. Her two brothers and people like me were privileged to spend some great times there too.

I developed close and personal relationships with her family members that exist even today. I would specifically like to mention Zahida here. Our relationship is more special mainly because she looks a lot like her Pappu *bua*. It is natural to remember Nargisji when you look at her. She even resembles her in her mannerisms and nature. Whenever I come to India, I make it a point to visit Zahida. To give an analogy, it's like anyone who goes to Agra has to visit the Taj Mahal. I consider myself fortunate to have had such wonderful people in my life. They are a gift to me from the Almighty just like my wife and my children are. Sahay *saheb* has a similar gift in the form of Zahida and she is fortunate too.

While reminiscing about Zahida, my mind went back to May 3, 1981, the black day in our lives when Nargisji left us for her final journey. That day I saw her in a sleep that was permanent. I remember sitting in front of her, trying to control my tears that promised to surge any moment. Just then, I felt someone's hands on my shoulder. It was Zahida, telling me tearfully, "Now no one will call you *ullu ka pattha*, Raaj." At this point, the tears just broke all the dams and spurted out in full force. I simply broke down and it felt as if along with the tears, our entire relationship was washing away.

Prakash Mehra

This is the story of a man, who despite being named Prakash (light), battled with pitch darkness for a very long time. He had complete faith in God and it never wavered regardless of the testing situations he found himself in. He had the same dogged faith in his abilities too. Considering it a period of struggle ordained upon by God, he continued his fight. However, no one could fathom why success was playing truant for this well-meaning, hardworking and God-fearing man. It was only when he was on the verge of giving up his fight did lady luck smile on him. The darkness that had enveloped him eventually cleared, leading him to a path that was as bright as his name and was strewn with sanguine luminescence. His first film as a director was *Haseena Maan Jayegi*. The film was a hit and he met with sweet success that had been eluding him for a long time.

The following bit is best said in Hindi: *Pareekshaon ki zanjeer uss ne tod di aur kal tak jo lawaaris tha aaj apna khoon paseena baha ke aur bina kisi hera pheri ke is maya nagri mein muqadar ka sikandar ban gaya.* (Breaking the shackles of his tribulations, he who was a vagabond till just yesterday, has today, with blood and sweat, and without treachery or deceit, in this city of dreams, conquered fate.)

It was only that it took some time for his fate to unravel its real plans for him. He was a very discerning man and had an innate ability when it came to ascertaining the difference between real and fake. It was a God-given gift. After all, like a true jeweller, he managed to polish the raw diamond named Amitabh Bachchan in such a beautiful way that he shone like a true star, spreading light in all directions.

When we became friends, he was still single. We had a common friend named Sateeyan Chaudhary. When you understand the other person, they become your friend for life and if you can't, it doesn't take much time or effort for distances to emerge. The three of us were rather different from one another. Prakash was a poet at heart. Sateeyan possessed a very clear thought process. Though intrinsically a poet, he didn't indulge in poetry. He had the gift of the gab though. As for me, I stuck to my work and considered love and hard work my religion. And I could never understand people thoroughly. I took them at face value. The three of us got together and became friends, but the uncertainty of when things might change always loomed large over our friendship. There were two incidents in our alliance that made us unhappy, where we displeased each other.

Prakash Mehra was born on July 13, which is also my wife Shashi's birthdate. So every year on that day, a bouquet from Prakash's house would arrive at my place in Bandra. Once it so happened that when Prakash's driver dropped the bouquet at my place, I noticed that it was the same one that I had sent him in the morning. When he got to know that I was hurt, he apologised, putting the blame on his driver. Apparently, while he had asked the driver to pick up a bouquet on his way to Bandra, he decided to pocket the money and recycle one of the several bouquets that Prakash had received. He didn't even see our card that was kept with the flowers. Prakash was so annoyed with the driver that he sacked him the next day. When I got to know this, I felt sad for the driver and after much cajoling from my side, he rehired him.

Prakash Mehra would often write the songs for his films along with lyricist Anjaan. When I announced my second film, *Thikana* in the film journal *Screen*, I added Prakash Mehra's name as the lyricist without informing him. When Prakash saw the ad, he was not only surprised but also distraught. He telephoned me and told me, "Don't you know that I don't write songs for any films other than mine? Then why have you included my name in the ad?" Now, it was my turn to face his resentment. Without wasting any time, I reached his bungalow at around nine in the night. To placate him, I said, "Prakash, when your films become successful, I feel as happy as you because I don't consider them as just your films, but as mine too. And I feel proud of your success." When he heard me, he went silent for a while and called for a glass for me too. Just after two drinks, he said with a laugh, "Let's start a school like Asha Chandra, not for acting, but for fooling people." Moments later, letting go of his ire, he added, "When are you introducing me to your director, Mahesh Bhatt?" Believe me, from that very minute, my friend and well-wisher Prakash Mehra came closer to my heart. He was the one to write the title song for my film. What happened was, one day post-midnight, he called me on the phone and asked me to write down the *mukhda*. He said he was actually four drinks down and wasn't sure if he'd remember the lines in the morning. The *mukhda* went something like this:

Aasman ho chchat meri, dharti mera sirhana ho
Jahan mile pyar mujhe woh mera thikana ho

(Let the sky be my roof, the earth where I lay my head,
Where I find love, is where I am home.)

Ever since we became friends, he had always been ahead of me. The success he had been running after for years was now following him. The love for poetry held Sateeyan and Prakash together. I was focussing steadfastly on work too, hoping I would be face to face with success one day. My determination and work earned me people's love alright, but money still remained a distant dream. Carrying on with my dream, I started a movie titled *Taaqat*, with Narendra Bedi, Rakhee, Vinod Khanna, Parveen Babi and Pran. I had only ₹5,000 in my bank account at that time. When I got an advertisement designed to be carried in *Screen*, I got to know that I had to pay ₹20,000 along with the design. I had taken a chance with this move and I could clearly see myself losing the bet already. When Nargis *bhabhi* came to know of my predicament, she immediately called the General Manager of *Screen* and Indian Express, JC Jain, and told him to accept my design without charging me a single paisa and to print it that very Friday. She assured him that he would get his money within three months. "If it doesn't happen, call me and you will find your cheque on the table the same day," she told him. Even if I were to spend my entire life thanking Nargis *bhabhi*, I would still not have paid off all my debts to her.

My relationship with my friends was such that they always stood me in good stead. The day the ad appeared in *Screen*, I got a call from a distributor in West Bengal, Bansal, telling me, "I agree to all your terms, but I will be the distributor of your film in Bengal." Sateeyan Chaudhary and Prakash had called up all their distributor friends and even before the movie could begin screening, it was making money. My bank account soared from a meagre ₹5,000 to a massive ₹7.5 lakh. It seemed like I was also on the path to success now. There were hurdles on the way, but thanks to the support of friends, they vanished into thin air even before they could rear their ugly heads.

An individual supports himself in life in two ways – either through *aap kamai* (one's own earnings) or through *baap kamai* (father's earnings). The three of us were proud to belong to the former category. Only those who have experienced this will understand the importance of being self-made. With his hard work, Prakash accumulated a lot of wealth, property, cars and servants and left it to his three sons as *baap kamai* and turned to the merciful one who had blessed him for the goodness of his heart. Success never left his side till the end. A man makes mistakes. He is able to accept them sometimes and at other times, he can't. Even Prakash Mehra found himself embroiled in the matters of the heart. He was, after all, only human, not God. This clash of hearts was so intense, it reminds me of something Ghalib said:

Dostdaar dushman hai eitmad-e-dil maloom
Aah be-asar dekhi, nala naarsa paya
Rishte woh nahin jis mein roz baat ho
Rishte woh bhi nahin ke roz mulaqat ho
Rishte toh woh hain jis mein bhale hi kitni dooriyan hon magar dil mein
Hamesha un ki yaad ho

(To my beloved enemy whom my heart refuses to trust

My cries and sighs are rendered effectless
A relationship is not made by talking every day
It is also not made by meeting every day
A relationship is that in which, despite the long distance,
the memory of the person always remains in your heart)

This was the relationship I had with Prakash Mehra and I still cherish those memories in my heart.

Rajendra Kumar

Yaad a rahi hai... teri yaad a rahi hai
This famous line is from a song from producer Rajendra Kumar's film *Love Story* in which he launched his son Kumar Gaurav. The film was a super hit and the hero, played by his son, and the above-mentioned song was declared the very reason for its success. This father-son success story was the only topic of discussion for many years. And once again, today, as I write this very interesting chapter on Rajendra Kumar, I go back to those heady days.

At the time of partition, Rajendra Kumar, along with his parents, three younger brothers and two sisters left his ancestral city of Sialkot, which, after being on the map of India for hundreds of years, suddenly found itself in Pakistan. As destined, the family landed in a new and unknown place as helpless refugees. They started staying on the ground floor of a tiny old building in the Sabzi Mandi area of Delhi.

Neither did he have a job nor any money in his pocket. This problem haunted Rajendra Kumar for quite some time. With nowhere to go and no one to pass his time with, he would take refuge in the only talkies in the area, Robin Talkies. His only pastime was watching films of his favourite actors like

Ashok Kumar, Moti Lal, Dilip Kumar, Nargis, Suraiya, Noor Jahan, Nadia and John Cawas, Gope and Yaqoob.

As they say, '*Allah meherbaan toh gadha pehelvan.*' (If God is kind, even the impossible is possible.) This maxim proved to be true in Rajendra Kumar's case. God had decided to change his fate. It was as if the Lord decreed, "You have been blessed with such good looks, make use of them, help yourself. I am with you. Do something which will end your struggle." And lady luck smiled on him.

His father had gifted Rajendra Kumar an expensive watch on his birthday. That was it. In a few days itself, he sold the watch at Chandni Chowk for ₹63. He bought a train ticket for ₹13, kept the remaining ₹50 securely in his pocket and with just a couple of shirts and pyjamas and a single pair of trousers, he got into the Frontier Mail's Class III bogey meant for poor passengers and arrived in the city of dreams, Bombay, to realise his dream.

According to Rajendra Kumar, there was a man called Sethi, also from Sialkot, living in Kurla, who had good contacts in the film industry. He was quite popular too. On arriving in Bombay, Sethi was the first man Rajendra Kumar met. He became Sethi's shadow.

In a unique coincidence, another aspiring actor came to Mr. Sethi and shared the room with Rajendra Kumar. He was Balraj Dutt, who later came to be known as Sunil Dutt. Both the young boys were busy chasing their dreams in the city of glamour. And, Sethi *saheb*'s caring concern for them and contacts in the industry helped the young men tremendously. They remained grateful to Sethi *saheb* till the day they lived. Who knew then what heights these two boys were meant to attain in the film industry!

According to Rajendra Kumar, though he wielded a great deal of influence with the film folk, Sethi *saheb* worked at the ticket window of New Empire Cinema near VT. The cinema house used to screen English films and often, by the time the stars would reach the theatre, the tickets would be sold out. On such occasions, thanks to the stars' acquaintance with Sethi *saheb* and his influence, he would organise extra chairs for them so that they wouldn't be disappointed.

It's a miracle of sorts that he could take Rajendra Kumar from a room in Kurla to Marina Guest House near Bandra *talao*. Soon, the owner of the guest house became like a mother to him. Now he had the flexibility to pay rent whenever he could. It was here that this young man met the famous and much-in-demand writer Rajendra Krishan. He got him a job as assistant director under producer-director HS Rawail for a monthly salary of ₹150. Rajendra Kumar was always fond of turning out dapper. A silk shirt of Bosky and a pair of crisp, white trousers were his choicest attire. His boss HS Rawail used to often remind him that he was the assistant and not the hero! The films he was associated with as the assistant director were successful ones: *Saaqi*, with Prem Nath and Madhubala; *Shokhiyan*, with Prem Nath and Suraiya, and *Patanga*, with Premnath and Nigar Sultana.

In all the three films, Rajendra Kumar was the second assistant director and the clapper boy. One day, when he was coming down the stairs of Mahalaxmi's Famous Studio, successful producer-director Devendra Goyal spotted him. He stopped him and asked, "You have the looks of a hero, why don't you give acting a try?" In reply, Rajendra Kumar said, "A number of people make this suggestion, but no one gives me any work." Goyal *saheb* asked him to come to his office the next day. He bunked HS Rawail's shoot and reached Goyal *saheb*'s office the following day. He was given a signing amount of ₹101 and finalised as the hero for his next film. The film *Vachan* started after a year and Rajendra

Kumar continued working with Rawail *saheb* till then.

For the premiere of the film *Vachan*, Rajendra Kumar reached Krishna cinema in Lamington Road with his boss HS Rawail in his car. The hero was welcomed with huge applause for his first show. When the movie ended, he was surrounded by fans. When Rawail *saheb* saw the crowd and realised that Rajendra Kumar would take a long time to reach the car, he left his assistant behind and drove off.

A time came when HS Rawail went through a bad patch. However, his assistant clapper boy didn't disappoint him. He took his boss in his own car to actress Sadhana's house, gave her the signing amount from his own pocket and convinced Naushad *saheb* to give music for the film. When the film released, it turned out to be a blockbuster and HS Rawail was back in the running as a great filmmaker. The film was *Mere Mehboob*.

After the success of *Vachan*, V Shantaram hired Rajendra Kumar for a monthly salary of ₹350 for playing the hero in *Toofan aur Diya*. A week before the premiere of the show, Shantaram's manager asked the hero of the film, Rajendra Kumar, if he wanted to invite his friends or family for the premiere of the film. The hero requested that ten tickets be reserved. The manager was kind enough and happily complied. After the premiere, when Rajendra Kumar went to collect his salary, he saw that they had deducted money for the ten seats. Rajendra Kumar always said that the incident was a great lesson for him. This was a lesson that held him in good stead when he became a producer. He used to narrate an episode about how during the shooting of *Naam,* in Hong Kong, the film's heroine Amrita Singh made international calls to Delhi, Bombay and London. When he saw the bill, he recalled Shantaram*ji*'s example and deducted the amount from the heroine's fees. He also learnt to first get the bill and then get the receipt signed. He made this approach a cardinal rule as a producer.

Mehboob Production used to hire the staff, including actors, on monthly salaries. For the film *Mother India*, Sunil Dutt and Rajendra Kumar were paid ₹1,000 each; Raaj Kumar got ₹750, and Mukri, ₹400. Kanhaiya Lal, who played Sukhi Lala in *Mother India*, used to get monthly bus fare from Sion to Bandra and back along with his salary of ₹350. Interestingly, for the same project, Nargis was paid ₹5,000! The film was such a hit that Mehboob *saheb* and his family are perhaps still reaping its rewards. It was iconic. The credit for Rajendra Kumar meeting Mehboob *saheb* goes to comedian Mukri. Nargis, Sunil Dutt, Rajendra Kumar, Raaj Kumar and Kanhaiya Lal were the film's main characters. Faredoon Irani was the cameraman, Shakeel Badayuni the lyricist and Naushad the music composer. The film owes its success to all of them.

Interestingly, there was a phase in Rajendra Kumar's career when all the movie theatres in Bombay would be showing his films and most of them would be celebrating their silver jubilees. This was the reason he was dubbed 'Jubilee Kumar'.

When producer, director and actor Raj Kapoor began his film *Sangam*, he required two heroes. He thought of Dilip Kumar but somehow things didn't work out and his search turned frantic. He was looking for someone who would not only fit the role, but also look like Dilip Kumar, his first choice. When the name finally struck him, he rushed to Mohan Studio where a handsome young man was shooting. He agreed even without hearing the story and continuously thanked Raj Kapoor for the opportunity. The hero, of course, was Rajendra Kumar. After the success of *Sangam*, Rajendra Kumar's success peaked and the Mount Everest almost paled in comparison.

This led to film producers from the south making a beeline for the star who had just shot to fame. They came with suitcases filled with money and due to this, Rajendra Kumar even began speaking Tamil. The producers from Madras, after signing Rajendra Kumar, would consult him on everything – who the heroine would be, who would be the music director and even who would play the roles of the father or mother. Heroine Waheeda Rehman used to quip, "It looks like he is not only your hero, but also your production controller. Two jobs in one pay!"

When with huge success, his confidence grew multi-fold; it was as if KL Saigal's hit song '*Ek bangla bane nyara*' was echoing in his dreams. It was fulfilled when he found out that a seaside bungalow owned by a Parsi on Bandra's Carter Road was for sale. He was determined to buy it. The owner asked for ₹65,000 for the house. *Aadmi jis cheez ko pane ki thaan leta hai toh koi na koi len den ke dhandhe ka pathan mil hi jata hai.* (If a person makes up his mind to achieve something, then he invariably finds a benefactor to help him.) And, it so happened that BR Chopra came into the picture as the Pathan. Rajendra Kumar signed two of his films, *Kanoon* and *Dhool ka Phool*, for ₹65,000 on the condition that he would be paid the said amount in advance. In those days, he was charging this amount for one film, but Rajendra Kumar agreed to two because he was hell-bent on buying the house. As soon as he got the cheque, he proceeded to the bungalow and possessed the key to his dream house the very next day.

He settled in with his wife and children in the house but didn't stop dreaming. Within a week, he was determined to buy an even bigger house in Pali Hill, Bandra, which cost ₹17 lakh. So he sold the sea-side bungalow on Carter Road to Rajesh Khanna for ₹3,50,000. When Rajesh Khanna asked if he could pay in instalments, Rajendra Kumar agreed without a second thought. As soon as Rajesh Khanna paid the first instalment, Rajendra Kumar handed over the keys to him. While taking the key, Rajesh Khanna bowed his head for Rajendra*ji*'s blessings. That's why he named the bungalow Ashirwad.

I was already acquainted with Rajendra Kumar, but we grew close after his son Kumar Gaurav (Bunty) married Sunil Dutt's daughter Namrata (Anju) and both the boys from Kurla became in-laws.

Whenever Sunil Dutt would stand for the Lok Sabha elections from Bandra, Bombay, we would talk every day from morning till late in the night. The office of Ajanta Arts used to be converted into a party place. During the election campaign, Rajendra Kumar was entrusted with the job of keeping the books. Expenditure towards posters, vehicles, food and petrol, etc., had to be taken care of. I had one car in my possession. My job was to go door-to-door and urge people to vote for Sunil Dutt. I also had to take care of the driver and the two other men who used to accompany me. Lunch and tea were also my responsibility. Once or twice, I fuelled the car with my own money. The following week, when I asked Rajendra*ji* for reimbursement, he asked for the petrol bill, which I didn't have. I never received the money. Rajendra Kumar was called High Command and I the Deputy High Command. The lesson that Rajendra Kumar learnt from V Shantaram, I learnt by sacrificing my ₹500. It later helped me when I turned Producer.

Rajendra Kumar and I grew closer when he was making *Naam* and I was simultaneously making *Thikana*. Since both the films were being directed by Mahesh Bhatt, we used to talk often. Rajendra Kumar was quite interested in poetry and so was I. So, often when we met during the shoots, we would talk for hours about films, literature, history, etc. But most of all, we used to avidly discuss politics and listen to each other's views.

Then we got into a new routine. Every morning at 5:30, we would meet at Bandra's Joggers Park, take a stroll, return to his house for tea and biscuits, and read newspapers. This would lead to numerous conversations, and at times, arguments on the various news items and at eight, I would bid adieu with the words penned by famous songwriter, Anand Bakshi: *Achcha toh hum chalte hain*. (It's time to say goodbye now.) This continued for almost two years. He would often talk about his wife during our walks. "Next to my faith in God is my faith in my wife. She has the perfect temperament towards our children, our staff at home, her friends, and some of mine too. She is caring and scary, and that makes her the perfect home minister. Children treat me as their prime minister, not knowing that this title is just to keep peace at home. The actual boss is not this so-called prime minister, but their mom – the best home minister on earth."

Occasionally during our evening sessions, we'd have discussions on politics and films over a drink or two. I found him tensed and tired once and upon my asking him the reason behind the fatigue, he replied, "As my wife Shukla has gone on a yearly visit to Los Angeles to be with Dimple, our daughter, I thought I'd surprise her by presenting a brand new home with new paint, upholstery, etc. All this took three weeks, with ten workers on the job round the clock. All the work got completed to my satisfaction only last night. After that, all the vouchers for the material bought by the workers had to be signed and their wages had to be paid in cash." And before I could leave with a broad smile, he said, "Shukla*ji* is arriving tomorrow night. Let's have one last one for the road. A double peg will make you feel single again. After all these sleepless nights, I am itching to get some sound sleep.

From tomorrow, you will find me fit, fine and kicking but no morning walk for the next two-three days." Rajendra*ji* knew that Grover too was sailing in the same boat of belonging to Shashi, his wife for life.

Since both of us were interested in poetry, we would sit and read each other our poems, admire what the other had written, have a couple of drinks to add to the occasion and then it was the same, '*Achcha toh hum chalte hain.*'

Dehradun-based poet Kanwal Ziai was a close friend of Rajendra Kumar. He was a refugee too and after coming from Sialkot, had settled in Dehradun. The style in which he wrote about Rajendra Kumar was rather interesting. I am sharing a part of his work with you:

Kuch paththar umar bhar paththar rahe
Aur kuch paththar shivale ho gaye
Tum samandar ke kinare ja basey
Hum pahadon ke hawale ho gaye.

Tere hothon ke tarazu pe ae dost
Apne lafzon ko kabhi tolunga main
Mera vada hai ke agle janm mein
Lab toh tere honge aur bolunga main

(Some stones remained stones all their lives;
Others turned into temples
You settled by the seaside
I surrendered myself to the hills.

On the scales of your lips, my friend
I will never weigh my words
It is my promise that in the next birth
It will be your words and my voice.)

Rajendraji remembered his good days as 'healthy days'. While talking about the great times gone by, he would say, "*Chinta ki koi baat nahi, bas samay ko thoda sa nazla zukam ho gaya hai. Theek ho jayega.*" (There is nothing to worry about. It is just seasonal cold. I will be fine soon.) However, when his health started deteriorating, it led to rounds of doctors, then hospitals. The combination of the numerous medicines prescribed to him made him uncomfortable. During this difficult time, his wife Shukla was by his side always. She would try to console him but the effect was only momentary.

On July 9, 1999, I reached Breach Candy Hospital at five. I was with him throughout the visiting hours, from five to seven, and kept him busy in conversation. I asked him what was worrying him. "God has given you so much that it will provide for generations to come." It was natural for me to feel sad upon seeing his condition. He was sad too because I was supposed to return to New York the next day. This was the last time I was meeting him before going back, but I didn't imagine it would be my very last meeting with Rajendra Kumar. He had told me, "*Kuch bhi ho, Raaj. Main apni saari daulat kharch karne ke liye taiyar hun. Tum mere liye thoda sa swasthya khareed kar bhej dena. Waise mujhe lagta hai ke parson, 11 July ko, putra Bunty ka janmdin manane ghar chala jaunga.*" (Whatever it is Raaj, I am ready to spend my entire wealth. Just buy some good health and have it sent to me. That way, I feel I will be home to celebrate son Bunty's birthday day after, on July 11).

But, who can alter fate? I had reached New York. On July 12, my friend Tirlok Malik told me that Rajendra Kumar had passed away. All the memories I had shared with him went past me like a slideshow. The meetings at Joggers Park, the poetry sessions, the arguments – everything came back to me in a gush of emotion. I just caught my head and sat and kept remembering the way I used to bid him adieu: *Achcha toh hum chalte hain.* Now the same words were reverberating within me.

Even though nothing is in our hands, I would still hold Rajendra Kumar responsible for his physical sufferings and failing health. He was being treated by one of the city's top doctors, Dr. Kanu Bhai Shah at Vile Parle, and after the doctor's demise, under his son, Dr. Sunil Shah, who was a doctor to many film celebrities. Despite knowing well that the medicines and injections took a little time to take effect and get the body back to normal state, Rajendra Kumar was so impatient that after just two days of medication, he would change his doctor, which would also include some *hakeem*s and homeopaths. He would also keep shifting from one hospital to the other – Breach Candy and Hinduja in Bombay, Escorts in Delhi, and if he wasn't satisfied with any of them, he'd go to Los Angeles to get admitted in one of the best hospitals there. His dear daughter Dimple lived there with her husband Raju Patel – a successful Indian-American film producer in Hollywood. He eventually flew back from the US to get readmitted in Breach Candy Hospital, his last and final station in the ever-moving train of life. Rajendra Kumar finally got down to go to his guide – the God Almighty. It's true that *Vaham ek aisi bimari hai jiska koi ilaaj hai hi nahin.* (There is no cure for misconceptions of the mind.)

He completed his journey from Delhi to Bombay by selling the watch his father gave him, but his final journey was according to the time set by the one above, who is watching over all of us.

Rakhee Gulzar

You all must have heard the story about a few blind men trying to identify an elephant by touch. The person who gets hold of its tail thinks it is a rope, while another who feels its legs thinks it is a tree trunk and the one who touches its ears thinks it is a fan. You must be wondering why I am referring to this story. The fact of the matter is, very few people have the vision to understand a person like Rakhee. Getting to know her is somewhat like the story above. People have attempted to define Rakhee by decoding just one aspect of her personality. That is the reason she has always remained an enigma. In reality, she is like the deep sea and it is impossible to determine or achieve the depth she possesses.

Let me begin by saying that I have known Rakhee for the past forty-five years – from the time she became a part of Sunil Dutt's film, *Reshma aur Shera*. When Sunil Dutt cast her in one of the main roles, some people in the unit, including editor Pran Mehra, cameraman Ram Chandra, and a few others, weren't in favour of the decision. I was the chief assistant and production in-charge for Sunil Dutt, who was the producer and director. So the entire responsibility of the production was on me, and Sunil Dutt and Nargis *bhabhi* would consult me on everything, even casting.

The shooting for *Reshma aur Shera* took place in the deserts of Rajasthan continuously for three months. There were few options for transport in the desert and since there were no hotels near the location, fifty-two tents were put up for the cast and crew there itself. Rakhee's scene had her dressed up as a bride, waiting for her husband Ranjit's *baraat* when news comes in that he has been shot dead by the enemies. On hearing this, the bride starts crying inconsolably while running and stumbling. The camera was panning her manic sprint and fall continuously. When the camera stopped and the scene was completed, we realised that Rakhee, dressed as a bride, was actually in a semi-conscious state. To run helter-skelter was vital to the scene, and this new actress had done it beautifully. There was applause from everyone present. Pran Mehra and Ram Chandra had to eat their words. Dutt *saheb* was complimented by all for his choice of actress. When we returned to Bombay from Rajasthan, Rakhee invited me to her house. Taking her up on her invitation, I went the very next day. Rakhee, carrying a silver *thali* with a lighted *diya*, burning incense and some sweets, walked towards me. First, she applied *tilak* on my forehead, touched my feet, and considering that day was *Rakshabandhan*, tied a rakhi on my wrist. She had given me the stature of her brother and made me promise to honour this delicate relationship all my life. Since that day, our relationship became strong and invincible. No one could dare to destroy it.

When I had started the film *Taaqat*, apart from Sunil Dutt and Nargis *bhabhi*, it was only Rakhee who supported and encouraged me. From what I know about Rakhee, once she takes a decision pertaining to her personal life, no person or force in this world can make her budge. Because she is the kind of woman who is capable of taking on the world on her own terms. When Rakhee was offered the role in *Taaqat*, I wasn't sure if she'd accept it. But not only did she say yes to it, but also displayed extraordinary interest in the difficult character she was to play. I had asked her brother Shibranjan Mazumdar (Shibu) to be my associate producer in the film. As per ritual, a brother gifts her sister something on Rakhi, but here the roles were reversed. Rakhee didn't charge a single penny for her work in the film. In a time and age when man doesn't do the smallest of things without being paid for it, don't you think this gesture by Rakhee speaks volumes about the kind of individual she is and how much she values relationships? Once she brought a girl from Calcutta to take care of her household needs. The girl was sharp and understood Rakhee's needs and other household work. She was pleased with her. One day, Rakhee called me to ask if I could lend my driver to her for a few days since hers was on leave. I happily complied. When a couple of days turned into a week, I hopped into a rickshaw to go to Rakhee's house to enquire if all was well. On the way, I saw her in her friend's car. We both saw each other and stopped midway to meet. When I enquired about my driver, she said that that's exactly what she wanted to ask me about. It turned out that the driver, along with Rakhee's girl from Calcutta, had been missing since the last two days. Both of us really regretted this incident. For a few weeks, I depended on taxis and autos for transport because I can't drive. Rakhee too managed with her friend's car till she found a new driver. When the new driver got married, Rakhee enrolled his wife into service too to take care of the household and Rakhee's personal work. The guy still drives Rakhee's car and the lady continues to work at her house till this day.

Rakhee was born on July 26, 1947, in Sylhet, Bengal. It was

a part of India then. After 1971, it became a part of Bangladesh. Rakhee's family were an integral part of this journey. Her parents did their best to provide her and her two brothers – Shibu and Shanker – a proper upbringing. However, when she entered her youth, Rakhee stepped out of the comforts of her home and family, and landed in Bombay, the *Maya Nagari* (the Land of Illusions.) When she started getting one good offer after the other, she never looked back. Work was worship to her and she ploughed on single-mindedly. Along with fame came wealth, property, cars, a farmhouse and every other luxury that she had always aimed for.

Rakhee's first marriage was with the wrong man – it hurt her, but she ended it rather soon. After this incident, she met writer, producer and director Gulzar. While one of them was a victim of the partition of Bengal, the other was uprooted because of the Punjab partition. When they got together, it was as if they shared the same pain. They fell in love. This was followed by their wedding at the Mahalaxmi Race Course in Bombay, where Gulzar proudly rode on a mare to marry the love of his life. It was definitely a memorable wedding. Then came along Bosky, the most precious addition to their lives. When Rakhee brought Bosky home from the hospital, as planned, I was already present there. As per our custom, when a new mother enters her home with her child for the first time, the *mama* breaks a coconut at the threshold of the house. After the completion of this ritual, the proud parents stepped in with their baby girl.

Bosky is an intelligent girl and quite similar to her father in her thinking. Gulzar is very dignified and successful, apart from being a straightforward man. I don't know why and how distances crept up between Rakhee and Gulzar. It just kept widening, eventually leading to their separation. Bosky lived with her dad, fell in love with Govind and married him. Today, she has a son, and Gulzar and Rakhee are proud grandparents.

In these forty-five years, I have come to realise that if you are in Rakhee's good books, she will do anything for you, even give her life for you. But if not, she can take your life. It's a different thing that she hasn't done it so far! But it's true that once she ends a relationship with someone, it is forever. It is always black or white for Rakhee, no shades of grey whatsoever. Most people know that after she divorced her first husband, Ajay Biswas, she went to Calcutta and stayed in a hotel there. When Ajay tried to speak to her on phone, she coldly told him, "Who Ajay Biswas? I don't know anyone by that name."

Stories about Rakhee's mood swings abound the industry. Once, even Shakti Samanta bore the brunt of her moodiness. The shooting of *Barsaat ki Raat* was in full swing in Darjeeling. One day, Shakti Samanta advised Rakhee to go to bed early as he wanted to start shooting early the next day. This was enough to make him the subject of Rakhee's ire. She point blank told him that he should not be concerned about whether she slept at night or stayed awake. She said he should only be bothered about whether she reached the set at seven in the morning or not. You will be surprised to know that because of her obstinacy and to prove a point, she neither slept all night, nor did she allow others to retire for the night. She played cards all night and reached the set at 7am sharp. She couldn't even keep her eyes open and wasn't fit to shoot that day. She felt guilty. Whenever Rakhee realises her mistake, she accepts it graciously.

Once she had taken her daughter for a stroll and saw a toyseller on the way. Although Bosky wanted to buy all the toys, Rakhee was only willing to buy her one. Bosky cried; Rakhee scolded her but did not budge. She could have easily fulfilled her daughter's whims. But she didn't. She didn't want her daughter to turn into a spoilt brat. She said, "Aren't there children who can't buy even one toy?" Same was the case with Gulzar. He even named his house after his daughter. It is called *Boskiyana*. Incidentally, Bosky Gulzar is a great cook!

Today, the people of the film industry address Rakhee as *didi*. She hears out her colleague's issues, and even helps find solutions to their problems. Her advice has bailed out many from difficult situations, but Rakhee's biggest weakness is that *she* never asks anyone for help. When I found out that she still loved Gulzar, I tried to intervene, hoping that both of them would resolve their conflict and reunite. Unfortunately, neither of them was willing to step down or have a conversation about it. I have felt the sadness Rakhee experienced every time one of Gulzar's films flopped. She wouldn't entertain any negative comments about him. Even today, there is a picture of Gulzar in her bedroom. Very few people know how despondent she actually is without him. Once when I had talked to Gulzar about the love and warmth that Rakhee still harboured for him, he said he was in the same boat. However, he also added that he would eventually get over the feeling. Rakhee should follow the same philosophy. No one has found out or fathomed the real reason for their conflict nor has anyone understood what's good or bad for the couple.

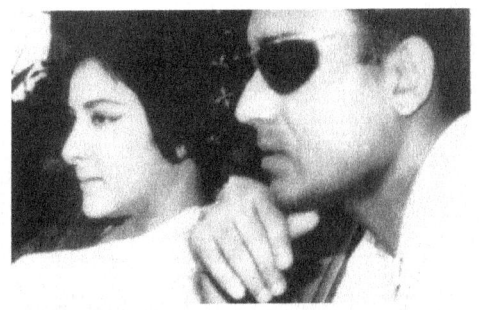

▶ Nargis and Raaj Grover

▶ Ajanta Arts Welfare Troupe boarding a chartered flight to Bangladesh to perform for the soldiers

▶ From left to right: Shammi, Nargis & Punita Dutt (Som Dutt's wife)

▶ Raaj Grover at his engagement with Rosy

▲ Rajendar Kumar's family. Left to right: Kumar Gaurav (son), Rajendra Kumar with Kajal (younger daughter), Shukla Ji (his wife) & Dimple (elder daughter)

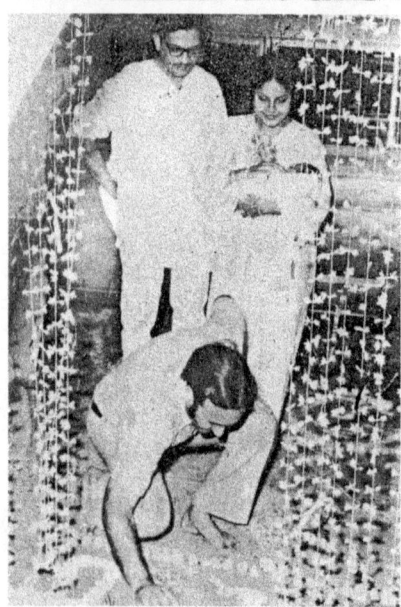

◄ Raaj Grover welcoming Rakhi & Gulzar along with their newborn daughter Meghna by breaking a coconut at the threshold of the Gulzar family home, in the role of the maternal uncle

▼ From left to right: Tosh Ji (Balraj Sahni's wife), Raaj Grover, Shashi, Balraj Sahni, Shashi's father Acharya Jialal Vasant & Dinanath Grover (Raaj Grover's father) at Raaj Grover's wedding

▼ *Shashi Kapoor with Raaj Grover and wife Shashi on their wedding day*

▼ *Yash Chopra with the newlyweds Raaj and Shashi Grover*

▶ *Raaj Grover and wife Shashi along with Prem Chopra and Mrs. Chopra on the Chopras' wedding day*

▲ *Raaj Grover's daughter Jalpa's first birthday. From left to right: Nargis, Prem Vasant (Grover's sister-in-law), Shashi (Grover's wife), Jalpa, Raaj Grover, Sunil Dutt & Priya Dutt*

▲ *Field Marshal Sam Manekshaw and Raaj Grover*

▼ *Raaj Grover with Lt. Gen. Jagjeet Singh Arora, the hero of the Bangladesh War*

▼ *Raaj Grover (sitting on the ground) with Sunil Dutt (left), Indira Gandhi (middle) and Nargis (far right) after visiting the Prime Minister at her residence in New Delhi*

◀ *Producer Raaj Grover with Maharaja Arvind Singhji of Mewar (on the right) on the location of* Taaqat *in Udaipur*

▲ *Thikana's poster with Raaj Grover's name as the producer*

▲ *Raaj Grover (producer) & Kaka Thakur (DOP, Cameraman) on the location of* Taaqat *in Udaipur. Top: The poster of* Taaqat.

▼ *Nargis and Baby Sanjay Dutt*

▼ *Sunil Dutt with son Sanjay Dutt*

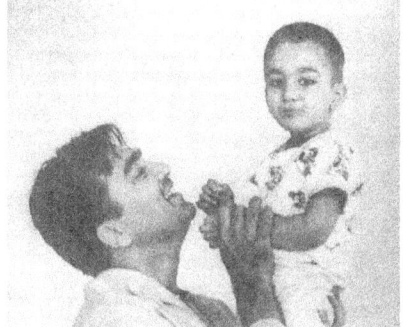

▲ *Rajesh Khanna with Raaj Grover*

▲ *Sunil Dutt dancing with daughter-in-law Richa Sharma during one of Sanjay Dutt's birthday celebrations*

▲ *Dimple Kapadia with Raaj Grover*

▼ *Raaj Grover with Jaya and Amitabh Bachchan in New York*

▼ *Raaj Grover with wife Shashi, daughter Jalpa, son-in-law Rajiv Thapar, son Sugriv and daughter-in-law Steuart Osha Grover along with grandchildren Avijit & Riya Thapar and Uma & Pavan Grover*

▲ *Dilip Kumar with wife Saira banu*

▲ *Ajtabh Bachchan's daughter Naina's wedding reception in Delhi. Left to Right: Kunal Kapoor (the groom), Naina Bachchan (the bride), Ajitabh Bachchan (father of the bride) & Raaj Grover*

▼ Raaj Grover with Ina Sharma (Richa Sharma's sister) and Trishala Dutt at Trishala's Sweet 16 celebrations in New York

▼ With Sanjay and Manyata Dutt

▲ Manoj Kumar and Raaj Grover

▲ From left to right: Dharmendra, Raaj Grover and Gurpal Singh (Kaka)

◀ Raaj Grover with Nobel Prize winner biochemist Dr. Har Gobind Khorana at his house in Boston, USA. Grover's father Dinanath gave shelter and helped a young Khorana to achieve the education that would later produce a Nobel laureate

◀ Soni Razdan and Mahesh Bhatt with daughters Pooja and Alia Bhatt

▲ The entire Dutt family now with the next generation and at the helm, Sanjay Dutt

Sanjay Dutt

The first example of boundless love that I had witnessed as a child was my parents' love for me. Though I didn't realise it fully then, I understood it completely when later in life, I got acquainted with Sunil and Nargis Dutt, when they became one after their marriage on March 11, 1958. Their love story will always remain the ideal love story in my eyes. Though their identities have now become memories, their love will remain alive eternally. Within a year of marriage, on July 29, 1959, amid the raging Bombay monsoon, they were blessed with a bundle of joy, Sanjay Dutt, and their happiness knew no bounds. The newly minted father excitedly told his mother, "*Tu dadi, aur tera Balla baap ban gaya, maa.*" (You have become a grandmother and your Balla has become a father.) For the first time, he saw his otherwise quiet and reticent mother look up at the sky and say, "*Mera baba aya, Baba tera aya.*" (My grandson has arrived, and yours too.) It was as if she was informing her husband that he had become a grandfather. When she couldn't control her emotions, tears just flowed, unabated.

There is also an incident behind Sanjay Dutt's name, which was told to me by Baby Tabassum. Nargisji used to love

Tabassum so much that people would even call her Chhoti Nargis. She told me that a lot of thought had gone behind the name – the letter S was taken from Sunil Dutt's name, N from Nargis' and Jay was added to denote the victory of their love. This led to the name Sanjay! At home, he became Sanju, but his grandmother continued to call him Baba and he became Sanju Baba or just Baba among his acquaintances and friends. Once I had asked Dutt saheb why Sanjay, at forty, was still being referred to as Baba. He smiled and said, "This has something to do with the family. His mother, even after she had three children, was still called Baby by her friends. Especially by actress Shammi and Kusum, and Indra Sindhan from Delhi. They are Sanju's aunts and my sisters-in-law, who I got as dowry. Similarly, if Sanju is still called Baba, it's no big deal."

Baba's mother never let her son out of sight as if he was a flower that might wilt. Both the parents never compromised on his upbringing. The proud Nargis proved to be a soft mother, while the father, at times, lost his temper. If Sunil Dutt scolded the child on matters of discipline, the mother would be upset. Every year, Sanju's birthday was celebrated with such grandiose that it felt like Diwali or Eid celebrations. On that day itself, they would start planning his next birthday – the guest list, the menu, and what Sanju would wear!

The parents were so devoted to Sanjay Dutt that this would lead to fights between them. They would stop talking to each other for some time, but it would pass. My association with the Dutt family is as old as Sanju Baba and in these years, I have learnt a lot from them about the intricacies of married life. I was already close to Nargisji, her brothers and their children, but became close to Dutt *saheb* after he started Ajanta Arts. I became so friendly with his brother Som Dutt that Nargisji used to shower me with as much love and respect as she did with her brother-in-law. Once Dutt *saheb*, Sanju Baba and Mrs. Dutt had to go to Delhi to attend the wedding of the well-known lyricist and scriptwriter Rajendra Krishan's daughter. I knew Rajendra Krishan well and was invited to the wedding too. So Dutt *saheb* booked my tickets along with the others. It was December and Delhi's winter was at its peak. Nargis *bhabhi* had picked up a very expensive suit for Sanju Baba from London. He wore the same suit and believe me, everyone at the wedding only had eyes for the young boy. It was so cold that people were shivering despite wearing multiple layers. Suddenly, I saw Sanju Baba shivering. He was wearing only the trousers and the tie but the coat was missing. I immediately hugged him tightly. On seeing this, the mother was perplexed and the father angrily asked him about the coat. And the eight-year-old boy answered, while still shivering because of the biting cold, "Outside the bungalow, a child was shivering in the cold. I couldn't bear to see him and gave my coat to him." Nargisji was overcome with emotion; she hugged him and sobbed uncontrollably. The father too couldn't control himself and embraced his son. All the guests, including the priest, stopped to witness the emotional scene that unfolded before them.

Nargis *bhabhi* often used to say, "My Sanju has a heart of gold. So does his father, but while his is 22 carats, Sanju's is 24 carats – absolutely pure." She used to narrate this incident to everyone with great pride. When Sanju grew up, just like his father had planned, he attended the Sanawar boarding school in Shimla. There are only a handful of schools in India that have produced great students who hold important positions in the country today. It was only natural for the parents to take Sanju to Shimla for his admission. But when it was time to leave him, their emotions took over. While the father stoically controlled his tears, the mother couldn't bear the thought of parting and sobbed copiously. As the father offered her his handkerchief, it got completely drenched. This state of mind continued till much after she returned to Bombay. Once she got a call from Sanju's school saying he had hurt his hand, leading to a lot of blood loss. He was continuously asking for his mother. They then added that things were under control and that they had taken care of him.

But it was too much for Nargis *bhabhi* to take. She immediately rushed to the airport, flew to Delhi, took a private taxi to Shimla and reached the school. After giving Sanju a loving *jhappi*, she enquired what had happened and found out that Sanju had cut his finger while sharpening his pencil with a blade. The bleeding stopped after the teacher applied ice to the wound. It was a minor accident, but was too much to handle for a mother's heart. Perhaps, it is true for all mothers. I have seen my mother getting perturbed over small things too. My father, on the other hand, would always remain calm and strong, and would dismiss such behaviour from my mother by calling it, "*Auraton ke baaton ka batangad banana.*" (A woman's habit to make a mountain out of a molehill.) I had seen the same strength in Dutt *saheb* too, but not more than my father's. Dutt *saheb* never approved of such pampering. But I don't agree with it. I have seen how much he loved his mother. Once, in rustic Punjabi, she said to him, "*Baliya puttar, tu apni tarah Som nu vi hero bana de.*" (Baliya, son, make Som a hero just like you.) On her request, the very next month, under the banner of Ajanta Arts, he announced the film *Man ka Meet* with Som and two newcomers, Vinod Khanna and Leena Chandavarkar.

In those days, Dutt *saheb* was terribly busy with films being made by big producers and was shuttling between Bombay and Madras, and wasn't able to dedicate enough time for his own production. So he handed over the responsibility of the new film to me and I put in all my soul to make sure it was completed successfully. Whenever he got a little time, Dutt *saheb* would come to the shoot. The famous director Subba Rao even hired dance master Hiralal to choreograph a song with the two newcomers in Darjeeling. Now, a fight scene between Vinod Khanna and Som Dutt was about to be shot, when Sunil Dutt turned up with his eleven-year-old son. He expressed happiness at the pace of the work and patted my back. Meanwhile, the fight scene was to be filmed on the top of a hill and below it, at the end of a steep slope, river Teesta flowed with splendour. It was windy too. For the scene, after punching the hero Som Dutt, the villain, Vinod Khanna, had to push the hero down with force. The hero had to roll down the slope and reach the river, come back up and bash up the villain.

Before the scene, the director Subba Rao and the fight master explained the scene. When the hero found out what he had to do, he froze and refused. Dutt *saheb*, who was watching all this, got furious. The first target of his outburst was me. He blamed me for not having rehearsed the scene. The second target was Som Dutt, who had just refused to do the scene. When the hero, in a scared voice, told the producer and brother Sunil Dutt that it was a very risky shot, the latter grabbed his son with both hands, turned around and with all his might, threw him down the slope to the river. Sanju rolled down the hill and as he reached the river, he stood up. He wasn't hurt at all. On seeing this, Som Dutt was embarrassed and immediately agreed to do the risky shot. But before that, he ran down and brought Sanju back to the top. He apologised to the director and the fight master, and in his broken English, said, "I am ready, Sir. Call Vinod and let's complete the scene today only, sir."

In the ten to twelve years of knowing Som Dutt, this was the first time I had heard him talk in English. Though not very fluent, it made sense alright! We managed to finish filming the scene well before sunset. The hero of the film may have been Som Dutt, but the real hero that day was the eleven-year-old Sanjay Dutt!

When Sanjay was around twenty, his father started the film *Rocky* with him and Tina Munim. Sanjay had left his childhood behind and had stepped into youth. After the success of this film, he never looked back. But despite his strong exterior, deep inside, he was still the same person whose heart beat for the cause of others rather than himself. He made new friends, not to mention, there was a stream of girlfriends too. One couldn't imagine whom he would choose to be his wife.

Rocky wasn't even complete yet when Sanjay's mother had to go to the USA for cancer treatment. Sunil Dutt's problems just kept escalating, without an end in sight. It was his strength of character that helped him brave such storms. It was as if he had forgotten to smile and a tense demeanour was taking over his persona. At times, when he would look up at the sky, looking for answers, it was as if he said to God, "*Ya Khuda! Mujhe ab bina kisi hetu se muskurane ki shakti pradan kar kyunki main apne aansuon ko ponchte ponchte thak chuka hun.*" (Oh Lord! Give me the strength to smile without reason. I am tired of wiping my ever-flowing tears.)

God heard his prayers, and we all heaved a sigh of relief when Nargis *bhabhi* returned to Bombay. *Rocky* released on May 7, 1981 and the premiere was supposed to be at Bombay's Ganga Cinema. The hall was booked. It was Nargisji's wish to see her son's debut film in a theatre. But, as they say, man proposes, and God disposes. On May 3rd, she departed from this world. Today, you can see Nargis' reflection in her children, Sanjay, Namrata and Priya clearly.

It is famously said that 'the show must go on'. Remembering this, Dutt *saheb* stuck to the date of the movie premiere. The hall was teeming with people. Dutt *saheb* had booked three seats for himself in the last row. He sat on one, Sanjay on another and Nargisji's photograph occupied the middle seat. Whenever the hall would echo with applause, the father and son would look at the photograph and weep silently. According to media reports, the film was a hit. It should have been a good reason to forget the sad moments, but it was clear that in the absence of his mother, all happiness seemed meaningless to Sanjay.

As is common in the film world, after the success of *Rocky*, all eyes were on him. He hadn't even fully emerged from the tragedy of his mother's demise and there was a queue of small and big producers at his door. Even those producers who were strangers sympathized and tried to become friends with Sanju and because of his inexperience and soft heart, he signed several films – some of them worked, but the others just tanked at the box office. Simply listening to the heart proved to be a disaster. Now Sanju had to use his brain to make decisions that would avoid further damage. Perhaps, had his mother been alive, she would have guided him, for she was well-versed with the whims of the industry. But she wasn't around, and his father was busy completing films with other producers and couldn't devote much time to his son. The father's long absences from home created an atmosphere of carelessness and negligence. It was the delusional sense of freedom and guilelessness that led to Sanju making wrong career choices.

When a person crosses over from his childhood to adulthood, one sees a change in their thinking and behaviour. We had seen a similar change in Sanju too. When his family, well-wishers and friends started saying, "We are proud of you Baba," and kept heaping praises, he was bound to change. Unfortunately, it wasn't a change for the good. This proves that a mother not only plays a big role in bringing up her children, but also nurtures them. This crucial element was missing in Sanju's life. The love from his father and sisters could never fill that void. When Sanju realised that people were distancing themselves from him, he became quiet and lonely but kept treading the path he had chosen. He had no idea about the destination yet. When he felt tired on this trek of life, he halted for a bit and found a companion in a girl on the way. Being two young people following the same path, they got talking. Sanju found out that she was also from a rich family and that her name was Richa Sharma. As they got to know each other better, they felt they were meant for one another. Predictably, they became life partners. Just a year after marriage, a daughter was born to them, and Sanju and Richa became proud parents. Suddenly, there was happiness all around. They named their daughter Trishala.

Everyone knows that Sanjay Dutt is the son of respected and famous parents, and that he is kind-hearted and emotional. Several people, on the pretext of friendship, have literally duped him. Once a producer's wife tied a *rakhi* on Sanju's wrist and called him her brother. And the husband, taking advantage of this, began shooting a film with Sanju, who was a rising star then. The film was completed and released but Sanju was never paid his fee. As per custom, when a sister ties a *rakhi*, the brother gives her a gift, either in the form of cash or something in kind. Perhaps this non-payment was his *rakhi* gift to her. Of all of Sanju's films, this is the only one I haven't seen. But my ears have heard several stories about it.

Thanks to his hard work and simple nature, Sanju earned

a great name for himself as an actor with films like *Rocky, Sajan, Sadak, Vastav, Munna Bhai MBBS* and *Lage Raho Munna Bhai*. I want to share with my readers certain things that I know about Sanjay Dutt. While he was a hero on screen, he was actually a zero when it came to understanding what was good and bad for him. Like I said before, some of his friends took extreme advantage of his goodness. In 1993, some of his fraud producer friends went over to him and handed over some guns, saying they were meant for hunting. These were the same people who had used Sanjay to make big bucks and were enjoying the good life but Sanjay became a victim of their wicked conspiracy. When the guns were found in his house, the media went berserk. Due to all the negative publicity, Sanju had to pay the price for an act committed with total innocence and got arrested. Imagine the plight of his father. He did all he could to get Sanju out of the mess. He even met the then chief minister of Maharashtra, Sharad Pawar, who had some silly differences with Dutt *saheb* so his request was ignored.

At that time, opposition leader Bal Thackeray's clout was what helped in the situation and Sanju was released from prison, while the case continued as per the law of the land. Meanwhile, he continued doing films but Sanju missed his mother a lot in those trying times as well as his daughter, who was now in America with her maternal grandparents. The child must have been secure there but surely must have missed having her parents around. As he continued on his journey, once again, life brought him face to face with another co-passenger, just like the previous one. For Sanju, it was no less than experiencing déjà vu. He felt blessed, as if God had sent some succour to all his problems in Manyata's avatar – a new mother for his child. They married and Manyata became Mrs. Dutt. And again, the next year itself, they were blessed with twins – son Shahran and daughter Iqra. Things were going as per his wishes, but he still had to pay for the crime he committed in 1993, even if unknowingly and without any motive. Now, neither did he have his parents for support nor the old benefactor.

After the trial, in 2013, the court ordered a punishment of five years of imprisonment to Sanju. And Sanju, without any hesitation, bowed to the ruling and went off to jail to complete his sentence. At this point, I am reminded of a saying in Hindi, *'Ek toh andhe se apni izzat lutvayi, phir use ghar tak chhodne bhi jana pada.'* (First of all, you had your pride shorn off by a blind man, and to make matters worse, you even had to take him home.)

However, I consider all this God's grace. I don't have any complaints with the law. I only know that Sanju deserves a lot of kindness. He went through a trial by fire and only emerged purer and cleaner, just like pure gold.

Sanju baba loved his mother too much and her absence at crucial turns of his life affected him. One day, he saw her in his dreams and started talking to her. What I write below is an imaginary conversation he had with his mother.

An Imaginary Letter to Mother

Mom! My adorable mom!

I am remembering you a lot right now. Even today, I find myself very lonely without you. When you were with me, I loved you a lot and in return, would take your love. Now that you are not here, your memories are all I am left with and they fill up the void that your leaving has left. I remember the days when you would dream about my marriage and about bringing home a beautiful bride. You would be so immersed in your dreams for me. It is the cruelty of time that you are no longer with me, in front of me and I only get glimpses of you in my imagination. When you make an appearance in the garden of pleasant memories, I feel we are all happily together again, but when you leave, I cannot bear the pain it causes me.

Anju, Priya and I were like your playthings, with whom you spent such beautiful times, dreaming their dreams. With the flow of time, we lost you, and your daughters, who used to wait for you for everything, are today busy playing with their tots. Anju has two daughters – Sachi and Siya, who are lucky to have loving parents like Anju and father Bunty. Priya's two sons Siddharth and Sumair are also in love with their parents. My daughter Trishala had her mother snatched away from her too early. She must be somewhere close to you up there. Maybe I am not destined to have a normal life. I hadn't even gotten over your loss when Richa was also taken away from me. Tell me, mom, what kind of a dilemma is this? Your loved toy, me, just kept disintegrating. Dad tried to pick up the pieces several times. Mom, don't worry, in your absence, dad hasn't raised his voice at me even once. He has been dealing with me with great love and care and trying to make me a better person. I did change, but little by little. If God had been kinder and allowed you to live with me a little longer, I would have never taken a wrong turn. Look what your absence has done to my life.

Mother, you know I miss you a lot and keep searching for you in the sky, amongst the stars and I am intoxicated with your memories. Even when I dream, I dream of you. When there is a fire in my heart, you come and turn the raging fire into beautiful lamps and fill me up with happiness. And when I wake up, everything is gone, my dream is shattered and your toy, which dad went to such pains to put together is broken once more. I want to cross this threshold and act like a grown-up, but this world doesn't allow me to grow up. People keep calling me Baba or Munna. I don't know what to do. I am terribly disturbed.

Today when I look at Priya's children, I can see a glimpse of Dad in them and Anju's daughters and Trishala have reflections of you in them. I keep oscillating between happiness and sadness, and keep wondering when I will grow up and see my kids settled. When I look at the situation at home, I am amazed at how it has made me the oldest person in the family – the patriarch. I promise you that I will take care of the family until all the children are settled, just like you and dad took care of us. I will continue to have loving relations with them till the end. I will never scold them or get angry with them. You know I lose my temper easily, but I will try and control myself now. I remember how if dad ever scolded me for my own good, you would be so upset that you wouldn't talk to him for days. I know your concerns very well, maybe that is the reason you have called him to be with you. How can I forget all these things?

I know I still lack the quality to understand a person for what he is, I am paying the price for my mistake by being behind bars. I hope this punishment will prove to be a blessing in disguise for me and I will emerge as a wiser man. Keep faith in me, mother. While atoning for my mistakes, I always say this to myself, '*Na jane kab se main ek bhool yeh karta raha, ke dhool toh mere chehre par thi aur main sheesha saaf karta raha.*' (I can't remember for how long I have been making the mistake of cleaning the mirror, when the dust was on my face all this while.)

India is my country and I love it as much as I love you,

Mother India. I want you to make a request to God on my behalf: *Mujhey jeene do* and keep me in your loving care till I am done with my duties towards all your unseen grandchildren.

Always in love with you.

Sanju
Your Baba

Shabana Azmi

Names like Jaya Bhaduri, Shatrughan Sinha, Paintal, Subhash Ghai, Asrani, David Dhawan, Binod Pradhan, Shabana Azmi, Zarina Wahab and Rita Bhaduri are celebrated names in the film industry. They are people who, after passing out from the Film and Television Institute of India in Pune, have made a name for themselves with their unparalleled talent and dedication. They stand as examples for those venturing into the cutthroat world of films. Pune became well-known because of the iconic institute and the great people who have graduated from it. In those days, anyone entering the industry was asked this question in the interview: "Have you completed a course from FTII?"

The story I am about to narrate is an old but a rather interesting one. Once, it so happened that the owner of Filmistan Studio, Tolaram Jalan, took a liking for the personality of a Punjabi boy. He asked him the same question about the institute and if he was from Pune. When he replied in the affirmative, without wasting a moment, he was signed as the hero. Within a month, it was the new film's *mahurat* and the shooting commenced. In only three days, the director of the film, Kanak Mishra, was fed up with the boy. He went and told Tolaram, the producer, that neither does the boy know how to deliver dialogues nor does he know the ABC of acting. Angrily, he vented, "Pune film institute *se kya yeh ghanta seekh ke aya hai?*" (What crap has he learnt from the Pune film institute?)

The shooting was called off immediately and the boy was shown the door. On his way out, he told Tolaram, "You asked me if I was from Pune and I said yes. I never said I was from the institute. How is it my fault?" One can gauge the value of the institute from this incident. And why not? It gave the film industry actors who were unrivalled in their talent. There was a time when there was no such institute to train people interested in films. Great actors like Motilal, Dilip Kumar, Nargis, Meena Kumari and Guru Dutt were all self-taught and self-made. They did it all on their own. People could learn a lot by just watching their work a couple of times. They didn't need to go to an institute and spend lots of money to learn their craft.

While Shabana is from the institute, two other institutes too have played a major role in her success as an actor. These are her father, Kaifi Azmi, and her husband, Javed Akhtar. Apart from the world of films, these two gentlemen are intellectuals and experts in Urdu, and Shabana has learned a lot from their thoughts and their perspectives towards life. She is not only a great actor, but is also a devoted social activist and is associated with many NGOs.

Though I have never been that close to the Azmi family and its son-in-law, Javed Akhtar – pure diamond, it is a fact that all the Azmis are highly admirable, talented and well-respected people.

I can never forget my meeting with Javed Akhtar at his house in Bandra around forty years ago. Surprisingly, even he remembers it till date. It so happened that Idris Dehlvi of *Shama* magazine had given me a packet to be delivered to Javed in Bombay. When I went to his house, my five-year-old daughter Jalpa came along with me. When Javed gave her some chocolates, she hesitantly accepted them and instead of feeling happy, burst out crying. Wiping her tears, she said, "Mummy *gussa karegi*." (Mummy will scold me.) Even today, whenever I meet him or speak to him on phone from the US, he starts the conversation by enquiring about Jalpa. He is such a wonderful and talented man – a worthy addition to the Azmi family. Shabana and he are certainly a couple who are made for each other. I feel proud to know them both and that they know whatever little of me – as a person from the film industry.

Later, as per my good fortune, I got a book on poems and ghazals of Kaifi Azmi, put together by his dear daughter. On seeing that, I felt any parent would be proud of having such a child – a God's gift – at their home. She had written a few lines in it that were heart-wrenching. I kept reading them again and again and just cannot resist sharing them in this chapter.

"When Javed and I started getting close to each other, my mother was not happy with the development because he was already married. I went to my father to take his opinion and he said, 'Javed is fine but his circumstances are far from fine.' And, when I told him about him having compatibility issues in his marriage, I saw him dive into the deep pool of his understanding, experience, sense of loyalty and intelligence to find an answer, and when he emerged from the pool, even from his silence, I knew that he had fathomed the abiding trust his daughter possessed. Father had always taught his wife and daughter that having self-confidence was as important to live as the beating heart. Once equipped with that, there is no dream that cannot be fulfilled.)

"There are many similarities between Abba and Javed. Both are particular about manners and decorum and both are interested in politics. Earlier, I didn't have an iota of interest in politics, but thanks to being in the company of the two men, I can say I became a part of the web of politics.

"Abba was always concerned about the poor labourers, farmers and artisans – he always yearned to see them witness happy days. Though he didn't have much to complain about the capitalists, he did want to point out to them and tell them that, 'the workers simply spread a sheet of newspaper on the footpath and sleep, they never resort to sleeping pills."

About her Abba, I will quote the same lines I did for Lalaji, my father:

Rukey toh chaand hai, chaley toh hawaon jaisa hai
Woh – jissey kadakti dhoop mein dekho toh chhaon jaisa hai.

(When he is still, you can call him the moon, when in motion, he is like the wind
If you look at him in the burning sun, he is like the shade.)

Before ending I want to say that all those aspiring actors who have watched her in the film *Neerja* need not bother joining an acting school. The portrayal of her role is equal to all the lessons that you will learn in a school. Her work in films is a school in itself, indeed!

Shashi Kapoor

Well, there are plenty of stories in my treasury – some sweet and some savoury.

Shashi Kapoor's first film as a hero was *Char Diwari*. Krishen Chopra was the director, Nanda was the heroine and I the Chief Assistant Director. It is from here that my friendship with Shashi Kapoor took seed. He would often tell me about how both his elder brother and I had the same name, Raj. "It is just that one is a Kapoor and the other is a Grover," he'd say. To carry the coincidence further, the girl I married is named Shashi! To tease him, I would tell him how he was Shashi and so was my wife. "The only difference is, one is a Kapoor and the other a Grover." He would be in splits on hearing this. Shashi was a very humorous and fun-loving person.

Once when he called, I told him my wife had gone to Delhi. On hearing this, he said, "*Oye, toh main aa jaun? Kya fark padta hai? Mera naam bhi toh Shashi hai!*" (Oye, so should I come over? What difference will it make? My name is also Shashi!) This was followed by rapturous laughter that was very characteristic of him. There is no fun in friendship if it doesn't have a good dose of teasing, fun and laughter.

Then Shashi became a busy man, thanks to a stream of successful films. Though our meetings became a bit irregular, it wasn't like we were unaware of what was happening in each other's lives. Like Ghalib has said:

*Go main raha rahi-ne-sitam haye rozgar
Lekin tere khayal se ghafil nahi raha.*

(Though I remained trapped in the tangle of earning a livelihood
Your thoughts always remained with me.)

There was not a single memorable occasion when we didn't get together. Shashi was head over heels in love with his wife Jennifer, but was equally scared of her wrath. Well, he certainly wasn't the only man to be scared of his wife!

Shashi Kapoor belonged to a film family. When Raj Kapoor asked his grandfather Dewan Baseshwar Nath to enact the role of a judge in his film *Awara*, he agreed. Shashi Kapoor began his career as a child artiste and because he was specially endowed in the looks and the brain department, he soon became the audience's favourite artiste. He was a very talented actor and it was in his genes. So apart from Hindi films, he also made a name for himself with English films, which he made along with Ismail Merchant and James Ivory.

I remember this one time, we were chatting at his Juhu home opposite Prithvi Theatre. Two of his friends, Tiger and Ashwini, were also there. Though we were speaking softly, the speed with which we were guzzling down our drinks was rather fast. When the Black Label got over, everyone was worried about how they would reach home. I was single back then. So it was just the remaining three who were worried about getting home. Shashi took me to his house.

On reaching the twelfth floor of Atlas apartment, when he rang the doorbell, it was midnight. The door was opened by none other than Jennifer Kapoor. The minute she looked at us, she knew the drunken state we were in. When Shashi asked her if there was anything to eat, she simply lost her cool. Flinging a hundred rupee note on his face, she said, "This is not a hotel where you can get what you want any time of the day. Go to hell. Eat somewhere else. Don't wake me up. Take the key and don't ring the bell again." And the door was slammed shut.

What else could we do? Shashi asked the driver to take us to a place which was open all night. Once we reached there, he told him, "*Ek plate apne liye aur do plate anda, bheja fry aur char pav hamare liye lao.*" (Get one plate for you, two plates of egg, bheja fry and four breads for us.) Since we were drunk, without any calculations, we flung the 100-rupee note at the vendor, who, in the same way, flung it back at us.

A hero's popularity is directly proportional to the success of his films. Shashi's success streak continued, and he bought a beautiful flat on Altamount Road. The day he shifted to the new house, he invited a few friends over. We all left around 2 am. When the couple was left alone, the wife asked the husband, "How is it that I never saw Raaj leave?" Even Shashi was perplexed because he knew I would never leave without a hug and a goodbye. Anyway, when they returned to their room, they saw Raaj sprawled on their bed, sleeping!

When I woke up at six the next morning and stepped out of the bedroom, I saw Jennifer sleeping on the sofa while Shashi was on the floor, sleeping on the carpet. I was getting worried about the repercussions of my actions. I was still in the bathroom when they woke up. When they saw me, they burst out laughing. They served me breakfast and when I was about to depart, Jennifer *bhabhi* said something to me that I will never forget in my life. She said, "Don't worry. Until you get married, consider this your home. And when you marry, do call us over. We will repay the loan by sleeping on your bed on your first night together with your wife." This was followed by, "When do we see you next?"

I was married on August 18, 1968. On my wedding reception, Shashi came alone since his wife, Jennifer, was away in London with her family. We met after that too but somehow, I never found the same warmth and smile on his face. I could never find the reason for this change.

Several years later, when I moved to the US to be closer to my children, Shashi Kapoor visited the country on an invitation by the Indian community. A function was organised in his honour. I don't remember the date, but I was present at the function too. It was supposed to begin at 3 pm. The hall was packed with guests and the wait for Shashi Kapoor began. His car arrived around 4, I opened the door and saw that Shashi had a glass of vodka in his hand. In a slightly stern tone, I asked him, "What is this? People have been waiting for you for so long and you are so late... And why are you having vodka in the afternoon? It's not sundown yet. What will people say?"

As soon as he heard this, he hugged me and said, "*Kya karun yaar, woh mana karne wali ab jo nahin rahi toh yeh aa chipki. Main majboor ho gaya hun. Kya karun, woh toh chhod kar chali gayi, ab yeh chhodthi nahin.*" (What do I do, my friend? The person who would stop me is no more and this [alcohol] has become my companion. I am helpless. She left me but this [alcohol] is not ready to leave me.)

I became emotional on hearing him and both of us entered the function with moist eyes. The hall erupted with the sounds applause as we entered. At that time, I saw the same smile on Shashi's face that had abandoned him years ago and it was only then that I understood the real reason for its disappearance.

Yaar toh hain kuch aur bhi yahan
Tumsa magar ab main dhoondoon kahan?
Shakl teri kissi mein jhalakti nahin
Teri yaadon ki khushbu jo mili mujhe
Maut bhi kabhi isse chheen sakti nahin

(Friends, there are many
But, where do I look for one like you?
There's none who is a reflection of you
Even death cannot take away the fragrance
of your memories.)

In the Bollywood industry's hundred-year-old history, the last eldest member from the Kapoor family, son of Sikandar, Prithviraj Kapoor, bid adieu to the life of falsity, and became one with the Goddess of Truth. As he departed on his new journey, he left behind several other Kapoor elders, those who were young until now: Randhir Kapoor, Rishi Kapoor, Rajiv Kapoor, Aditya Kapoor, and Kunal and Karan Kapoor.

I am assured that these new 'elders' will have the blessing of the entire film industry so that they continue to inspire the next generation with their invaluable experiences. The very same experiences that have kept the Kapoor flag flying high for years, even today, in full glory.

May the noble soul of Shashi Kapoor, the last elder, rest in peace.

Sunil Dutt

Every Indian city has seen dreamers and aspiring artists, who in search of happiness, arrive in the city of dreams – Bombay! Perhaps, that is the reason it is called *Maya Nagari* (Land of Illusions). The city had people preoccupied with their respective professions for generations, but the newcomers are invariably those who want to try their luck in the film industry. This process has continued for ages. While some realise their dreams, others get a severe beating for their decisions. For those who make a name for themselves in the industry as stars, it is an abundance of luxuries, wealth, name and fame.

The film industry folk typically lead their celebrated lives in the Bandra, Juhu and Versova areas of the city. I lived in Bandra. I got married there and both my children were born there too. Unsurprisingly, since all these stars and I were neighbours, we very quickly became friends. But I was particularly very close to Dilip Kumar, Rishi Kapoor, Nargis, Sunil Dutt, Rajendra Kumar, Johnny Walker, Rajesh Khanna, Pran and writer Salim Khan. However, my proximity to Nargis and Sunil Dutt was of a different level altogether. Though we were neighbours, we were like family.

Even if we started out as just neighbours, I could feel warmth emanating from them. It was natural for this feeling to take effect. If two hearts are on the same path, they are bound to meet. We became friends and so deep was our love for each other that I am sure it will last forever.

The incidents of Dutt *saheb*'s life are exciting, to say the least. I have heard several stories – some from him, some from his brother Som Dutt, and others from his mother. Besides these, I have myself witnessed some great ups and downs in his life. I dedicate some of those stories to you, my dear readers.

The Dutts have had centuries-old ties with the city of Jhelum in Punjab, which became a part of Pakistan after partition. It was a city where Hindus and Muslims lived peacefully, with only love for each other. Interestingly enough, there are some families there known as Hussaini Brahmins, a Mohyal community with links to both Hinduism and Islam. Besides, there was also a Majlis by the name of Munjhal where both Hindus and Muslims used to meet. They would even perform *puja*s and *namaaz* together. But the British created such an ugly divide between the communities that it saw the destruction of the Majlis.

Dewan Raghunath's wife then found herself coming to India's broken Punjab with her daughter Rani and two sons Balraj, who then came to be known as Sunil, and Som. The kids didn't have a father figure to look up to and so it was the elder son Balraj's responsibility to be the father figure. With a widowed and uneducated mother, a younger brother and sister, he was at a total loss. But he had to face the situation. So with deep faith in God, and keeping his family under the supervision of his uncle, he went to Lucknow in search of a job. With great difficulty, he had found a room to stay. Just then, the partition happened. And Pakistan was born. Thanks to the cunning politics of the British, the two countries were faced with gory and bloody communal riots. People were seen tragically scramming from their houses – Hindus and Sikhs were fleeing Pakistan and the Muslims, India. Terrible scenes of exodus were rampant, and the troubles just became more intense and grave. There was no light in sight to the problems being faced by Balraj. All his hopes of starting life afresh had crashed. There was no news of his family's whereabouts. He was desperately looking for them. Not to mention that he was broke. In the ensuing melee, he had to stay in the waiting room at Lucknow station. Here, he met another person in the same predicament as him – Kalim. This young man had reached Lucknow from Aligarh to meet his parents but had found a lock on their door. He got to know that when his family found the chance to leave for Pakistan, they took it. No one knew where they had gone. Though Balraj and Kalim did not have much in common, their situations were the same. They didn't know where to find solutions to their problems. Meanwhile, conditions only worsened. When Balraj saw piles of dead bodies, he found himself getting crushed by the burden of worry.

Only some time ago he had left his family in Jhelum to look for a job in Lucknow. And while in Lucknow, he had to leave the place to look for his family. The irony wasn't lost on him. He went from place to place looking for his mother and siblings, without money, without food. He reached Delhi and found a refugee camp in Kashmiri Gate where several people who had run from Pakistan were taking refuge. The camp resembled any city in Pakistan, with people from different cities like Lahore, Multan, Peshawar, Rawalpindi, Jhelum and Chakwal, finding space and some solace.

Clinging to hope, Balraj looked through every tent in the camp swarming with desolate people, hoping to find his lost family. He would describe his family members to the people and ask if they had seen them. Perhaps God took pity on his desperate state because he finally found his mother in one of the tents, holding on to her other two children. It looked as if being separated from one of her sons had led to the fear of losing the other two.

The mother was uneducated, and parting from her son Balraj had left her in a complete state of disarray. The eyes that had gone dry waiting and crying for her lost son danced with life when they saw Balraj. She embraced him and said, "*Mera Balla, mera puttar aa gaya.*" (My Balla, my son has come.) She then looked up at the sky and said, "*Aa gaya tera Balla, hamara chhota dewan.*" (Your Balla is here, our little prince.) Balla was Balraj's nickname coined by his mother.

Sunil Dutt was infused with a new life upon finding his family. His first reaction was to hold them in the tightest embrace as if he feared losing them once the grip loosened.

Being educated helped him. After great efforts, the government gave him a piece of land in the Mandoli village near Ambala. It was a village consisting mainly of farmers, and farming was the chief profession of the people there. Balraj's mother, though technically uneducated, was rich with life's experiences. She took on the challenges fate had ordained upon her with a smile and started farming the small land. And life was back on track.

After some time passed, Balraj took his mother's blessings and departed for Bombay for further studies and in search of a job. He promised his family that he'd take all of them to the big city once he had secured a stable job. He left on his big journey, armed with little money to see him through for a few days, a shoulder bag with a couple of *kurta pyjama*s, and a tiffin box with *aloo paratha*s which his mother lovingly packed for him.

On arriving in Bombay, two problems stared him in the face – accommodation and college admissions. For a week, he made VT Station's waiting room his home. While roaming around the city, trying to sort things out, Balraj met a barber from Punjab, who had a salon in Colaba. The two soon struck a friendship and Balraj even got permission to sleep in the salon at nights. It turned out that the barber, Akram, was from Shimla, and had come to the big city to pursue an acting career. After wasting five precious years in trying to fulfil his dream, finally good sense prevailed and resulted in the opening of the Shimla Hair Cutting Saloon. Lucky for him, it took off well.

Now, Balraj was faced with the problem of college admissions. There is an interesting story behind this. In a club in New York, where we are members, my wife has a Sindhi friend called Jyoti Vaswani. When she got to know that we shared a close relationship with the Dutts, she was surprised. She narrated an incident relating to Sunil Dutt's college days. Jai Hind College in Bombay benefitted tremendously from the Sindhi community's contribution towards the field of education. The principal of Jai Hind was also a Sindhi. His niece Rukmini and Jyoti would head to the college canteen whenever they had time between classes. And the canteen, like all other college canteens, was bustling with students sipping coffee or Coke, and having a nice time. In those days, a particular student would go to college regularly and sit all by himself; I am talking about young Balraj. Thanks to his height and handsome face, the girls couldn't keep their eyes off him. One of the victims was the beautiful Rukmini. She gave him several hints that she liked him, but Balraj ignored them. When Jyoti got to know of this, she formally introduced Rukmini to Balraj. They started talking and the conversation continued even outside the canteen. In a few days of knowing her, Balraj confided in Rukmini how he had gotten nowhere with his college admission, and that he was only hanging around in the hopes to get admitted. Rukmini promptly passed on the message to her uncle, the principal. Things worked out and Balraj became a student at Jai Hind. Now all that was left to be done was to find a job so that he could fulfil the promise made to his mother – the promise of bringing his family to Bombay.

Once he completed BA Honours, he found a job too. It so happened that Radio Ceylon had just started Indian programmes. One Mr. Chandran was the head of Radio Ceylon India, with his office on Pedder Road. He liked Balraj's personality and voice so much that he handed him an appointment letter for the position of a radio announcer even without an interview. All Balraj had to do was sign on the dotted lines and start working. His job involved interviewing cinema stars for Radio Ceylon.

His first interview was with Nimmi. It was a great success and there was no stopping Balraj. Then came Dilip Kumar and Dev Anand's interviews and on the latter's recommendation, even Suraiya agreed to an interview. Balraj's voice and interviewing style became so popular on the radio that it could be heard in almost every household. He would earn ₹25 per interview. During this period, another heroine, who was as famous as Suraiya, gave Balraj a tough time. The interview was fixed by the actress' brother at a certain time, only to be rescheduled for the next morning at 10 because she had to suddenly go for a shoot. Balraj reached at 9:45 am the next day. Her brother accompanied him to a room and after waiting till 11 am, the servant came in to say that since madam wasn't well, she had gone off to sleep. Balraj was asked to call after a few days. The servant even enquired if Balraj would like some tea. But even before he could answer, the door was rudely slammed shut on his face. Balraj was humiliated. There was an Irani restaurant at the intersection of Marine Drive and Churchgate, which Balraj frequented. That was where he headed. Upon sitting at his table, he requested in a polite tone, "Can I have some tea and bun maska, please?" The waiter took his order and left. It was still afternoon and Balraj had time till nine in the night, as he could only get into his barber friend's salon after nine. A sense of adventure took over him and he went over to Eros cinema. He bought a ticket for the 3'o clock show and went into the theatre. Raj Kapoor's *Awaara* was being screened and he watched it.

In a couple of days, Mr. Chandran sent a letter to Balraj at the barber shop, ordering him to reach office the next day before 10 am. As per orders, Balraj reached the office before time. When Mr. Chandran entered the office, he looked extremely happy. He told Balraj that madam had called him for the interview at nine the next morning. He asked him to be well-prepared for it. Balraj was taken by surprise and said, "I will do any interview you ask me to, except this. You do this interview yourself. Please excuse me this time. I will do all the research and give you the questions for the interview. That will be my responsibility." It was quite a sight to see Mr. Chandan's plight at the time. His order turned into a request and Balraj couldn't say no. The next day, Balraj reached madam's house a little before time and was surprised to see her ready for the interview. She addressed Balraj as *aap*, apologised for the earlier fiasco and asked the servant to bring some tea for him. Balraj said, "It is my good fortune that I am sitting in front of you having tea. Now that you have touched it, what is the need for sugar?" It seemed as if this one line shredded the veil of formality between them. The interview was great. Then she asked her driver to drop Balraj at Colaba. The driver was the same guy who had slammed the door on Balraj's face. His name was Kasimbhai, and the heroine was the famous Nargis!

It had become Balraj's routine to reach Churchgate station every morning between 7 and 8 from his friend's shop. Normally, people wake up and go to the bathroom, but this is possible only for those with homes. Balraj wasn't one of them. He was living in a shop! He didn't have money to rent a place for himself. He made friends with a newspaper stall owner at Chruchgate station. Both belonged to a region in India where no conversation was complete without using mother/sister cuss words. In other words, two true-blue Punjabis had come together. Thanks to his new friend, Balraj's problem of morning ablutions got sorted. At the station, he made friends with the guard outside the men's room and so he would go in, relieve himself, brush his teeth, have a bath, change into the fresh clothes that he would have kept in his bag, have breakfast at the Irani hotel and get back on the road, looking for a job. He did this for two months, but when nothing worked out, it was his new friend who came to his help. He found him a job at the Bombay Electric Supply & Tramways Company Limited (BEST) office located near the salon where he was put up. His job was to keep account of the amount collected by the bus conductors every day. His duty hours were from 3 pm to 11 pm, for which he was paid ₹120 per month. It was quite a decent amount in those days. Since Akram's shop closed at 10, Balraj had been given a spare key to come in after his duty hours.

They say friends are more helpful than relatives in one's life. And Balraj understood this quite clearly through various experiences. All the friends he made in his initial days even in a strange city like Bombay stepped in to help him in the different stages of his sojourn in their own unique way. Be it the waiter at the Irani hotel, Bashir, the newspaper stall owner, or the watchman outside the men's room at the station. Because they were all Punjabis, the friendship grew faster.

The fourth Punjabi whom Balraj befriended was a man called Sethi. Everyone called him Sethi *saheb*. Though he used to work at the ticket window at New Empire cinema, he also had quite a bit of clout in the film industry. Whenever Punjabis from the film industry, which were quite a few, came to see a movie and saw the 'Houseful' sign in the theatre, it was Sethi who would go out of his way to organise seats for them to watch the film. Quite often, when there were no seats available, he would get extra chairs for the special guests. As a result, they started respecting Sethi *saheb* for his generosity. He used to live in Kurla and was also a man with a proclivity for poetry.

Balraj was Punjabi but he wasn't your typical Punjabi, the kind to use cuss words in every sentence. His language was clean. Sethi had once told me that Balraj was so impressed by the etiquette he observed at Nargis' place during the two-hour interview that the same civility became second nature to him. It was Nargis who induced the element of grace in Balraj.

Sethi was quite like Balraj when it came to behaviour and the display of manners. When he got to know that even Balraj was into poetry, he was beyond himself with happiness. While Balraj was only interested in listening to good poetry, Sethi *saheb* even recited poems occasionally but hadn't really found the right audience. When he found Balraj, his search came to an end. They became great friends. He would recite poems quite enthusiastically and so many times, Balraj would just nod off during the session. If Sethi *saheb* didn't meet Balraj for a few days, he would get restless and anxious to have a poetry session with him.

In Sethi *saheb*, Balraj found a friend who ended up finding solutions to almost all his problems. Firstly, he thrust Balraj with a duplicate key to his house, which became a common meeting point. It was as if indulging in Sethi *saheb*'s poetry was Balraj's way of paying him rent.

Balraj had another friend by the name of Narang. He had nothing to do with the film industry, but they ended up forging a great bond of friendship. *Dost No. 1*, which sounds a lot like one of David Dhawan's film titles, would have been apt to describe their connection. They were each other's confidants in the true sense of the word. It was an ideal equation between the two. Balraj was exemplary when it came to handling his associations with people. When he introduced me to Narang, to give an analogy of the song, '*Deep se deep jalate chalo*', our friendship blossomed too. Our topics of conversation used to be largely two things – one, the 1947 debacle, and how our friend, Balraj, a crude stone once, metamorphosed from Balraj to Sunil Dutt – a pure, shining diamond.

Sunil Dutt was a simple, friendly and warm person by nature and was good to everyone he met, but some people had a special place in his heart. They were yours truly, actor Manmohan, film producer Yash Johar and Harbans Kumar. They were his closest friends. Harbans Kumar started his career as an assistant to director Nasir Hussain in the Filmistan Studio film, *Tum Sa Nahi Dekha*. With his hard work and sincerity, he managed to win many hearts and garner respect among the fraternity. Soon, he also built a great rapport with some international distributors. This led him to earn some invaluable experience in the field of filmmaking and marketing. He met Sunil Dutt through the famous advocate CB Wadhwa, the former offered him the job of manager at Ajanta Arts, which he accepted. Since those days, I was working at Ajanta Arts as production-in-charge; we became colleagues and later great friends too. You can gauge our closeness from the fact that just like him, I shifted to New York too and we remain friends here.

Sunil Dutt's entry into the world of films is rather exciting too. Amongst all the Radio Ceylon programmes, the one which broadcast the interviews of film stars was most popular. While the audience was familiar with the stars, they could only hear the voice of the interviewer, considering that it was on radio. One day, Balraj had to go to Central Studio to interview Dilip Kumar where he was shooting for producer-director Ramesh Sehgal's film *Shikast*. When it was lunch time, Dilip Kumar insisted that they have lunch before starting the interview. Even the thought of sharing lunch with an actor like Dilip Kumar sent Balraj into a tizzy. Though the food was right in front of him, Balraj was lost in a world of his own. It was an unforgettable and momentous day of his life. After all, he had eaten lunch with the reigning actor of the time.

On the other hand, there was Ramesh Sehgal, who had heard about the magical voice of the person doing the interviews on Radio Ceylon, but had never met him. Now, when he saw Balraj with Dilip Kumar, he was so impressed by his persona that he invited him to Central Studio in Tardeo the next day. This time, it wasn't for an interview, but for a screen test. When Balraj heard this, he couldn't contain himself. He felt drunk with happiness. Next day, he reached the studio for the screen test. He was wearing a *kurta pyjama* even though Sehgal had a suit in mind. But when he saw Balraj, he didn't say anything. Then he called the dress man and told him to give the suit reserved for Dilip Kumar to the new boy. When this lanky guy appeared in the suit, it looked like it was on a hanger. But Sehgal *saheb* got what he wanted. The very next week, he signed a contract with Balraj and gave him a signing amount of ₹500.

Ramesh Sehgal was also from Multan like my ancestors. I got to know him because he studied in the same school where my father was the headmaster and was his favourite student. So he had the same respect for me as he had for my father.

The film was to start the following month and Balraj Dutt was rechristened Sunil Dutt. Not only was the name more *filmy*, but there was also another superstar by that old name already creating waves – Balraj Sahni. Dutt *saheb*'s first film as the hero was *Railway Platform* with two heroines – Nalini Jaywant and Sheela Ramani. The film just took off at the box office and then there was no looking back for Sunil Dutt. He also launched his own production house by the name of Ajanta Arts and made several films under its aegis.

One of the films was *Reshma aur Shera*, of which I was the production in-charge. Let me tell you some interesting incidents related to the film. The film was being shot for three months in the village of Pochina, eighty miles from Jaisalmer, in Rajasthan. This village is around four kilometres away from the Pakistan border. On the first day of the shooting itself, there was panic across the border on hearing gunshots. They retaliated with fire. Our BSF soldiers had to placate them saying it was only a film shoot and not any military movement. On knowing this, they wanted to know who the actors were. When they got to know that Waheeda Rehman, Vinod Khanna, Sunil Dutt, Rakhee and Amitabh Bachchan were shooting, their behaviour changed from hostile to friendly.

There is a scene in the film where an ornaments-seller is sitting in his shop in an inebriated state when the heroine visits it. Jankidas was supposed to do the scene but he missed his flight. The scene was ready and in the absence of Jankidas,

I had to do the scene. When I reached the set as the drunk shopkeeper, everyone burst out laughing.

Coming back to the film, we had booked five camels from the chief of the village as they were essential for some scenes. There was one camel atop which Waheeda Rehman shot many scenes. It became so familiar with its routine that as soon as Waheeda*ji* would approach, it would sit, allowing her to alight it. And as soon as it heard the clap, it would get up, as if on cue. It was no less than an actor! Most of the shooting used to happen in moonlit nights in the desert. There was a scene that went on from nine in the night to six in the morning. It had three actors – Sunil Dutt, Waheeda Rehman and the camel. It was important for all three of them to be present. For two nights, everything went smoothly. On the third night when we found out that the third actor, the camel, was missing, there was panic. When we went in search of it, we realised that it had crossed the border and reached Pakistan since clearly it didn't need a visa to cross over.

On the third night, the shooting got over by 10 pm and all of us returned to our tents. Dutt *saheb* gave me the responsibility of finding a solution to this issue by hook or by crook. He then left for a hunting expedition in his vehicle along with actor Ranjeet, dialogue writer Ali Raza and dialogue director BS Thapa because anyway, the shooting would only be at night – if the camel was found, that is. When they returned from their hunt at around four in the morning, another serious issue had cropped up. While everyone else got off the jeep, there was no sign of Ranjeet. No one knew about his whereabouts. Everyone stayed awake in a tense state and then at around six, Ranjeet returned, but in a totally dishevelled state. Apparently, he fell off the jeep when Dutt *saheb* applied the brakes and since he fell on the sand, it didn't make a sound and Dutt *saheb* continued driving like nothing had happened. Ultimately, it turned out that though the hunters came empty-handed, it was Ranjeet who had become the hunted one.

Since I was responsible for getting the lost camel back, in the morning, waving a white flag, I walked towards the border along with two BSF jawans. The Pakistani soldiers requested if they could move closer to us. When they did, we saw the camel following them. I thanked them and brought the much-needed actor back to the camp. Problem solved, we finished shooting the scene perfectly in two hours. From 11 to 2 in the night, the crew only celebrated. Everyone had a couple of drinks, but the camel guzzled half a bottle. Of course, rum bottles exchanged hands when the camel returned, and the Pakistani soldiers became friends. In fact, on a couple of occasions, I even brought them along to watch the shooting and to meet Sunil Dutt and Waheeda Rehman. Once it so happened that six soldiers walked across to meet us. And among them was one who got a special embrace from Sunil Dutt. That jawan belonged to Jhelum and was Dutt *saheb*'s compatriot. Ever since, there was a festive atmosphere on both sides.

Another interesting incident took place during the shooting for *Reshma aur Shera*. We had created a temporary office in the village of Pochina, which was around 80 km from Jaisalmer. It took care of our food and laundry needs and also relayed messages. The man responsible for handling this office was an elderly gentleman, who retired as Mehboob Khan's chief assistant director. Nargisji and Dutt *saheb* called him Chinu *Mama*. Ali Raza had brought him along. These relationships developed on the sets of *Mother India*.

Every day, Ali Raza would write one letter to his wife Nimmi and send it to Chinu Mama in Jaisalmer. Then Chinu Mama would post it to Bombay. One night, beneath a magical moonlit sky in the desert, a romantic scene between Sunil Dutt and Waheeda Rehman was to be filmed. I handed over two pages written by Ali Raza to Waheeda*ji* without reading it. She read the scene and couldn't control her laughter. The reason was that she was reading Ali Raza's love letter to his wife, while his wife had received the scene. It became a reason for great mirth on the sets.

In *Reshma aur Shera*, Amitabh Bachchan, who was just beginning his career, played acharacter who was mute. Sukhdev was going to be the director of the film. So before starting the film, he suggested that Amitabh's character should be mute. He said it would win the audience's sympathy since he was supposed to get the heroine in the end. While not everyone was convinced, Sukhdev was gifted with the power of convincing and eventually, Sunil Dutt agreed with him. Three people who didn't approve of this decision were Nargis Dutt, the cinematographer Ramchandra Singh and I. In retrospect, Mr. Dutt admitted that it was a mistake. We don't know what Amitabh felt, because back then, he had no choice in the matter and had to accept it. He was in no position to refuse anything that came his way. He has always been silent about the film, but I just want to say, I can hear his silence.

The success that Sunil Dutt received in the film world is no secret. The list of his films is endless – *Railway Platform, Ek Hi Rasta, Gumrah, Waqt, Usne Kaha Tha, Khandan, Main Chup Rahungi, Milan, Geeta Mera Naam, Heera, Ghaban, Mujhe Jeene Do, Yeh Raste Hain Pyar Ke*, etc. However, his career took a new turn during the shooting of *Mother India*. The movie had a scene in which the heroine gets trapped in a raging fire in the field. But unfortunately, instead of being merely a film scene, it turned into a horrifying reality. Nargis, who was the heroine, found herself surrounded by a furious fire that enveloped her, leaving her no way out of it. Panic spread in the set as wildly as the fire. It seemed like Nargis would succumb to the tragedy soon. Everyone could hear her desperate pleas for help, but no one had the courage to do anything to save her. Just then, one saw Sunil Dutt emerging from the crowd and plunging himself into the fire and bringing Nargis to safety. When they emerged from the fire, they had severe burns. The shooting was halted. Meanwhile, there was another fire that had set off in both their hearts. Now the question was who would bell the cat. It looked like Nargis had made up her mind that she would not blink first. The unnerving silence between them was deepening when the shoot resumed. Then nature took it upon itself to break this deafening silence. It so happened that one day when the shoot, which was going on in Mehboob Studio, ended. Nargis' car, a Jaguar, broke down and her driver had to take it to the garage. So getting home, which was at Marine Drive, was an issue. When there seemed to be no solution in sight, Sunil Dutt modestly asked her, "If it's okay with you, can I drop you home in my humble Fiat?" It was a black Fiat which Sunil Dutt had bought on instalments. I even remember the number: BML-1933. Nargis' problem was solved. It would take about an hour to reach Marine Drive from Bandra. Taking advantage of the time available to him, Sunil Dutt asked her, "I want to talk to you about marriage. Whatever you decide, I will respect it. Please think about it and let me know."

When they reached Marine Drive, the only thing Nargis offered was a 'thank you'. Nothing more, nothing less, and Sunil Dutt drove back in his car. He kept cursing himself for this rash move as he was sure that she would refuse. This particular car is still parked in Sunil Dutt's garage because of sentimental value – he had proposed to Nargis in that car, after all. His children refer to it as, 'Papa *ki gaadi*' and it has a special place in their hearts.

Two days later, when Sunil Dutt reached his home, he found his sister in a bewildered state. When he asked her, she said, "The heroine Nargis had come over around 5 pm and had said, "*Apne bhai se keh dena ki jo usne mujhse poocha tha, maine haan keh di hai.*" (Tell your brother that my answer to his question is a yes.)

One can easily imagine Sunil Dutt's mood on hearing this. It was as if he had touched the sky in one leap. The sizzling fire that had consumed them all this time finally took the form of holy fire that was witness to their becoming life partners the very next month. The next day, newspapers carried headlines, which read, "Nargis marries Sunil Dutt." From love to wedding bliss, it augured good tidings for the couple. The symbols of their love are their three children, Sanju (Sanjay), Anju (Namrata), and Priya. However, just when it seemed like they had a fulfilling and content life, they were cursed by some evil eye. The brightness in their lives was beginning to get swallowed by an ominous darkness. Nargis was only fifty-two when she became a victim of the deadly cancer. On their doctor's advice, her husband took her to New York for treatment.

For Sunil Dutt, the status of his mother was always above everyone else and Nargis shared the same sentiment. When she understood that she wouldn't live too long, she told her husband, "*Jab main duniya mein ayi thi toh pehli goad mujhe meri maa ki mili thi. Meri ichcha hai ki antim goad mujhe unki hi mile, isliye marne ke baad mujhe meri maa ki kabra mein hi dafan karna jahan woh hamesha ki neend so rahi hai. Agey aap ki marzi.*" (When I came into this world, my mothers lap was my first refuge. It is my wish that even in my last journey, I be buried next to her. The rest is up to you.) Sunil Dutt decided to fulfil his wife's wishes and did exactly what she had requested. But the next day, a controversy erupted, and one could hear voices shouting slogans of 'Sunil Dutt *murdabad*'. (Down with Sunil Dutt.) Some parochial Hindus believed that being a Hindu, Sunil Dutt should have cremated his wife rather than burying her. It was natural for anyone to get perturbed in the face of such upheaval. However, Sunil Dutt was content at heart. The next day when I reached his house, I saw his close friends Narang, Murli Deora, Dilip Kumar and Ram Mohan who had come to give their friend courage to deal with the tragedy. What Dutt *saheb* said as an answer to those who raised objections about Nargis' last rites was worth its weight in gold. He said, "*Mohabbat khud ek alag aur pak mazhab hai jis ka koi rasm-o-rivaj nahin hota. Maine jise jalti bhadakti aag se zinda bacha ke nikala tha aur phir havan kund mein jalti aag ke gird saat phere lete hue hum zindagi bhar ke liye ek duje ke hogaye the, usey khud aag ke havale kaise karta?*" (Love itself is a unique and pure religion that doesn't follow any customs and rituals. I had saved her from a violent blaze and then went around the holy fire seven times to become one with her. How could I surrender her to fire once again?)

When Nargis was being treated at the famous Sloan Kettering Hospital in New York, she was admitted there for ten months. Sunil Dutt was a permanent presence by his wife's side in those months. I think it was the first time and perhaps the last time that the nurses and doctors there saw a husband so dedicated and in love with his wife. Perhaps that was why the American hospital's dean's wife said, "If there is reincarnation, I would love to have an Indian husband in my next birth."

The doctors did their best to save Nargisji, but who can question fate? May 3rd, 1981 was the last day in Nargis' life. After a brave fight, she eventually gave up in the fight against cancer. She was fifty-three.

Their bungalow in Pali Hill, which was witness to the birth and childhood of the three children, the home that Nargis personally decorated, had turned into a place haunted by her memories. It was best to move away from it. So it was demolished to make way for Imperial Towers, a ten-storey building. Sunil Dutt kept four flats on the top two storeys of the building. He kept one for himself and gave the other three to his three children. While the children moved in soon after the construction was completed, the father decided to enter his flat only on June 1, the birthday of his beloved wife. While the interiors of the house were being done, Sunil Dutt made sure it was just how Nargis would have liked it. The furniture was bought from Delhi and great thought went into every accessory in the house. When the flat was ready, the wait for June 1 began. But fate played its cruel game once again. Just a week before his wife's birthday, on May 25, 2005, it snatched Sunil Dutt away from the world. And it was only his photograph that made it to the house. It was hung next to his wife's on a wall in the living room.

Sunil Dutt had borne a lot of burden in his life, but he never gave up. He always shared whatever he earned with people he cared for. His popularity can be gauged from the fact that when he stood for elections, he won by a huge margin of votes. He became the Union Sports Minister and left an indelible mark in the political sphere too. The unfortunate part is that though he got into the sports arena, he didn't manage a century and got run-out at seventy-five, leaving us only with a bundle of unforgettable memories.

I would like to end this chapter with this poem:

Yaad aapki bekarar karti hai
Nazar aap ko talash baar baar karti hai
Gila nahin ke hum door hain aap se
Aap ki toh judai bhi hum se pyar karti hai

(Your memory makes me restless
My eyes keep looking for you all the time
There is no regret about us being apart
For, this separation loves me too)

Tabassum

The Indian film industry is a magnificent cricket ground that has witnessed several champion players test their skills in it and score centuries. They have enriched the film industry with their invaluable contribution. Among them, Meena Kumari got out at forty-five runs, Nargis got out at fifty-three, Dev Anand made eighty-six, Sunil Dutt seventy-five, Rajendra Kumar batted for seventy-two runs and Rajesh Khanna called it quits at sixty-nine. They all returned to the pavilion after their priceless innings, but the two who have continued running on the crease are two of my favourite players – Dilip Kumar not out at ninety-five, and Tabassum not out at seventy. I pray to God that they make their centuries before calling it a day.

It is important for me to talk about Tabassum, because for me, she is just as important to me as Nargisji and Nimmiji. People have known Tabassum since she was a four or five-year-old child, and a child artiste in those days. Be it Meena Kumari, Nargisji, Nimmiji or Madhubala, their childhood version had been played by Baby Tabassum. She became popular by this name in the country. Even though her face glowed with innocence, one could also easily see the maturity and intelligence that governed her personality. When she grew up, she went to Aligarh Muslim University for a BA degree in Urdu, and once done, returned to the world of camera, light, studio and sound, and lost herself in it completely. Work and struggle in the industry became her life, her world. Then there was her parents' concern to see their daughter settled. After all, like all girls, Tabassum must have dreamt of a fairytale wedding and a beautiful life with her partner too. Fortunately, she found her life partner in Vijay Govil and their union was like Kamal Haasan's film *Ek Duje ke Liye*. While that was just a film, here it seemed like they were truly made for each other.

Many years ago, when Tabassum had already been married for a while, I remember an incident that took place at CSIA. I was going to Delhi, and Tabassum and her husband were going to Shimla. Suddenly, Tabassum got up and walked towards someone, trying to introduce herself. Just then, the person cut her short and said, "I know, you are Baby Tabassum." This person was none other than India's former PM, Rajiv Gandhi. There is a strange attraction in Tabassum's face. There is so much positivity, goodness and sincerity in her words that one inevitably gets attracted to her. She is a popular figure not only in the film industry but in other fields too. *Shama* magazine's editor and owner Idris Dehlvi and Tabassum were so close that she was a part of every celebration at his house. She may not have a big body of work in the film industry, but she has maintained great relations with most of the stalwarts and they respect her too. She has very close associations with actors like Dilip Kumar, Shatrughan Sinha and Amitabh Bachchan.

Every parent in the world wants the best for their children, but at times, children fall into bad company, resulting in the crashing of the big dreams their parents had for them. I thank

God that I found my sister Tabassum's son an obedient and well-behaved child. If he is good looking like his mother, he is also strong and healthy like his father.

I have to say that I am quite pleased to see Tabassum having grown from Baby to *Bebe*, but even today, I find a child-like quality about her, which is very heartening. She may be a grandmother today and has a somewhat serious demeanour now, but her innocence is intact.

The heroes and heroines in our industry often play hide and seek with their real ages. When they turn twenty-nine, they will remain twenty-nine for a few years, and then the same at forty-nine, and so on and so forth. They celebrate their forty-ninth birthday at least three to four times. Just the thought of saying that they are fifty makes them nervous. Not so for Tabassum. On one occasion, the topic veered towards her age and I guessed it to be sixty-five. But she immediately got back to me saying she was seventy and not sixty-five! This is what she is all about – realistic to the core. She is in love with the truth and doesn't believe in a make-believe, unreal world.

Be it the big screen in cinema halls or the small screen in your house, Tabassum's smiling face, her affectionate banter, her chirpy and magical voice will let you forget all your worries for the time being. You will find yourself mesmerised by her magic.

Even though I am now settled in New York, closer to my children, much to their relief and happiness, I often miss my home in Bandra. When I think of the old days, neighbours and friends, I feel sad and find it difficult to sleep. But sometimes I take advantage of the sleeplessness and watch *Abhi toh Main Jawan Hoon,* a TV show created by Amitabh Bachchan and HR Shah, a New Jersey-based businessman. I forget all my fatigue and worries after watching that. The popularity of this programme can be compared to Sachin Tendulkar's in cricket or Amitabh Bachchan's in films. It has been ages since we used to be crazy to hear Ameen Sayani's magical voice on Radio Ceylon. It was his disciple, Shiraz Sharif, who started this programme on TV Asia. Thirteen years after taking care of the show, taking it to the pinnacles of success, on his retirement, he handed over its responsibility to my sister Tabassum. This hour-long programme is so popular in the USA that all the Indian, Pakistani and Bangladeshi families gather around their television sets to watch it exactly at 11 pm. It is my favourite programme too. After hearing Tabassum's beautiful voice for an hour, sleep embraces me like a warm hug. When Doordarshan had just launched in India, one of its most popular shows was *Phool Khilein Hain Gulshan Gulshan* hosted by Tabassum. She opened the show with her dimpled smile, and amicably chatted with the guest of the day, and even interspersed the conversation with some unforgettable songs.

Tabassum and Nargis were like mother and daughter. They both loved each other. Just like Nargis had a mixed parentage – Jaddan Bai and Mohan Babu, Tabassum was from a similar background. Her mother was Asgari Begum and father Ayodhya Nath. Such stories often find a place in the chapters of a novel or in films but are rare to find in real life.

May 3rd is Nargis *bhabhi*'s death anniversary. Last year, on this day, Tabassum played songs dedicated to Nargis in the programme, which was very well-received. When I watched the show, I was wrapped in a cloud of memories and I found myself lost and getting sucked into timeless nostalgia. It felt as if I was trying to find myself amongst the crowd of memories and could see Nargis *bhabhi* saying:

Daem abaad rahegi duniya
Hum na honge, koi hum sa aur hoga

(The world will remain eternal
I may not be around; there will be someone else like me)

In the end, I must add that as good as Tabassum may be at making people smile, she also has the ability to make people cry. I say this because when I was watching the programme, tears were welling up in my eyes. But they were tears that cleared all the mistiness in my mind and heart. When the seventy-year-old Tabassum said, "*Abhi toh main jawan hoon,*" somehow it felt right. She really is young, at heart!

The Legend of the Kapoors

As I was reflecting upon my precious reminiscences and memories, I chanced upon a special story about a mischievous boy. I was at Hotel Sun-N-Sand in Juhu, having a chat with my friend Rajendra Nath (also lovingly known as Jinder) by the poolside. We were drinking beer when we got into a bet – the person who drank lesser beer would pay the entire bill.

Rajendra Nath was one of the first people I befriended in Bombay. He was the popular star Prem Nath's younger brother and they were, in fact, Raj Kapoor's brothers-in-law – *saalas*. Anyway, we were in the middle of our beer session when a chubby and mischievous looking child came up to Rajendra Nath and asked him for 100 rupees. It seemed as if Rajendra Nath actually owed him the amount. When the child kept on pestering him while addressing him as Mamu, Rajendra Nath admonished him, "Chintu, *tang mat karo. Jab dekho kabhi yeh de do, kabhi woh de do. Abhi jao swimming karo. Ek ghante tak aa jaana* for lunch with us." (Chintu, don't trouble me. You are always asking for something or the other. Now go and swim. Come back in an hour for lunch.)

The problem with beer is that you have to go to the bathroom too often to relieve your bladder. Jinder had already made three visits to the toilet. The fourth time he went, he took the beer bottle with him. And he was gone for a long time. I finally walked to the bathroom to check if everything was alright. When I got there, I saw that even though he had relieved himself, he was still standing there. With his right hand resting on the wall, he was holding the bottle upside down with his left hand, emptying it and muttering, "You're cheating me; you're indirectly going down the drain anyway... I know you well, my dear bitch... now go directly."

I was still in my senses, but realised that my friend certainly was not. He had lost the bet. When I helped him to our table, I saw that while the car keys were still there, the wallet was missing. When we asked the staff, they told us that the kid who was with us had taken it. About ten minutes later, one of the staff members came with the wallet and said the child had asked him to return it to his Mamu, who was seated by the poolside. When Jinder Mamu opened the wallet to check the contents, he realised that only hundred rupees were missing. Thanks to the missing note, at least Jinder came back to his senses and paid the bill of ₹400 from the remaining money. This little brat was none other than Rishi Kapoor, who later became a successful hero, with several hit films with heroines like Madhuri Dixit, Poonam Dhillon, Sridevi, Jaya Prada and Dimple Kapadia. But one heroine with whom he did a number of films – all of them super hits – was Neetu Singh. She was also the lady who stole his heart. When they realised they were in love, the family supported them and the two got married. The groom's father, Raj Kapoor, hosted a reception for the newlyweds at RK Studio. It was a grand affair. I was invited both by the groom's uncle, Shashi Kapoor and

Mamu, Rajendra Nath.

I had been to many weddings as a guest, but this one was something. No one who attended it would have been able to forget the grand spectacle. Now, *jeeja* Raj Kapoor had given his *saala*, Prem Nath, a strange duty. He was supposed to open every bottle of Johnnie Walker Black Label at the party and taste it to verify that the liquor was indeed authentic. Only then was it to be served to the guests. Prem Nath took his job very seriously and dutifully tasted the scotch. He would take some in the lid and swallow it. He managed to do it with twenty bottles but soon after that, he was clean-bowled and had to be carried away.

Meanwhile, at the party, people were drinking as if there was no tomorrow. Tipsy guests, on their way out, would thank Prem Nath instead of the actual host, Raj Kapoor. As for us, we bade farewell to Shashi Kapoor, who was totally in control, and Rajendra Nath, whose condition was similar to that of his brother's!

Around the same time, Rajendra Nath's sister, Uma Chopra, was set to marry the famous movie villain, Prem Chopra. Hotel Sun-N-Sand was duly booked to carry out the nuptials in the day and the reception in the evening. Rajendra Nath had been accorded the duty to take care of the guests. But since he wasn't confident of handling it single-handedly, he urged me to help him. How could I refuse a friend? After the rituals and lunch, it was decided that some of the guests who had come from Delhi, Chandigarh, etc., and were staying in the same hotel, would retire to their rooms and would come to the evening reception.

Considering that both the parties were from the film industry, there was great camaraderie between some industry people with both the Prems (Prem Nath and Prem Chopra). Among the special guests, there was also a film producer,

CM Thakkar. He used to live in Santacruz. He was among the first ones to arrive at the wedding. Since he was coming from Santacruz, there was no room booked for him at the hotel. We were in a dilemma as to where he would rest. So we decided to leave this producer of the super hit film *Mr. X* at the bar. We took him to the bar and after finalising all the work that needed to be done, left, leaving him there. We got busy with the preparations outside and he, inside!

After completing all the work, before going to our rooms for a break, we decided to check on Mr. Thakkar. On reaching the bar, we saw that he was snoring on the bar chair, completely sozzled. We carried him outside, put him in a taxi and told the taxi driver to take him back home. We told the driver, Thakkar would help him with the directions to his house. Once the taxi left, we retired to our rooms. In the evening, when we came down for the reception, what we saw left us gaping in amazement. We saw Thakkar sitting in the bar, sharing a drink with the taxi driver! We found out that they were on their third drink. Perturbed, Jinder asked the driver what was going on. He replied, "*Sahab, ek ghante tak Santacruz mein unka ghar talash karte rahe; kabhi yeh gali kehte, kabhi woh gali batate, magar unka apna ghar hi nahi mila. Maine socha wahin kahin utaar dun, lekin jab kiraya manga to yeh saheb mujhe wapis yahin le aye. Main marta kya na karta, majboor ho kar sath chala aya.*" (Sir, for one hour we kept looking for his house in Santacruz. He took me into every bylane but never found his house. I thought I'd drop him off somewhere there, but when I asked him for the fare, he brought me back here. I was helpless and came along with him.) When we heard this, we felt helpless.

Thakkar was in such a state that he didn't even remember he was a guest at Prem Chopra's wedding. With a wave of his hand, Jinder left. I tried my best to explain his whereabouts to Thakkar. I asked him to come to the party and stay with me throughout. By then, he was feeling a little better. He told me to carry on and that he would join me after a visit to the bathroom. So I proceeded to the party without him and met Jinder. After about ten minutes, when Thakkar came to the party hall, we saw that he was once again accompanied by the same driver. He looked perfectly fine now, but it was time for both of us to reach for our smelling salts. Thakkar went on the stage, congratulated Prem Chopra, only to then ask, "What is happening? Which film...?" After witnessing this episode, I excused myself and stood in a corner. Jinder and the driver then managed to take him to the taxi. Once in the taxi, he very innocently asked who'd pay for it. "I don't have a penny in my pocket today." Jinder asked the driver to drop him and come back to the hotel for his bill.

While leaving the party, I told my friend Rajendra Nath, "*Yaar, filmein toh aksar over budget ho jati hain, lekin aaj yeh dekh kar hairaan hun ki shadi bhi over budget ho jati hai!*" (Buddy, I have heard of films going over the budget, but it is the first time that I am seeing a wedding go over budget.)

Prithviraj Kapoor

This is the story of the unique friendship between famous producer and keen astrologer Mohla *saheb* and the real Sikandar of the film world, Prithviraj Kapoor. In the drama that is life, they played the parts of Mohla-Krishna, Prithvi-Sudama, Prithvi-Krishna or Mohla-Sudama at different times.

Raj, Shammi and Shashi Kapoor were still quite young when Prithviraj Kapoor found that Mohla guru's predictions about them were rather accurate. This further deepened their friendship. What's more, Prithviraj Kapoor's wife became Mohla *saheb*'s Rakhi sister and the friends became *jeeja* and *saala*.

The following month itself, Mohla *saheb* announced the film *Insaan*. The hero was Prithviraj and heroine Naaz, who had close relations with actress Mumtaz's mother, while the director was Kedar Kapoor (the father of Madhu Kapoor – a heroine with Rajshri Productions). In those days, he was also famous actor, producer and director Jagdish Sethi's chief assistant director. The film's *mahurat* was held at Andheri's Prakash Studio. Owing to their friendship, the hero didn't demand a single paisa as fees. And the film continued without any glitches.

However, there was an unwritten agreement between the *jeeja* and the *saala* that on the last day before the shoot could begin, the *saala*, Mohla *saheb*, would hand over ₹10,000 to the hero and *jeeja* Prithviraj Kapoor or else he wouldn't come to the sets and shoot. So, on the last day, Prithviraj Kapoor was ready with his makeup and costume at seven in the morning, waiting in his makeup room for Mohla *saheb* to fulfil his verbal promise of handing over the money so that he could start shooting.

But when Mohla *saheb* heard this, he started sweating as if he were standing under the scorching sun in May, even in the cold month of December. After much consideration, the producer asked the director to continue shooting the scenes that didn't require the hero and that he would be back by lunchtime. It was 11 am then and sharp at 2 pm, the producer arrived and the hero had received his ₹10,000 as promised on the last day of the shooting at Prakash Studio,

Andheri. It felt as if light (Prakash) had arrived and darkness (Andheri) had gone.

Along with the cash, *saale saheb* also gave his *jeejaji* a box of sweets. When he handed over the cash, he said, "*Yeh lo cash, shooting karo aur phir karo aish.*" (Take this cash, start shooting, then you can have fun.) At 6 pm when the shooting was over and the film was wrapped up, the producer and the hero hugged each other tightly. With a smile on his face and a bundle of crisp hundred-rupee notes, Prithviraj Kapoor reached home and handed over the money and the box of sweets to his wife when she asked, "Why was Mohla *saheb* so upset today? When he came in the afternoon, he looked sad. As a sister, I gave him courage, fed him lunch and gave him sweet lassi to drink. And when he asked to borrow ₹10,000 for a few days, I gave him that too!"

When my friend Rajendra Nath, Prithviraj Kapoor's son, Raj Kapoor's real *saal*a, narrated this incident, I wondered how *hairan* and *pareshan* the hero of *Insaan* would have been on finding out the truth about his fees of ₹10,000!

Vinod Khanna

When my family and I arrived in Delhi from our native place, Multan, after the partition, my father, Lala Dinanath, found a place for us in the new city, and as a means of subsistence, opened a school in his name. Since he was the headmaster of a school back in Multan, he thought this would be ideal to make a living. My younger sister Sheeli and I were the first students of the school. A Khanna family from Peshawar had recently become our neighbours. Their kids were admitted in Dinanath High School. My father was respected by everyone in the community. He was known not only as the headmaster of many schools in Punjab, but also for his unusual way of teaching the children.

The senior-most member in the Khanna family, Kishanchand Khanna, was aware of my father's reputation, and given the way he looked after his children, he was treated as no less than God. Khanna *saheb* tried to start his family business in Delhi too, but when he felt it wasn't working out, headed to Bombay. The children continued to study in Delhi for a few years. When he tasted success in Bombay, he moved the family too. He used to stay away from films and film folk, as a rule. By then several people from Peshawar had made a name for themselves in the film industry, such as Prithviraj Kapoor and Dilip Kumar (Yusuf Khan). He didn't regard the film industry as a noble profession. He only believed in old-fashioned rituals, worship and being involved in the functioning of the Arya Samaj.

He had two sons and two daughters. Even after the daughters were married, he was worried about his sons. When the elder son spoke about choosing modelling as a career, the father was completely against it. Though the son respected and loved his father, they were as different as chalk and cheese when it came to attitudes and choices. The boy had unique characteristics. He befriended actor Manmohan. Their likes and dislikes were quite similar. Manmohan had won the hearts of many through his performances. One of them was Sunil Dutt. His friendship with Manmohan set an example of what friendship meant in the film industry.

One day, when Sunil Dutt, after a hectic day of shoot, returned to his home in Bandra, he was visibly tired. Around 9 pm, when he was planning to retire to bed, Manmohan reached there unannounced. When he told him the reason for dropping by, Sunil Dutt looked at the clock and excused himself, saying he was tired and couldn't go out with him to meet anyone then. But Manmohan convinced Sunil Dutt to go with him to a big party in town. It was 11 pm when they arrived at the venue and it looked like the party had just begun. Dutt *saheb* had finished just one drink when he spotted a young, handsome man in a smart suit. He couldn't stop looking at him. To introduce the young man to Sunil Dutt was the reason Manmohan had dragged him to the party. He thought since Dutt *saheb* was planning a film with his brother Som Dutt, the young man might get lucky and land a role in it. As soon as they were introduced, Dutt *saheb* asked him if he would like to work in films. The boy said yes but he was worried about his father's reaction. He was confident that his father would never agree. Dutt *saheb* then asked him to come to his office the next day at 2 pm. He then left for home.

The next day, Dutt *saheb* told me about the boy and said that in the Ajanta Arts film *Man ka Meet*, Som Dutt would be the hero, the new girl, Leena Chandavarkar, the heroine and a new boy Vinod Khanna would play the villain. When the film started, Dutt *saheb*, with full confidence in me, handed over the responsibilities of taking care of the budget and of co-ordinating with director Subba Rao, writer Rajender Krishan, music director Ravi and editor Pran Mehra to get the best out of them. Besides this, I also had to handle the marketing of the film.

When the young man arrived at the office in the afternoon, we were speechless after seeing each other. While in Delhi we were neighbours, we hadn't yet met in Bombay. Both of us simultaneously said, *"Arey, tu yahan kaise?"* (How is it that you are here?) Though we were acquaintances in Delhi, we weren't really friends. His sisters were in the same class as my sisters in Dinanath School. When the school's average result was announced as 95% the next year, everyone was ecstatic and forced my father to have a celebration for it. The programme was fixed for the following week. The chief guest was Prithviraj Kapoor. Khanna *saheb* was invited too but he didn't make it to the function. Perhaps it was because of his views on film stars and the profession. He used to say, *"Film line kanjaron ka dhandha hai."* (The film line is for those without scruples.) However, both his daughters were present along with their friends.

Now, after he signed the contract with Ajanta Arts for the film and had taken an advance of ₹500, Vinod Khanna was tension personified. I understood his predicament and he probably sensed that I did. So while leaving with the advance, he invited me to his house the next day. I was surprised at the invitation, considering we weren't friends then. Anyway, as promised, I reached their Nana Chowk residence. I knew about his father's opinion on actors and the film industry.

It was only after he introduced me to his father that I understood the reason for Vinod Khanna's invitation. He said, "This is Raaj Grover. He is our Delhi neighbour Lala Dinanathji's son. He works with Sunil Dutt."

I have already mentioned that my father was the headmaster of the DAV School in Multan. Today, it is known as the Muslim High School. Since education has no religion, his photograph still hangs on the walls of the school along with those of the other headmasters.

When we were in Delhi, I had never met Vinod Khanna's father. So he didn't recognise me. On hearing that I worked with Sunil Dutt, he didn't seem interested for reasons already mentioned. But when he heard the name Lala Dinanath, he asked me, in native Punjabi, "*Bachche, tu apne marzi naal aisi line ich aya hai?*" (My child, have you willingly chosen this line of profession?) Clearly, I was supposed to say yes and I did. Then he enquired about Sunil Dutt. The conversation continued at the dining table over lunch. After the meal, he told his wife, "*Jay, Lala Dinanathji da jatak, ais line ich unnan di marzi naal kaam karda ae. Te phir lagda ae ke sab tai nahi, kuch toh theek theek changey bande Sunil Dutt akan vi hain is line ich jo Raaj ne dasya ae mainu. Han, Sunil Dutt de bare ich. Changa ae phir.Mere kaam ich te zara vi shauk nahin ennu.*" (It seems not all in the film industry are bad. There are some good people too like Sunil Dutt, as Raaj has told me. It's good then, anyway, he [Vinod] is not interested in my business.) Both Vinod and I overheard this conversation that was likely to clear the path for Vinod's future.

Then he lovingly saw me off, requesting me to give his regards to my father. When I saw Vinod's face, it was plastered with a big smile and relief. I realised that apart from his good looks, he was also a clever individual for having used my father's reputation to convince his father.

Vinod Khanna played the villain in many films that were commercial successes. He starred opposite Dharmendra and even Rajesh Khanna as the villain many times. But thanks to his tall Punjabi structure, and handsome and macho countenance, the audience, distributors and even the media felt that he was hero material. As a result, he soon found himself in leading roles. He found great success after this. He acted along with stars like Hema Malini, Asha Parekh, Saira Banu, Sadhana and Nanda, and was well-accepted.

After my visit to his house, our friendship deepened with time. Today, we are both close to seventy, but the tales of our youth have kept our friendship alive and young at heart.

He did a lot of favours for me. One day, after the debacle of Ajanta Arts' film *Reshma aur Shera*, Sunil Dutt summoned all the staff for a meeting and said, "I have incurred a huge loss with this film. Besides, even my other films are not doing as well as before. So with a heavy heart, I must tell you all that I have decided to close Ajanta Arts. I request you all to find another job in a month's time."

On hearing this news, we were all dumbstruck. Apart from being an important part of Ajanta Arts, I also held a special place in Dutt *saheb*'s family. Nargis *bhabhi* accorded the same love and respect to me as she did to her brother-in-law Som Dutt and nephew Sarvar Hussain. This announcement by Dutt *saheb* made me emotional, and without even consulting the other staff members, I said, "I am sorry Dutt *saheb*. This office will not shut down. If you are doing this because you feel you can't pay the staff its salaries, we don't want it. We will take it as it comes. We will not give up. Not only we, but also the whole industry has learnt the fighting spirit from you." Everyone agreed with me and I could see the happiness on their faces.

Dutt *saheb* had earlier heard a story from one of my friends that he had liked. It had two heroes. The very same evening, without informing Dutt *saheb*, I went to meet the writer to take the story, whose script was ready, forward. I also told him about Dutt *saheb*'s announcement. A drinks session ensued and by the time we reached the second round, it was decided that work would start the very next day.

The following day, we found out where and for which film Vinod Khanna was shooting. After finding out Vinod's whereabouts, we reached Modern Studio in Andheri at around 3 pm to meet him. The hero was busy filming a scene with his heroine Saira Banu. After around twenty minutes, when the scene was completed, before they could start the next, Vinod ushered us into his make-up room. He ordered some tea and biscuits. We told him about Sunil Dutt's predicament and his decision about Ajanta Arts. On hearing us, he first spoke to Saira Banu and then to the director. It was around 4 by then. Immediately, the shooting was stopped for the day and the three of us reached the Ajanta Arts office in Bandra. Once again, Vinod was sitting across the table where he had signed his first film, *Man ka Meet*. On that day, no one knew him, but then, the whole world did.

When we reached the office, Dutt *saheb* was busy with his accountant. My writer friend put the script of the story, which Dutt *saheb* had already read, on the table. Then he touched Dutt *saheb*'s feet and when they embraced each other, both had tears in their eyes. Vinod held Dutt *saheb*'s hand and didn't let go of it until he had embraced him too. This writer friend's name was KK Shukla. Wiping his tears, he first smiled and then told Dutt *saheb*, "Last night, when Raaj came to my place, as usual, he addressed me as KK. When I asked him the reason for his visit, he said, 'When I said KK, I wasn't taking your name, I was asking you, *'Kya karun?'* After searching for the answer to his question all night, I have kept the solution on your desk." That evening was spent in KK's house over drinks.

Within a month, all the necessary groundwork was done and the *mahurat* and shooting of the film *Nehle pe Dehla* began. With Sunil Dutt, Vinod Khanna, Saira Banu, and Prem Nath as the leading cast, and the efforts of director Raj Khosla and writer KK Shukla, the film was a hit. Ajanta Arts was debt free and the staff received their salary. Happily, I again said, "KK," and my friend turned around. This time, I said, "*Kamaal kar diya*" (You did a great job) and my friend just burst out laughing.

It was a coincidence when two renowned writers got married and became brothers-in-law. One of them was KK Shukla, who married Daisy Irani and Javed Akhtar tied the knot with her sister, Honey Irani.

I have received a lot of love in my life and I have loved a lot too. I am very lucky in this regard. Aided by this love, in 1978, I brought Rakhee, Vinod Khanna, Parveen Babi, Pran, director Narendra Bedi, Anand Bakshi and Lakshmikant Pyarelal together. Even though I had just ₹5,000 in my bank account, I started the film *Taaqat* on March 21, 1978, with all of them, without having to give a single paisa as the signing amount. It was our love for each other that made it possible. The film was completed; it released and ran but not as well as I had expected it to. Towards the end of the film, it was the love and effort of Rakhee, Vinod Khanna and director Narendra Bedi that kept me going.

Vinod's second favour to me is exciting and still holds

great importance in my life. Those days, his popularity was at its peak. He had purchased a flat near Bandra station but he didn't require it anymore. He told his manager Gandhi to sell it off. The next day itself he got an offer for two lakh rupees and an advance of ₹25,000. He had bought the flat three years ago for ₹67,000. Around the same time as he was finalising the deal, he came to know that I didn't have an office. The *mahurat* of *Taaqat* was done on March 21, and I used to conduct all my work for the film at the office of Ajanta Arts, with Dutt *saheb*'s permission. So Vinod made his secretary Gandhi return the advance, and on May 1, handed over the key to the flat to me. Not only that, he offered me the flat at cost price and told me I could pay him whenever possible.

The third act of kindness by Vinod towards me is the one I can never forget. For the film *Taaqat*, the hero's fee was fixed. But even after half the film was complete, I was only able to pay him ₹10,000. I had promised him that during the outdoor schedule in Udaipur, I'd pay him an instalment of ₹2 lakh. I was scheduled to leave for Udaipur in two days with my hero but I faced a bad situation that gave me palpitations. The reason was that my overseas distributor, who had promised me an instalment of ₹3 lakh, was not able to keep it, and said that he'd give me ₹4 lakh instead of 3 only when I returned from the shoot. I was at a total loss. The entire unit was already in Rajasthan and I was supposed to join them with the hero in two days. So I borrowed the money from a friend. The next day, first thing in the morning, I handed it over the to the hero. Everything fell into place and we left for Udaipur the next day. When we reached the location, we realised that Narendra Bedi was shooting a scene that didn't require the hero. When we reached the hotel, Vinod called me to his room saying that he had something important to discuss and that we could have dinner together too.

When I went to his room, he firstly thanked me for keeping my promise about his payment. Then he handed over a suitcase to me that contained the amount I had paid him in Bombay. I was stunned. He smiled and said, "I know how you arranged this amount. My manager has even told me about the guy who helped you. They are childhood friends. I am grateful to you from the bottom of my heart for keeping your word, but I also know that even though there is money available for the shoot, it is not sufficient. So use this. I have also told Gandhi that if ever Raaj Grover requires money, it should reach him without any delay."

I cannot explain the emotions that ran through me at that moment. It was as if every pore of my body was screaming, "Thank you, thank you, my friend."

Apart from being a great human being, Vinod Khanna was also a great actor, a wonderful brother and an ideal father. But more than anything else, he was the perfect friend. However, once this friend put me and some other producers and directors in an awkward situation. In those days, Acharya Rajneesh's ashram in Pune attracted many people. I don't know what magical charm that man possessed. People would go to the ashram, listen to his lecture, take him for their guru and never return. Several people from the film industry had become his disciples too. Out of them, three names are important – Mahesh Bhatt, Vijay Anand (Goldie) and Vinod Khanna. Not only were they influenced by Acharya Rajneesh, but they were also quite close to him. Once Vinod took me to Pune to meet him. I spent the whole day at the ashram, observed the activities there. It was quite possible that I could have been taken in by the guru's charm too and he would have another disciple, but I understood the ashram's reality much sooner than Mahesh Bhatt, who took several years of association to understand it. I returned to Bombay immediately. However, Vinod Khanna said goodbye to *sharm* (shame) and took to his new way of life and became one of Acharya Rajneesh's closest disciples. I couldn't believe he could do it. Later, when Acharya Rajneesh opened another such ashram in the USA and attracted a lot of admirers, many Indians went along with him. Vinod was one of them. He sacrificed his career, wealth, respect and even his family to be with his guru in America. Acharya Rajneesh put the onus of taking care of this enterprise on him. And he obeyed his guru's command.

Like me, other producers too were waiting and hoping to complete their films. *Taaqat* was almost complete and what was remaining was the dubbing for which Vinod Khanna was needed. I kept making calls to Oregon, USA, to his guru's ashram, asking him when he'd be back. And he would always reply, "Next month." And that month would never come. When I began to lose my patience, Vinod suggested I come to Oregon and that he would make all arrangements for the dubbing at Hollywood in Los Angeles. After consulting my friends and giving it a lot of thought, I decided to go. I gave my flight details to Vinod Khanna. When he assured me that he'd receive me at the airport and take me from there, I heaved a sigh of relief. When I reached the Los Angeles airport, however, I was at a terrible loss. No one I knew came to receive me despite Vinod telling me that he would be there. I was about to cry at my helplessness when someone came from behind and gave me a tight squeeze. He laughed and said he was enjoying my plight vicariously. From the time he received me at the airport till the end of my work, which took an entire month, Vinod took great care of me and I will always remember it. After the three favours that he did for me in India, this was perhaps the fourth. Right from my first say in the USA, it seemed as if not Vinod, but my production manager was the hero. He had already booked the Paramount Studio for dubbing. He had even rented an apartment for a month for me to stay in. Now, only a week was left for the dubbing to begin. And in those seven days, just like Raju guide, he gave me a good tour of Hollywood's various studios and explained the way it worked, besides taking me around town. I was very happy but also a bit embarrassed because in Hollywood, time was of the essence. It was sacrosanct. The release of the film was decided the day shooting began and they always stuck to it. It's the same even today. Even the actors' time is almost insured. I was embarrassed because back in Bollywood, time meant nothing. This trip proved to be an eye-opener for me.

While Vinod had booked Paramount Studio, we couldn't get it at a stretch. The schedule was erratic. It was two days of *kaam* and three days of *araam*. But we didn't waste our free time. My hero even took his producer to Disneyland. Another day he took me to his friend Kabir Bedi's house where he was living with his American wife. It was my birthday that day. Vinod took off his new watch from his wrist and presented it to me. The next day he bought shoes for his sons Rahul and Akshay, which I was supposed to deliver to their Malabar Hill home once in Bombay. I asked him why he spent money on such expensive shoes without even knowing their foot size. He replied, "I am their father. Won't I know their sizes?" When I delivered the parcel to their house, the children weren't at home. Later, when I inquired over the phone, they said the shoes had fit them perfectly! Vinod loved his wife and children dearly, and would always buy gifts for them whenever he travelled. His wife, Kavita, has proved to be a wonderful wife and mother, making their home an ideal one.

Till the dubbing was complete, Vinod stayed with me in the rented apartment. We came to an agreement that while we would have home-cooked Indian food, we would only drink Johnnie Walker Black Label. Vinod took over the responsibility of cooking, while I cleaned the dishes. People know Vinod Khanna as a great actor, but very few know what a great cook he was, especially his *rajma chawal*. He could beat the best chefs with his recipe. After dinner, Vinod would spend his time in front of the TV, and as for me, I would wash the dishes in front of my imaginary Biwi (wife). I had never done dishes before, but at the end of the month, I was an expert in the cleaning department. It came naturally to me.

Armed with this new talent, when I reached Bombay, an interesting incident took place. My wife had hired a maid to do all the kitchen work. She did all this in the morning, but since I was so used to it by then, I would do all the dishes after dinner and arrange them in order. The morning after, the maid would be surprised to see a clean kitchen. Since my wife would watch TV every night, she didn't know what I had done. And, when she did, all hell broke loose. She said, "*Yeh saare kaam karne ke liye main bai ko tankha deti hun taki subah woh yeh sab kaam kare, magar tum raat mein hi saare kaam karne ke baad mere paas sone aatey ho aur aatey hi so jate ho. Main soch rahi hun ki kahin iss bai ke sath koi chakkar toh nahi chal raha.*" (I pay a maid to do all these chores when she comes in the morning. But you finish all the work at night and lie next to me and just go off to sleep. I am wondering if you are having an affair with the maid.)

I was in a tizzy on hearing this. My new ability had gotten me into trouble. I thought of Vinod, who had given me this new skill as a gift. When my wife got to know the real story, she had a hearty laugh. *Jai ho yaar Vinod Khanna, jai ho*!

(Victory to you, Vinod Khanna!)

Sometime before I sat to pen this down, I heard about my dear friend being admitted to the hospital. In the photographs, he looked frail and fragile. I was sad on seeing Vinod, from a handsome young man, so full of life, to that changed self. Not able to handle this turn of events, I immediately called his brother and my friend Pramod to enquire about him. He assured me that it was merely a case of dehydration and that Vinod was on his way to recovery. I was relieved. I told Pramod about my impending visit to Mumbai and to convey to Vinod that I'd be dropping in to meet him once in town. I was looking forward to the reunion. After all, we had spent some wonderful times and those were the golden days of our lives and careers. He had touched my life in so many thoughtful ways – something I would always be indebted to him for. The very thought of meeting him opened the floodgates of memories and I found myself more and more eager to meet him. There was also an unexplained remorse, which I couldn't understand. I was experiencing a strange sense of foreboding. At that time, I brushed it off as just an emotional surge and concentrated my feelings on the happy thought of meeting my old friend once again. But when the shocking news of his passing away came, I was shattered. It was a loss I wasn't prepared to accept. Questions which had no reasonable answers occupied my mind. *Why him? He was only seventy. Wasn't he recovering? How could he leave so suddenly when I was supposed to meet him shortly? For a person who was always on a journey of self-discovery, wasn't it too early for the almighty to snatch him away from his loved ones? Had he finally found himself?* All these thoughts, accompanied by a melee of memories, disturbed me for days. Depression descended upon me like a miasma. But then, Vinod's face, with his trademark smile and his joie de vivre, flashed in front of me. I asked myself, *would he want me to be in this state of mind*? The answer was a clear no. I gathered my emotions and the courage to call Pramod. What he said reverberated as the only truth all of us could imbibe in the given situation. "Let's celebrate his passing away." I agreed wholeheartedly, for I knew that was the only way to bid adieu to a person as lively, as compassionate and as kind as Vinod Khanna. And that's exactly what he would have liked. As Acharya Rajneesh would have said, "He has only left his body." His soul will live forever – for his family, fans, friends, and for me and whichever universe he inhabits now will be lucky to have him.

Goodbye, my friend. I will miss you from the bottom of my heart till the day I live and beyond...

Waqt toh tujhe saath liye maut ke samundar mein jaa dooba
Magar
Yaad teri merey iss behtey yaadon ke dariya main hamesha tairti hi nazar na aaye toh kehna
Vinod yaar mere Khanna
Mere iss dariya mein teri yaadon ka doobna namumkin hai aur na rahega kabhi mumkin
Raaj yaar shubh chintak tera Grover – never-over.

(Time may have drowned you in the ocean of death
Tell me if in the flowing pool of memories, you don't see my reflection
Vinod, my friend, Khanna
It will never be possible for your memories to fade away, especially for me
I will always remain your well-wisher – Raaj Grover – never over)

Zarina Wahab

Once, Sunil Dutt and I had to go to Pune to attend a close friend's wedding. We took a morning flight out as the wedding was in the evening. So on Dutt *saheb*'s request, I called up the Film and Television Institute of India (FTII), and told them he would like to visit the institute and meet some final-year students in the acting course. As scheduled, we reached there at 11 am. Just as we got out of the car, four female students came running towards Sunil Dutt. They were Shabana Azmi, Rita Bhaduri, Neelam Mehra and Zarina Wahab. One could see in their eyes the strong desire to become great actors. I can never forget their enthusiasm and the sparkle in their eyes. It is as if it was just yesterday.

We knew about Shabana Azmi, the daughter of the illustrious poet, Kaifi Azmi. We loved her conversational skills. Even Neelam and Rita were brought up in Bombay like Shabana, so they too were proficient when it came to communication. However, Zarina Wahab, the girl who came from the small city of Rajahmundry in Andhra Pradesh, remained quiet and displayed some diffidence and shyness. But her ambition was just as apparent as the other three girls. I was pleased to meet the girls, but Zarina Wahab found a special place in my heart for her simple and unassuming nature.

After the completion of their course, they set foot on the path that Jaya Bhaduri had taken. While Shabana Azmi and Rita Bhaduri found success as actors, Neelam Mehra fell a little behind. Though she found work, she didn't succeed with the flourish she had expected. She was dejected. She later married actor and producer Shiv Kumar. Zarina Wahab may have seemed self-effacing on the outside, but she was made of solid mettle on the inside, and was determined to fight her way to recognition as a talented actress. She networked with famous people in the industry to get work. In those days, an actor called Mahendra Sandhu was enjoying a good run. He gave her the much-needed encouragement and even promised to help her find roles. Staying true to his word, he introduced Zarina to Tahir Hussain (Aamir Khan's father) and gave a good recommendation. Tahir Hussain was impressed with her and would always compare Shabana and Zarina to Jaya Bhaduri, including them in the list of the talented girls to have graduated from FTII.

Though the networking didn't get her a lot of work, it went a long way in keeping Zarina's hopes alive. People like Jaya Bhaduri, Asrani, Shatrughan Sinha and some others kept her spirits up with their constant reassurances, especially Jaya Bhaduri.

I still lived with my family in Bandra at the time. One morning, Mahendra Sandhu's sister brought along a shy and reserved girl along with her to our house. It was Zarina. After welcoming them into my home, I put my hand on her head and said, "I know that you have what it takes to make it big in this industry." At that time, my four-year-old daughter Jalpa was sitting nearby, finishing her homework. I pointed towards her and told Zarina that from this second onwards,

I would love her the same way as I loved my daughter. On hearing this, Zarina was overcome with emotions and started crying. When I tried to console her, my wife suggested we let her cry and offload all her stress; she felt this catharsis might help her. Zarina just got up, went and hugged my wife Shashi. After crying her heart out, she looked at me and smiled.

Those days, photographer Dheeraj Chawda was a favourite of both – film magazines and film stars. I was quite friendly with him. I met him one day and asked him to shoot some nice pictures of Zarina. But he took me aside and said in a hushed tone, "You are wasting your and my time." However, on my insistence, when he looked at her through the lens of his camera, he was stunned. He said, "Wow! What a photogenic face!" I simply smiled, and Dheeraj took so many photographs that Zarina was tired at the end of the session. It wasn't for nothing. The next issue of *Filmfare* devoted two pages to just Zarina's photographs. When I took her to Nargisji along with those photos, she couldn't believe that they were of the same girl. After chatting with her for a while, when Nargisji blessed her and wished her success, tears welled up in Zarina's eyes. I even took her to meet another actor from Zarina's hometown, Rajahmundry, Waheeda Rehman. Blessings came from her too, but projects were still playing truant.

Zarina didn't have a good enough place to stay in those days – a home she could have people over. Since I had proclaimed that she was my daughter, I brought her to my place without any further delay. She became a part of my family. Occasionally, her sisters, Malika, Haseena and Shammi, would come over to meet her too.

A close friend of mine, writer and director BS Thapa, had started a film based on a story written by him called *Mere Pati ki Patni*. It had Sunil Dutt as the hero with three heroines.

Rekha played a Christian, Radha Saluja a Hindu and Zarina Wahab a Muslim. For some reason, the film couldn't get completed but Zarina developed an intimate bond with Rekha on the sets. So much so that their friendship became the talk of the film fraternity.

My relationship with the founders of Rajshri Productions was such that I didn't need to take an appointment to visit them. I got to know they were planning a film with Basu Chatterjee as the director and Amol Palekar as the hero, and that they were looking for someone to play the lead actress' role. Without wasting any time, I took the photographs of Zarina taken by Dheeraj and showed them to Basu Chatterjee and Kamal Barjatya. They liked them but felt they didn't relate to the simple village girl they had in mind. They had to take a call on the heroine for the film in two days. So the same afternoon, I met another photographer friend Girish Shukla and fixed a shoot for Zarina to capture the village-girl look. I called up Krishna, the costume designer at Ajanta Arts, and asked him to bring the *ghaghra choli* that Waheeda Rehman had worn in *Reshma aur Shera*. When Zarina wore the same outfit and posed for pictures, she looked every bit a village girl. Girish Shukla captured about ten to twelve images of Zarina, which I then gave to Basu Chatterjee. He was very happy to see them and immediately finalised her as the lead heroine.

The film released to great appreciation and brought the so far elusive limelight on Zarina. After seeing the success of the film, my friend and filmmaker Bheem Sen came to meet me. Zarina was at my place then. It was decided then and there that he would start a film, titled, *Gharonda*, with Amol Palekar and Zarina Wahab in the coming month itself. The film was completed in four months. It was such a hit film that it was fully booked in theatres for six months.

By then, Zarina had bought a three-bedroom flat on Mount Mary Road and had shifted there with her parents and sisters. Later, her sister Haseena shifted with her kids to settle down in the US where elder sister Malika lived with her family. Soon Shammi was married. Then it was only Zarina with her parents at home.

One fine day, Zarina came to my place with a handsome, young man. I wasn't at home then. Zarina introduced him to my wife, saying, "*Bhabhi*, this is Nirmal. We have got married." My wife Shashi was ecstatic on hearing the news. She immediately blessed the couple. Zarina settled into her new married life but acting in movies continued to remain her passion. Even today, she does justice to any role she plays.

Zarina is a great cook and the *Hyderbadi baingan* she cooks is finger-licking good. It was this dish that brought Shashi and Zarina closer. Even today, whenever we are visiting from the US, she never fails to pack our favourite dish for us.

A small mistake can lead to a big loss at times. And it becomes difficult to undo it. After *Gharonda*, Zarina won a lot of accolades, but she somewhat lost her way after that. After the success of *Gharonda*, two of my producer friends were rather keen on casting her with Shashi Kapoor and Vinod Khanna but they were forced to change their minds when they heard that Zarina had paired with Asrani for *Pandu Hawaldar*. The film was in its last phase. This choice of film derailed Zarina's career to a large extent.

Both my children got settled in the US after they got married. My wife and I soon shifted base there to be close to our adorable grandchildren. But our close bond with Zarina continues. When Zarina used to stay with us, she would pamper my daughter Jalpa. So when Jalpa came to Mumbai for the first time after her wedding, Zarina, along with her two kids, went to meet her. This time, it was Jalpa who pampered Zarina's children, Sooraj and Sana.

Zarina's husband Nirmal Pancholi is better known as popular actor Aditya Pancholi, and now even their son Sooraj has made his debut in films with *Hero*. He is fortunate that he not only has his parents' blessings but also that of a great soul called Salman Khan.

Let me just end this chapter by saying that though their children are now grown up, both Aditya and Zarina continue to look like a young couple, very much in love with each other.

Ajanta Arts Welfare Troupe

Our young and brave soldiers sacrifice their happiness, and stay away from their families for long periods to protect our country at the borders. And this is true for all the nations in the world. There is not a single country in the world that has an unprotected border.

Bob Hope, a popular Hollywood star, donated all his wealth, and dedicated all his time to the welfare of American soldiers. The American government lauded his selfless move and there was not a single country that did not appreciate his gesture. He was flooded with gifts from the forces posted on the borders.

The first prime minister of Independent India, Pandit Jawaharlal Nehru, was a great fan of Bob Hope and hadn't missed a single film he had starred in. Just like Bob Hope went from border to border in the US to entertain the soldiers, Nehru devised a similar plan for our forces. The year was 1962. The hunt to find the equivalent of Hope in India began. Since the PM couldn't devote as much time to this, his daughter Indira Gandhi took on the responsibility and called up her favourite actress, Nargis. Both were great friends. Incidentally, at that time, Nargisji, along with her kids, had reached Delhi from Shimla. She was staying at the Imperial Hotel in Janpath. So Indira Gandhi came to meet her at the hotel. They spoke about Nehruji's idea and Indira Gandhi requested Nargisji to call her husband immediately and tell him that her father, the PM, would like to meet him. The very next day, Sunil Dutt arrived in Delhi.

Indira had already arranged lunch for the Dutt family at her father's bungalow. Within an hour, Jawaharlal Nehru found his Bob Hope in Sunil Dutt. And within a week, Dutt *saheb* floated the idea of the Ajanta Arts Welfare Troupe in his production office and Nargisji handed over the responsibility of its functioning to me. She also gave me the official designation of General Manager, AAW Troupe – which I was using to look after the production work along with Som Dutt. Outside that office, my job was to give the details of the troupe to all the big actors and actresses. The Dutts would simply call and tell them, "Raaj will come and meet you, and give you the details of the troupe. He will take an appointment before dropping in."

Now, it was my job turn to do the running around. Within a month, we had a huge list of great personalities who had agreed to become members of the troupe including Lata Mangeshkar, Kishore Kumar, Waheeda Rehman, Madhumati, Mahendra Kapoor, Manhar Udhas, Johnny Walker, and Gopi Krishna. They were the "troopers" of the Ajanta Arts Welfare Troupe.

After the Indo-Pak war of 1965, the troupe put up such a wonderful show for the weary and lonely soldiers to celebrate the victory that they'd remember it for the rest of their lives. And on the very next day after the victory of the 1971 war, the troupe headed to the new nation Bangladesh's capital Dhaka for the performance of a lifetime.

The war was still on at both the borders – western sector of

Jammu & Kashmir and eastern sector of Bangladesh – when Sunil Dutt telephoned New Delhi to seek an appointment with the then prime minister, Indira Gandhi. He requested her to organise chartered aircraft to fly twenty artistes and twenty musicians from Delhi to Jammu and Srinagar, come back to Bombay and leave for Dhaka the next day to entertain the soldiers in both the places. He also requested that the pilot and crew of the aircraft remain at their disposal till the time they finish their duties and return to Bombay. Indira Gandhi asked him to come to Delhi to meet her. The day he was to meet her, he was down with severe flu and the job of meeting the prime minister and make the above-mentioned request to her was assigned to me. I reached Indira Gandhi's bungalow as ordered. Her secretary had assigned to me ten minutes of her time. Once the time was up, her secretary, who was standing behind the PM, gestured me to leave. I don't know how Indiraji saw the gesture, but she ordered for some tea and biscuits to be brought in. In this meeting with Indiraji that actually lasted for half an hour, the reason for which I was there took merely ten minutes. In just five minutes, two planes from the Indian Air Force were allocated to our troupe. My mission was successful. The remaining twenty minutes were spent in talking about the Dutt family. She appreciated the film *Mujhe Jeene Do*, especially praising the *lori* penned by Sahir Ludhianvi – *Tere bachpan ko jawani ki dua deti hun...*' She had also watched *Mother India* and said, "Nargis and Naushad *saheb* have done a commendable job."

I returned to Bombay the same evening. The aircraft were supposed to be ready at the airport, and as for us, we were ready to entertain the soldiers.

Our first programme was in Jammu & Kashmir's western sector. We were received at Srinagar airport by the high command of J&K, Lt Gen Candeth. The same evening, the programme took place in the open grounds of the Srinagar Army Headquarters. The first show had just started with Deedar Singh's Punjabi number when about one-hundred-and-fifty *jawan*s came on to the stage. They began dancing and while doing so also carried the singer on their shoulders. Deedar Singh, though a bit perturbed, continued with the tempo, and kept singing.

It was a super success. The *bhangra* performance by Madhumati and Manohar Deepak was so good that once again it saw the soldiers marching on to the stage and dancing with gay abandon. And even after Madhumati and Manohar Deepak exited the stage, the soldiers continued dancing.

Sunil Dutt had planned for a group photo with the soldiers and Lt Gen Candeth. Film industry's famous photographer BJ Panchal was with us as a member of the troupe for this very reason.

The second show the next day in Baramulla also saw the soldiers enjoying themselves to the fullest. When we reached Jammu, we were received by the forces' favourite officer, Brigadier Tiger, who proved to be a wonderful host. Our troupe put up a splendid show there too.

Brigadier Tiger had an amazing stupendous disposition. A towering personality, at six feet three inches, he was the man who had twelve bullets lodged in his body only ten days before. Out of these, eight were removed by the doctors at the military hospital but four of them still made his body their home. But he was unaffected by this and went all out to entertain us. If the soldiers came on the stage to enjoy their time, the Brigadier entertained us at the Military Club's bar. So much so, that some of our artistes were in rather high spirits by the end of the evening. Tiger *saheb* danced a lot, as did Dutt *saheb*, Manohar Deepak, BB Bhalla, Nargisji and even Mukri.

When the Brigadier got somewhat high, he came to Dutt *saheb* and said that had he met Nargisji before Dutt *saheb* did, she would be Begum Tiger today. Dutt *saheb* summoned the photographer Panchal to take a few memorable pictures with Nargisji and Brigadier Tiger.

After the successful completion of our mission, we bid goodbye to Brigadier Tiger and left for Bombay. It would be two days of rest and then off to Bangladesh for the next leg.

As per Nargisji's suggestion, Dutt *saheb* took me with him to meet Lata Mangeshkar at her house to invite her to be a part of the troupe to Bangladesh. We knew it was too short a notice for such a big personality but when she heard our proposal, she said, "*Haan, kab jana hai?*" (When do we leave?) Dutt *saheb* replied, "The day after, in the morning." She asked, 'What time and where do I have to come?" This time, I replied, "We are all meeting at Dutt *saheb*'s bungalow at five in the morning. The flight to Dhaka will leave at around 7 am." Lata, in her melodious voice, said, "I will be there for sure, but please don't talk about this to anyone because I have a recording with SD Burman on the same day. Naturally, he will be upset. But, you don't worry; *Burman da ko main mana loongi.*" (I will take care of Mr Burman.) We made a promise and took her leave.

The next day, after completing all the arrangements, I spent the night at Dutt *saheb*'s bungalow in Pali Hill because the artistes would start trickling in by 5 am. Besides, I also had to organise transportation from Pali Hill to the airport. But the first person to walk in at 4:30 am was none other than Lata Mangeshkar. She had fulfilled her promise to us.

Two aircrafts provided by the Ministry of Defence were ready for us at the airport. In one of them travelled all the dancers and musicians along with Mahendra Kapoor, Manhar Udhas, Manohar Deepak, BB Bhalla, Mukri and

Deedar Singh. Sunil Dutt personally took on the responsibility of everyone in the flight. The second plane had Nargisji, Lata Mangeshkar, Mala Sinha and her father Albert Sinha, Waheeda Rehman, Sonia Sahni, Madhumati and some more parents as well. When no one was ready to be the in-charge of this one, as always, the onus came on me.

As per schedule, we left Calcutta at 3 pm and landed in Jessore, Bangladesh, at 3:10. The show began at 4 pm. Much before that, Dutt *saheb* had asked me to go along with BJ Panchal, the photographer, to the city of Khulna. He wanted us to meet the people there and enquire after their well-being because they had been subjected to a lot of torment and agony. After a half-an-hour drive, we reached Khulna. We met a few people in Khulna who didn't know any other language apart from Bengali. But I could understand what they wanted to convey from the language their eyes spoke. When we were about to leave, the driver of our jeep showed us some ditches. These contained the skulls and bones of people who were alive just a few months ago. Panchal took a photograph of me near one of the ditches. Whenever I see it, I feel they are still alive.

Meanwhile, after the show in Jessore, we headed off to Dhaka and reached there by 8 pm. We got to know that the next morning's breakfast was going to be with Sheikh Mujibur Rehman at his place in Dhanmondi. At 9 the next morning, Nargisji and Dutt *saheb*, along with Lata Mangeshkar, the photographer and I, reached Dhanmondi. Sheikh Mujibur Rehman was a warm and cordial host. The conversation revolved around the troupe and cinema. Nargisji was busy with his children in the upper floor of the house. After mollycoddling his sweet daughter Hasina, she came down, only to hear Lata Mangeshkar sing one of Sheikh *saheb*'s favourite songs beautifully, even without any musical accompaniments. In fact, the song she sung, '*Allah tero naam, Ishwar tero naam*' is one of her favourites too.

It was 11 am by now and we left from Dhaka and started towards Comilla where the rest of the troupe had already reached. It was only meant to be a two-hour show. But thanks to the appreciation, it was extended by an hour and Mahendra Kapoor had to sing around seven to eight very popular songs.

There was a big-scale event organised for the next day at Dhaka and the same evening, the Chief of the Eastern Command Head Quarter, Calcutta, Lt Gen Jacob, had made all arrangements for the show at a football ground in the city. Unfortunately, that wasn't meant to be because, instead of Calcutta, we were asked to do the show in Chittagong for the Mukti Bahini soldiers. The orders came from the prime minister's office and also from the Ministry of Defence.

Without any hesitation, and respecting the orders of the government, at around 3 pm, we landed in Chittagong in the Air Force planes. It was pouring heavily. We had to wait in the planes for half an hour till Brigadier Pandey arrived with three big trucks and numerous umbrellas to receive us. He took us to the army canteen and served us hot tea, a real saviour. When I asked him about the hotel we would be checking into in order to get ready for the programme, his answer left me reeling in shock. He said because of the short notice, they couldn't find rooms in any of the three hotels in the city. They were all fully booked. He added that they had organised our stay at Chittagong's military hospital. He went on talking but my shock and dismay had tuned it all out.

I thought that this would tarnish my reputation, but Dutt *saheb*, especially, had taught me never to give up. And that helped me out of this situation. I reasoned that it was not Brigadier Pandey's fault that no rooms were available.

Thanks to him, the arrangements were now my responsibility. I still salute his ability to deal with crisis with such a calm mind. I also saw Sunil Dutt and Nargisji, expecting them to be hopping mad at the situation. But instead, they were laughing and chatting merrily. It looked like I was the only one who was tense. Meanwhile, fortunately for us, an hour before the show at 7 pm, the rain abated, as if it was tired. It also seemed like there was quite a neat arrangement between Brigadier Pandey and the rain. From the time the programme began till the very end, it was dry and the show was a stupendous success.

As soon as we stepped on the stage, we were greeted with applause and congratulatory greetings, and flowers were showered upon us. It was a beautiful ambience. I also received a hug from Brigadier Pandey, which was so tight, I will remember it forever. The programme began with a short lecture by Nargisji where she talked about the love Indians and the Indian government had for the people of Bangladesh. This was received with loud cheers and claps. Then she introduced each and every artiste. The maximum applause was for Lata Mangeshkar – it just wouldn't end and ultimately Dutt *saheb* took the mic and requested them to make way for the entertaining programme that was waiting to unfold before them.

This was probably the first time in Lataji's life that she had to sing at least half a dozen songs in one show. Especially three songs on special request, each of which she had to sing twice or even thrice – *Barsaat mein hum se mile tum, Aayega aaane wala* and, *Alla tero naam, Ishwar tero naam.*

After a tiring day, when we reached the military hospital, Pandeyji had already made all the arrangements for the night, even before I could ask him to. Sunil Dutt was to sleep on a stretcher. Mahendra Kapoor, Manohar Deepak,

Manhar Udhas, Deedar Singh, BB Bhalla, Shahid Bijnori and all the other musicians were to spend the night at the fabulous general ward.

As a manager, I could see anger simmering inside the silent musicians and I learnt that day that silence could speak a thousand words and in this case, it was also visible. I was facing this kind of a storm for the first time in my life. They went to Dutt *saheb* and said I wasn't a manager but a 'damager'. He didn't pay much heed to their complaints. He only said, "I know it is bad, but how can I blame only Raaj Grover for this?" My biggest concern was finding a place to put up Nargisji, Waheedaji, Hemlata, Mala Sinha, Sonia Sahni and Madhumati. Pandey *saheb* urged them to wait in the lobby of the hospital until he could make some arrangements for their stay. The women waiting patiently in the lobby took pity on me and didn't utter a single word. They kept chatting about some interesting incident or the other. Then, sessions of *Antakshari* kept them busy. It looked like they had even forgotten what Pandeyji had promised before he left. I was the only one who seemed to be waiting for him to return. Nargisji and Lataji, while seated on the sofa, kept nodding off.

Mahendra Kapoor had brought the senior *tabla* player, Gyani*ji*, with him. He was a veteran in the film industry. What do I say about his liking for drinks? I was sitting on a chair and taking a cat nap myself when Gyaniji, completely sloshed, shook my shoulder and asked, "Where is, what's his name, Sunil Dutt?" I asked him, "Why? For what? It is 2 am. Go back to sleep." "I need some money. The *lungi*s in Chittagong are famous and I want to buy a few," he said, his speech slurry. But I was fed up and tired. I just dumped him on the chair that I was sitting on and parked myself on a stool, trying to swallow my anger. Just when sleep was taking over me again, Gyaniji repeated his performance. This time it was, "*Mujhe bahut zor ka peshab aya hai. Kahan ja kar karun?*" (I am desperate to relieve myself. Where should I go?) When I glimpsed at the clock, I saw it was 4 am. I took him to the dark room where Mahendra Kapoor was snoring rather mellifluously, and told him to ask him where he should relieve himself. I left him there. Then, I could hear the commotion from the room. It turned out that Gyaniji, in his drunken state, did what he had to do on Mahendra Kapoor.

The next day, we reached the airport for our show in Calcutta that Lt Gen Jacob had organised at the football club. The timing of everything had to be managed with precision. At 11 am, we reached Chittagong airport. Dutt *saheb*'s aircraft, flown by Capt Giri, was parked a little far. Now I had seen Dutt *saheb* get angry several times, but that day, it was something else. The reason was, while everyone had reached the airport, two ladies – Lataji and Nargisji, were missing. Without informing anyone, they had gone off shopping with Brigadier Pandey in his jeep. When Dutt *saheb*'s volcano of anger erupted, all the lava fell on me. And then he, along with all the musicians, started walking towards the aircraft parked far away. I waited with the other ladies for Lataji and Nargisji. Just when I was about to lose my patience, the jeep arrived. Both the ladies could see Dutt *saheb* and even sense his anger from afar. Lataji had bought a small transistor, which she quietly handed over to me, saying, "Tell him (Dutt *saheb*) this is your gift from Pandeyji."

When I had told Nargisji about Gyaniji's request for *lungi*s, she convulsed with laughter. On reaching Calcutta, she brought out a lovely *lungi* and told Dutt *saheb* that he and I should present it to Gyaniji in front of Mahendra Kapoor. In Calcutta, Lt Gen Jacob had made superb arrangements. On landing, instead of taking us to a hotel to get ready for the show, he took us straight to the venue. At the airport, we were welcomed by a 1971 war hero, Lt Gen Jagjit Singh Arora.

Twelve tents were erected for us to take rest before the show. It was no less than a 5-Star hotel. General Arora, Dutt *saheb* and Nargisji happily chatted with each other and I went with Lt Gen Jacob to take care of all the arrangements.

The show started with a *bhangra* item by Manohar Deepak and Madhumati. When the audience erupted with applause, both Dutt *saheb* and Mahendra Kapoor jumped on to the stage for some more *bhangra*. When Manhar Udhas came on next, his *ghazal*s put everyone in a soulful and euphoric mood. So much so that I even forgot that the next item was Lataji's, followed by Mahendra Kapoor. While she started with *Ayega aane wala*, I went to the tent to inform Mahendra Kapoor that he was next. When I reached there, I realized he was worried because Gyaniji was drunk and had passed out in the neighbouring tent. I felt bad but when I saw Gyaniji, I found that he was covered, from head to toe, with the *lungi* from Chittagong. So to save the situation, we played the tapes of the song that Mahendra Kapoor was going to sing and had Dutt *saheb*, Nargisji, Manohar Deepak and Madhumati on the stage making Mahendra Kapoor dance. The crowd went berserk with happiness and the cheers seemed as melodious as the songs that were being played.

When at 6 pm, we wound up our musical instruments and reached the HQ of the Eastern Command, we found that Lt Gen Jacob had organised a party in our honour. It was filled with music and induced a certain dreamy intoxication. General Arora kept this tired manager of AAWT in good spirits with his conversation and, of course, the continuous clinking of glasses.

Suddenly, I saw a lone guy dancing with great exhilaration

– it was the *lungi*-clad Gyaniji. When he heard us clapping for him, he stopped and asked Dutt *saheb*, "Why didn't you bring dancer Gopi Krishna? We could have had a contest today."

Anyway, that saw the end of a great event and all of us got into the same two flights and were back in Bombay in two hours. Happiness and contentment were evident on all faces.

For a long time, whenever Nargisji and I spoke about the event, it would never be complete without touching upon Gyaniji's *lungi* incident and Lataji's transistor episode. And we would end up rolling with laughter every time. But that is the charm of old memories, isn't it?

The Story of Mohan Studio

Mohan Studio in Andheri had been the building that you saw upon entering the premises, a temple for film-making. It was famous for constantly bustling with film personalities as it housed several celebrities' offices. At one point, famous producer Savak Vacha also had his office in the same building. Anyone wanting to meet him had to first approach the peon, Ganpat, who would be seated on a chair outside the office, continuously muddling tobacco and lime on his palm. Anyone there to see Mr. Vacha had to literally wait till Ganpat had freed himself from his tobacco rigmarole. Once done, he would ask, "Who do you want to meet and what is the nature of your job?" Very often, even without hearing the visitor or noting down his details, he'd say, "*Saheb* is busy in a meeting with the writer. Call and come some other time." If you had to meet Mr. Vacha, you had to cross this hurdle because Ganpat was not only his peon, but also sort of his secretary. So one could only meet Mr. Vacha after several attempts.

One day a Bengali *babu*, holding one end of his *dhoti*, came to meet him. When he encountered Ganpat at the door, he was told the same: "*Saheb* is busy in a meeting with the writer. Call and come some other time." The next time the Bengali *babu* came, he was determined to meet Mr. Vacha. At first, he continued to request Ganpat politely, but when it didn't work, he raised his voice and said, "I have to meet him today." At this, Ganpat too raised his voice equally high and said, "Haven't I said he is busy? Come again later."

On hearing Ganpat's voice, suddenly the door inside opened and Mr. Vacha stepped outside. When he lay his eyes on the Bengali *babu* and noticed the sincerity and politeness on his face, he interjected and told Ganpat, "Let him in," and returned to his chair. When Babuji sat opposite Vacha *saheb*, Ganpat offered to get him a beverage. Vacha *saheb* ordered some tea to be brought in. They spoke for about two hours and the Bengali *babu* started coming in often for film-related discussions. Finally, he struck gold and achieved what he had been waiting for from the visits.

Producer Savak Vacha announced his new film, *Maa*. And the movie was to be directed by the same Bengali *babu*, whose name was Bimal Roy. He also set a condition that the unit will have his people. When Vacha *saheb* agreed to this, Bimal Roy brought all his people from Calcutta to Bombay for the film – Kamal Bose (cameraman), Sudheendo Roy (Art Director), Salil Chouwdhury (Music Director), Moni Bhattacharya (Assistant Director) and Hrishikesh Mukherjee. When the film released, people couldn't stop talking about Bimal Roy. He made film after film – *Parineeta*, *Bandini* and *Madhumati*. These films took Bimal Roy to the peak of success. He started his own production house, Bimal Roy Productions, took up the same office where Vacha *saheb* used to work and even retained the peon, Ganpat.

One day, a producer came to meet him and encountered Ganpat at the door. The producer asked him if *saheb* was inside and that he wanted to meet him. Ganpat said he was busy, but offered his seat to the guest, saying, "Please have a seat, I will check." Moments later, he came out with by Bimal Roy who bowed to the guest. It was producer Savak Vacha. He then took him in the office and made him sit on the chair that he used to occupy. Bimal*da* disrupted his discussion with his writer to talk to Vacha *saheb*. In the course of the conversation, he made a phone call to Dilip Kumar and a big decision was taken. Next week itself, *Yahudi*, a film starring Dilip Kumar, Meena Kumari and Sohrab Modi was announced. It was a successful film.

Even Bimal Roy's film editor and assistant, Hrishikesh Mukherjee, made the film *Musafir* under his banner with Dilip Kumar at Mohan Studio itself. The film did well and this started a string of films by Hrishikesh Mukherjee at Mohan Studio. However, he didn't give up his job with Roy and continued working with him as a film editor. After *Musafir*, he made some super hit films like *Anuradha*, *Anand*, *Guddi* and *Namak Haram*. Even the two films starring Amitabh Bachchan and Jaya Bhaduri, *Mili* and *Alaap*, were made from start to finish at Mohan Studio. These two films didn't do as well as the others but the Amitabh-Jaya love story took seed at Mohan Studio, after which Jaya Bhaduri started getting close to the Bachchan family. The climax of their love story took place at one of their close friend Kusum Pandit's house, who was also one of the favourite students at my father's school in Delhi. This happy ending was only the happy beginning for the Bachchan household when the two got married.

All the people who have worked with Bimal*da* learnt a lot from him; he was like the Paras stone. Anyone who was associated with him hit gold and earned name and fame, besides making an identity of their own. Gulzar was one such person to have benefitted from the association. He started his career as Bimal Roy's assistant and later made classic films like *Andhi*, *Mausam* and *Parichay* at Mohan Studio.

Film director Krishan Chopra made two films, *Heera Moti* and *Char Diwari* and then announced his third film based on Munshi Premchand's novel, *Gaban*, with Sunil Dutt and Sadhana. In all the three films, I was the Chief Assistant Director and my close friend Jitendra Billu was the dialogue writer for *Gaban*.

Just like how Mohan Studio has been a great part of my film journey, I can say the same for Krishan Chopra too. He has been my guru. I have learnt tremendously about filmmaking from him free of cost and all the lessons have stood me in good stead. The icing on the cake was that I also got to imbibe a lot from the very capable editor and director Hrishikesh Mukherjee (who is known in the film industry as Hrishi*da*) because he was editing *Gaban* and he had kept me with him on the job. I always felt like a younger brother when I was with him and I felt the same feeling with Krishan Chopra.

There were still a few more days for the film *Gaban* to wind up when we got some great news. Krishan Chopra had won the National Award for *Heera Moti* and was also invited to an international film festival in Rome. Krishan Chopra, along with the hero of the film, Sunil Dutt, left for Rome, Italy, the same week. After participating in the festival, when everything seemed to be going extremely well, we were hit by the terrible news that Krishan Chopra had had a heart failure. The Indian ambassador in Rome completed his last rites. This tragedy hit us all badly. I thought *Gaban* would never see the light of day. However, Hrishi*da* took on the responsibility of completing the film as I remained by his side. Next month, a set for the film was built at Mohan Studio. But Sunil Dutt, the hero of both the films, was shooting in

Chennai for *Main Chup Rahungi*. Another problem was to find an actor to play the scene along with the hero. The issue was solved when we found Kailash, a famous theatre actor who was also producer Soral *saheb*'s brother-in-law. I convinced him to play the role. Now we had to take care of Dutt *saheb*'s availability. When I spoke to him on the phone, he said he'd reach Bombay after two days in the afternoon, shoot the important scene and return to Madras by the 8 pm flight. Until then, we tried to finish all we could that didn't require Dutt *saheb*'s presence.

On the day he was supposed to arrive, we waited with bated breath for 12'o clock to strike. The shooting schedule was to be from 2 to 6 pm. We had to shoot the scene under any circumstances and had made all preparations for the same. I had already passed on the dialogues to Kailash the previous day itself and had asked him to be present at Mohan Studio exactly at 12.

The crucial scene had a troubled hero Ramnath going to his friend for help. The dialogue that followed was something like this:

Ramnath (the hero): '*Meri naukri khatre mein hai. Kya karun? Mujh se galti ho gayi aur teen sau rupaye ke gaban ka ilzam mujh par lag gaya hai. Kal tak agar woh vapis na hue aur munshiji ne kahin malik to bata diya toh meri naukri chali jayegi. Kya karun samajh mein nahi ata. Yaar, teen sau rupaye ka aaj hi kisi tarah intezam kar de, main tera ehsaan umar bhar na bhoolonuga.*' (My job is in jeopardy. What should I do? I made a mistake and have been charged with the crime of embezzling ₹300. If I don't return the amount by tomorrow and Munshiji tells the boss, I will lose my job. I am at a loss. Friend, please help organise ₹300 for me today itself, I will forever be indebted to you.)

Kailash (the friend): '*Itna pareshan hone ki kya zaroorat*

hai? *Biwi se baat kar ke us ke zevar girvi rakh de. Teen sau kya panch sau rupaye mil jayenge. Main karwa doonga tera yeh kaam, mamooli baat hai. Itna pareshan hone ki baat nahi hai yaar.*' (Why are you so perturbed? Talk to your wife and mortgage her jewellery. Why just ₹300, you may even get ₹500 for them. I will help you with it, it isn't a big deal. There is no need to get so disturbed by it.)

But, it was inevitable to have *pareshani* (trouble) for this scene. What happened was that it was already 2 pm, and there was no sign of Kailash. He wasn't even reachable on phone. We couldn't find a way out of the situation. Dutt *saheb* was ready on the set and only waiting for the person who would come and relieve Ramnath of his problem about the embezzled ₹300.

I had never seen Dutt *saheb* as tense as he was that day. The solution to this showed up when an actor dressed in a *dhoti* and *kurta* and wearing a moustache appeared from the make-up room. On seeing a bewildered Ramnath, the actor said, "*Aap hairan na hon. Main bilkul taiyar hun. Aap fikr na karen.*" (Don't be worried. I am fully prepared. Don't worry.) As soon as he heard this, Dutt *saheb*'s bewilderment turned into a smile which was lined with a certain impishness.

The scene began. Once Dutt *saheb*, who was playing Ramnath, finished saying his dialogue, the other actor began mouthing his. But when he reached the last line, he ended up saying, "*Itna pareshan hone ki aisi koi baat nahin hai Dutt saheb!*" (There is no reason to be so perturbed, Dutt saheb.) He simply couldn't get himself to utter the word *yaar*. Everybody was in splits. The person who laughed the most was Hrishi*da*. Eventually, the scene was completed with the right words and it was applauded by one and all present on the set. Once again, the person who clapped the hardest was Hrishi*da*. Both Sunil Dutt and Hrishikesh Mukherjee came and embraced me because that actor was none other than me! When I saw that Kailash wasn't showing up, I decided to do the role myself. This is how the film was completed.

Stories and incidents pertaining to Mohan Studio are endless but there are some that I have personally witnessed. In these *man mohini* stories of Mohan Studio, some real life and unforgettable characters have been Savak Vacha, Ganpat, Bimal Roy, Hrishikesh Mukherjee, Sudheendo Roy, Gulzar, Krishan Chopra and Balraj Sahni. All of them were famous, able and hardworking people who also valued the importance of time.

The studio, which once reverberated with the happy sounds of the roles played by these characters and shone with the talents on display there, has today sadly turned into an eerie graveyard, thanks to the cunningness and greed of some capitalists.

Meanwhile, thanks to old age, Ganpat retired, but his monthly wages kept reaching him till the day he lived. On his demise, his family asked for blessings instead of money and left town forever.

Two Neighbours – The Love-Hate Relationship

It seems India, since centuries, has been fated to encounter numerous upheavals. Time and again it has been ravaged by war, hatred, loot and plunder. In 1947, the country was partitioned and a new country was born – Pakistan, which was accepted by the world.

India and Pakistan may be two separate countries today, but they are both rooted in such strong common customs and values that they cannot really be isolated. Whether it is a happy occasion or a sad one, we follow the same traditions. Even the problems of the people of both the countries are the same. However, after independence, politics took on a different hue and instead of concentrating on growth, development and peace, politicians joined the race to hoard money in offshore accounts. The prosperity of the country remained a dream, and instead, one saw a rush to acquire ammunition.

The dreams that Mahatma Gandhi and Mohammed Ali Jinnah had for the country's development vaporized once they left this world and remained just dreams. The people who took over from them seemed relieved to have the coast clear for their selfish shenanigans. It was like, '*Papa toh ab ghar mein nahi, hamein ab kisi ka dar nahi.*' (Now that dad isn't home, we don't have to fear anyone.)

As if to atone for their insincere and dishonest ways, both the countries printed the photographs of Mahatma Gandhi and Mohammad Ali Jinnah on their currency notes. I am sure the two great leaders would have been ashamed to see the pathetic state of the nations they were so proud of, from heaven. I feel they would have wished for those in power to focus on peace and growth and for them to either bring back all the black money into the country or at least to have their photographs removed from the currency notes.

The partition changed the fates of the citizens drastically. Those who went from India to Pakistan were known as *Muhajhir* while those who came to India from Pakistan were addressed as *Sharnarthi*. Even though I can read and write in English, Hindi and Urdu, I don't think I have what it takes to read the horoscopes of both these countries. The truth is that the innocent people from both sides only desire peace, food and shelter, and pray for that in their own ways through *namaz* or *pooja*, whichever the case may be. Unfortunately, it is also true that manipulative political leaders from both sides want exactly the opposite. It suits them to have both sides in a war-like situation for personal gains. They probably pray for disharmony and tension so that their pockets are always full. Maybe they also tell God that they'd give him a share of the ill-gotten profit.

This world is inhabited by people of different beliefs and religions, but the law of nature is the same for everyone. The way we come into this world and the way we leave it is the same for all its inhabitants and will continue to remain so. Similarly, every individual follows his own heart when it comes to saying his prayers. Some go to temples, some take a dip in the holy Ganga, and some go to the mosque and for Haj, some to the church and some to the *gurudwara*, but their purpose is the same – to thank the creator for the gift of this life. And I have learnt this from my father and my teachers, not from any *pandit* or *mullah*. So whatever the place of worship, I bow my head in front of the Lord in complete obeisance. At times I do hesitate before entering these places because they are no longer as sacrosanct and pure as they used to be – trade has entered these holy precincts too. Sometimes my conscience doesn't permit me this indulgence. I believe that worship is love and you can never trade love. Loving people is the same as loving God. For me, love is the only religion and that is the reason for my identity, my family and work. It is the business of love that is the foundation of my achievements, which I passed on to my wife and children – love and only love. That is the only thing that is permanent.

In as commercial a place as Bombay, if people respect all religions, it is only because of love. Here people of various religions share a great bonhomie and there are also cases of them spending their lives together. Let me give you some examples. If you take Nargis, her maternal grandmother Dilipa Devi was Hindu and grandfather Miyan, a Muslim, her Mother, Jaddanbai, was Muslim and father Mohan Babu, Hindu. Nargis herself was Muslim and her husband Sunil Dutt, a Hindu. Nargis' niece Rehana was Muslim and her husband Sikh. And her other niece Zahida's husband, Sahay *saheb*, is Hindu. Film writer Salim Khan's first wife is Hindu and his second wife, Helen, is a Christian. Director Mahesh Bhatt is a Hindu but his mother was Muslim. Shah Rukh Khan is Muslim and his wife Gauri is Hindu. Both of Aamir Khan's wives, Reena Dutt and Kiran Rao, are Hindus. In all these cases, there is only one religion, and that is love. Our films are known to respect all religions equally. Stories, songs and scripts are penned in such a way that they don't hurt the feelings of any. There are many reasons for the huge success of the film *Baiju Bawra*. One of them is a *bhajan* from the film, which goes like this:

> *Man tarpat hari darshan ko aaj*
> (My heart aches to have a vision of Lord Hari)
> *Tumre dwaar ka main hun jogi*
> (I am an ascetic waiting at your doorstep)
> *Humri ore nazar kab hogi*
> (When will you glance at me?)

Do you all know that these lyrics were written by Shakeel Badayuni, a Muslim, the music director of the song was Naushad, a Muslim again, and it was sung by another Muslim, Mohammad Rafi? An interesting incident took place during the recording of this song. When Rafi *saheb* reached the lines, *Tumre dwaar ka mein hun jogi... humri ore nazar kab hogi*, he was overwhelmed with emotions, his throat went dry and he choked, and was unable to continue singing. The recording had to be cancelled. It was recorded the next day. Rafi *saheb* paid for the recording and refused his fees too.

I am reminded of another instance. Famous filmmaker BR Chopra made a television serial on the epic *Mahabharata*. It had a successful run and made a record, which I don't think anyone has been able to break. Before starting to work on the serial, intense research was undertaken, this took two years. Once done, the job of writing it was given to a Sanskrit scholar from Aligarh, Rahi Masoom Raza! His reputation in the film industry was such that if he was involved in any project, it was bound to be a hit. He played a crucial role in the success of BR Chopra's *Mahabharat* too.

An actor, whether he is a film actor or a theatre actor, Hindu or Muslim, he only worships his craft and the audience. The same can be said about sportspersons. So the studio, stage or ground becomes their temple, mosque, church or *gurudwara*. This is where they pray. I wish those with biased minds would realise how many fans artistes like Mehdi Hasan, Noor Jahan and Ghulam Ali have in India. Similarly, Lata Mangeshkar, Mohammad Rafi and Jagjit Singh have plenty of admirers in Pakistan. In fact, both Ghulam Ali and Jagjit Singh admired each other and shared a great bond with each other.

Many attempts were made to improve the relationship between the two countries, but sadly, the people on the hot seats only seem interested in displaying their military strengths. I am surprised that politicians from both the sides are only interested in playing the blame game – the public may go to hell. They seem to forget that it is thanks to the public that they occupy such important seats. And they have conveniently forgotten the promises of food, clothing and shelter they made to them in their manifestos. People keep waiting for those promises to fructify but to no avail.

In New York, rather coincidentally, I met Wahed Bux Bhatti one day. Both of us belonged to Multan. We met each other far away from our place of origin and soon became great friends and were inseparable. Though we were from different countries, our thoughts were the same. Both of us loved people and considered this love as our only worship. We were surely destined to meet and the person who facilitated it was Naseer Rana from New York's television channel, GEO. I can't thank him enough for being the all-important bridge that brought me to my friend. When I met him across the bridge, we felt we had always known each other. Our friendship only got more intense with time.

Our conversations often revolved around politics. It is so unfortunate that these politicians, who should be working for the welfare of the people, are only busy pursuing personal gains. These animals with six legs (two of their own, and four of the chairs they sit on to rule us) are so dangerous that once they dig their heels somewhere, it is impossible to dislodge them from there. In the same way, while all religions teach us to love each other and to make this world a beautiful place, our religious leaders propagate hate in the name of religion.

Divisions among Hindus – Brahmin, Dalit and several other castes
Division among Muslims – Shia, Sunni and Wahabi
Division among Sikhs – Jaat and Ramgarhias
Division among Christians – Catholics and Protestants

Both Wahed Bux Bhatti and I firmly believed love was God and God was love and also knew that apart from those in the realm of politics, people all over the world only longed for love. For the former, only money and power were love. They were against humanity. They created the divide of the rich and the poor for their own gains.

When a person is sick and requires a blood transfusion, one goes to the blood bank but no one cares to check whether the blood going to be used for the patient belongs to a Hindu, a Muslim, a Sikh or a Christian. In fact, blood is universal and cannot be differentiated based on caste.

The Bombay film industry has been my means of living. It was there that I earned a lot of respect and some name too. I have also been interested in hearing and sharing poetry. In India, I used to fulfil this interest in the company of my friend, actor, producer and director Manoj Kumar. Manoj Kumar is a discerning fan of poetry, but he used to tolerate an amateur like me too. In America, when I met Wahed Bux Bhatti, the old interest took seed in my heart once again. He was a prominent member of the society in America, besides being a member of South Asian Journalists of North America. He was also a poet, apart from being a great friend, philosopher and guide to me. Since both of us were from Multan, we would often speak in the Saraiki language and would be overjoyed in each other's company. Just like Manoj Kumar would put up with my limericks in India, Wahed Bux Bhatti played that role in New York. Since I spoke so much about them, both got eager to meet each other. I introduced them over the phone. In a very short time, they became so friendly that they would talk to each other for hours on the phone. Manoj Kumar was so impressed by Bhatti *saheb* that he invited him to his house in Bombay. It was decided that in the month of September, both of us would go to Manoj Kumar's house as his personal guests.

During one such phone conversation, Manoj Kumar presented some of his thoughts so beautifully in a poetic way that Bhatti *saheb* couldn't help but be impressed by him. And he told the gist of their conversation to me proudly. And when he didn't see the same appreciation coming from me, he was taken aback. The reason for my reaction was that I had already heard all of it from Manoj Kumar before. After this episode, the three of us became thick as thieves. Now we waited for the month of September to arrive with bated breaths. Manoj Kumar even promised Bhatti *saheb* that he'd introduce him to Lata Mangeshkar and Dilip Kumar. However, just a couple of days after this programme was finalised, all of a sudden, Bhatti *saheb* just got off this train of life without anyone's permission. I couldn't understand what had happened. When I called up Manoj Kumar with the news, he was speechless and couldn't believe what I was saying. But everyone must accept the truth. And, saying, "*Maut hi ek akela sach hai, baaki sab jhooth hai aur woh bhi safed... berang jhooth*", he accepted it too. (Death is the only reality, everything else is a lie, and that too a white, colourless lie.)

A few days before this tragedy, Manoj Kumar and Bhatti *saheb* had spoken on the phone for hours again. So grateful was Manoj Kumar that he called me to say, "Raaj, you are really lucky to have a friend like him. Also, I want to thank you for introducing me to such an honourable, sincere and selfless person. Do you know the beautiful thing he said to me today? He said that high up there, God is one. "You may call him Allah or Bhagwan – he is one and the same. One who accepts this reality is a human being and one who doesn't is a demon. There was only one country in the world that was called '*Soney ki chidiya*'. The English came and divided the nation but they couldn't divide the cultures of the two countries – be it their customs, attires, music, love for cricket, hockey, *kabaddi* or *bhangra*. They couldn't touch these. Ironically today, these western countries are dancing to the tunes of *bhangra,* even more than those in Jalandhar, Ludhiana, Rawalpindi or Lahore."

One can imagine the feeling with which Manoj Kumar narrated this to me. He may have never met Bhatti *saheb* face to face, but their love for each other kept them united. These emotions are common among the people of India and Pakistan and this is what brought these two great people together. The friendship between Dilip Kumar and Mehdi Hasan also has its foundation in the same emotions.

I don't call myself an extraordinarily knowledgeable person or a visionary, but at an age when I call myself an old man, waiting for the final call from above, I don't have any qualms in admitting that what's going on in the name of politics today is a terrible example of man's weakness and selfishness. The countries may be divided today but when it comes to the water of the river that runs between them and nurtures them, Jhelum, can you call it Indian or Pakistani? The British played the game of divide and rule with us and benefitted from it, leaving us bankrupt and to rot in the aftermath of partition. It spoiled relations amongst our own people and the river got sullied in the process.

I want to give another example of how the common people from both countries still have love for each other. After my birth in Multan, I was fortunate enough to be tied in the bond of love and relationship with many people, especially, Mr. Malik Fareed, Mr. Shameem Qureshi, Dr. Farooq, Zahoor Dhareja and Masihullah. Once when I visited Multan, there was a programme organised in my honour, wherein Pakistan's famous singer Suraiya Multanikar was also invited. When we met each other, like me, she too got emotional and we tied one another into a bond of brother and sister relationship. I asked her that since she was from Multan, she could have simply called herself Multani, why add the 'kar'. She laughed at my question and said, "That's because I am a huge fan of Lata Mangeshkar and wanted to add 'kar' to my name, just like hers." I was impressed with her love for Lataji. When her daughter Rahat Banu addressed me as Mamujaan, my happiness knew no bounds. I have four other nieces in Delhi too who call me Mamu and love me a lot but in Rahat's case, it was a special bond created by the word, *'jaan'*.

My meeting with famous poet Faiz Ahmed Faiz's daughter Salima Hashmi was a memorable one too. For this, I am grateful to Suchitra Iyer, the editor of *Society* magazine, published by Magna Publishing Company. It was because of her that I could meet such a big personality. Manoj Kumar got me acquainted with late filmmaker Agha Gul's son Sajjad Gul who lived in Lahore. He too proved to be such a great host that my list of fond memories keeps overflowing. Also, while in Lahore, thanks to Bhatti *saheb*, brothers Najeeb Khan and Parvez Khan gave me a bungalow for three days to stay in. I can never forget their kind-heartedness, or the care they extended to me as hosts.

We used to lovingly address Bhatti *saheb* as Baba. Today, I, along with my friend Lala Meeru, Bhatti *saheb*'s daughter Pami and Professor Hamad Khan, are in the same boat which is flowing in the tears we have shed for Bhatti *saheb*. The person whom Bhatti *saheb* considered his son, Hamad Khan, has kept his memory alive in the form of '*Babe di baithak*' sessions. In his memory, I will end this chapter by reproducing one of his verses:

Mujh ko kya padhegi bata ae nigah-e-waqt
Woh khat hun main ke jiska lafz hai mita hua
Sham thi gehra zakhm khaye hue, pyar ko faaslon ne ghera tha
Tumne dekhe nahi mere ansoon, yeh bhi achcha hua ki andhera tha

(How will you succeed in reading me, oh eyes of time,
I am the letter where the words are erased
The evening was deeply wounded, love was bounded by distance
You didn't see my tears, I am thankful that it was dark)

Epilogue

Today, I have crossed seventy-five. I spent the first eight years of my childhood in Multan, the city of my ancestors. The city had been a *Jannat* to and for my family's associations– both in terms of relationships and business – for over five centuries (500 years) or may be more. Despite their religions, the people of this region had been united in a feeling of brotherhood and oneness for centuries, until the British policy of 'Divide and Rule' turned effective in 1947, the year India got partitioned and the feeling of oneness turned into a separate feeling of 'twoness' – all to the liking of the *Vilayti Goras* of the British Sarkar.

My childhood will forever remain cemented with the never-to-be-forgotten bond. And now, at more than seventy-five years of age, everything seems to have gone for a toss – whether heads or tails, no one but God alone knows! Unfortunately, we had to leave our ancestral city of Multan, then a part of Punjab in India that after the partition became a part of Pakistan. Whenever I talk about my hometown, invariably, I hear the comment about the people there having hearts as soft as the cotton they deal in. And that their hearts are as sweet as the mangoes they grow. The sweet dialect of this region is called 'Saraiki'.

When I entered the world, it was my grandmother (*daadi maa*) who held me first. On the same day, five girls were born in the hospital. So my grandmother, out of happiness, held me to her heart and sang in 'Saraiki', "*Maidda Ranjhu aya... Ranjha luchcha maidda baal te naal apne hik nahi, panj panj hiran giddi aye.*" It meant, "My Ranjha is here and he has brought with him not one, but five Heers." Whereas this was just a loving joke, till this day, for this Ranjhu, his grandmother is his Heer. Though my grandmother was thrilled to carry me and was overflowing with love, I also received my first slap from her when I wet her clothes. She continued calling me Ranjhu and I also learnt from my mother that after I was born, she came to know that my *daadi maa*, her mother-in-law, was a great dancer too.

Apart from me and the five girls, another boy was also born on the same day at the same Mission Hospital, Multan Cantt. His mother was from Shujahabad and a Muslim. It was a practice at hospitals then that if there were multiple deliveries, the kids were given identity tags in the form of differently coloured threads that were tied around their wrists. The same rule was applied to all of us. Coincidentally, the other boy and I got the same red-coloured tags. When the head nurse saw this, she was initially perplexed, but then she saw that my little toe was wrapped around the neighbouring toe, which she had noticed earlier. That is how she differentiated between us and I was handed over duly to my mother. My grandmother became great friends with the head nurse after that. And I got as much love from her as I did from my mother and grandmother. This beautiful relationship continued even after my grandmother's demise but came to a halt on October 14, 1947, which turned out to be my last day in Multan, the city of my ancestors. That morning, the head nurse came to our house just an hour before we were to leave for the airport and bid adieu to our ancestral motherland for good. She became emotional and tearful as she looked at the little toes of both my feet, and between sobs recalled the entire story of my birth – that terrible confusion of the red thread around my wrist. She, in her choked voice, could hardly even utter 'goodbye', and finally left – never to be seen again. This left all of us in a state of shock and we were in tears throughout the flight.

My father, Lala Dinanathji, was the senior-most teacher of English and Civics at DAV High School in Multan. And by virtue of his innovative style of teaching and his popularity with all the students, he earned his promotion and went on to become the Head Master. He earned a lot of respect there and became quite famous in all of Punjab. When my father was the Head Master, a poor man from a village near the small neighbouring city of Layyah would sell peanuts and candies at the gate of a small middle school in that village to be able to provide his family two square meals.

One day, he brought one of his three sons to meet Lala*ji* at home. He told him about his son's passionate desire for higher studies. The man told my father about his inability to afford even a rupee for this purpose. The old man fell at Lala*ji*'s feet, requesting him to make his son's dreams come true, come what may. He suggested that the boy could also be handy around the house – doing the dishes in the kitchen, washing clothes and other household work. He was ready to do anything to have his dreams come true. After this emotional appeal, a touched Lalaji hugged the old man and said, "I don't want any servant here. If he is ready to stay here as a son, he is welcome to stay and continue his studies at DAV School and I will take care of his desire to pursue education. I would want this son to make his father proud not only in this region, but the world over too."

My father showered him with love, kept him at home and got him admitted in his school. After partition, the name of the school was changed to Muslim High School. The boy turned to be sharp and great in studies and was able to earn a name for himself rather soon. He lived with us for about ten years as a family member. After topping his graduation and earning top grades in science, he got noticed by the US Embassy in New Delhi. Just after one meeting with the boy, the bosses at the Embassy were so impressed that with their recommendation, this son of a peanut-seller got admitted to one of the most prestigious universities in the world – the Boston University in USA. So off he flew to Boston, eager to make his dreams a reality. The amount of effort he put in there and the fame he received are an example for others to follow. The boy became famous across the world as the Nobel Prize-winning scientist, Dr. Har Gobind Khorana. Old memories were refreshed through my conversations with him. I was surprised to know that he remembered even the tiniest details about those wonderful days. The letter below which he wrote to my father from America is an example of the respect and dedication he had towards my father:

Dear Dinanath*ji*

I am delighted and touched by your letter and the cutting from the newspaper there describing the interview you gave. Your affection, as you can well imagine, meant a lot to me. I remember everything so vividly. My long stay at your home in Multan as a student. The time at DAV High School under your leadership as the senior-most teacher there. So prestigious across Punjab. My brother Ram Chand's stay there with you for quite some time too remains unforgettable. Those were the best meals I have ever eaten in my life. The food tasted so good and I remember it so well – my sitting with dear *Bhabhiji* by the fire in the cooking area. I can never forget her warmth and affection towards me. I am embarrassed by all the noise about me there in India. I have been and am still shy, as you know. I would never want to get involved in any discussion in public, such as what India should or shouldn't have done – 1948 and 1949 were trying times for the country. All this aside, I need stern discipline and humanity to function and rededicate myself. The years ahead are crucial. I enclose a recent picture of my wife and myself looking at a model of DNA in my office. It's taken by a newspaper photographer.

With love, regards and good wishes for your health and that of *Bhabhiji* too.'

Yours
Gobind (Khorana)

Dr. Khorana wrote this letter from Boston on December 3, 1966. He had been living there with his Swiss wife for a long time.

Meanwhile, after ten years of childhood in Multan, my next eight years were spent in Delhi. They were good days, but nothing compared to the time we had in Multan. While love was an overriding emotion in Multan, Delhi was more business-like. But we didn't complain, just took everything in our stride, convincing ourselves that it was the will of God. To tell you the truth, my soul is still wandering in the by-lanes of Multan.

In Delhi, I made two friends and found their love similar

to what I had experienced with people back home. I want to thank both Idris Dehlvi and Jitendra Billu for becoming my friends. Though we had our differences in opinion, there was a certain madness that was common to the three of us. All of us loved Urdu. The luckiest of us was Idris, who, along with his father, Janab Yusuf Dehalvi, had become a beacon of this beautiful language. Unfortunately, by the quirk of fate, one sad day, Idris was no more. Life goes on, but nothing has been able to fill the void that Idris' demise left in my life.

Now, there were just the two of us – Jitendra Billu and I, Raaj Grover. We had met when we were around sixteen. It was an age when we neither knew much about love nor the importance of relationships, but somehow, we came together and became close. And we are, to this day – even though we are balding and over seventy! We have always been madly besotted with Urdu and she has been our actual lover over the years. But this love helped Jitendra Lamba (his original name) in more ways than one. He embraced Urdu and became an author, having written several stories and novels in the language. He even took the name Jitendra 'Billu' for this purpose. His writing became popular on both sides of the border. 'Billu' was his pet name, just like mine was Ranjhu.

I was interested in poetry too, but the *filmy* style *tukbandi* (rhyming), not the literary kind. I would colour my thinking and fulfil my desire for poetry in my friends' company. I would force them to listen to my half-baked compositions, or would listen to the works by famous poets and enjoy myself, even trying to memorise some of them. My love for Urdu will never die. The only difference is that Jitendra Billu became a name to reckon with in the world of Urdu literature and I remained just an ardent fan of the language. He has his own style and I have mine, but at times, I colour my thinking with that of some prominent people in the world of literature. Sometimes I feel like their thoughts are mine. People like me, who are interested in literature, but are not capable of great literary writing, tend to get by this way. So do pardon me if you find such adulteration in my writing and please accept it for what it is.

My ambition to make a life and money in Bombay saw fruition with the help of my father's old neighbour and friend's son. He was already in Bombay, enjoying a flourishing career in films. The person was Balraj Sahni. He was highly respected in the film industry. That I was fluent in Hindi, Urdu and English worked in my favour. Besides, Balraj Sahni's exaggerated words of praise for me were like the icing on the cake. Balrajji had an old friend by the name of Krishan Chopra. He used to assist successful director Zia Sarhadi and then became a director himself. Zia Sarhadi had cast Balraj Sahni in the film *Hum Log* as the hero. When Balraj got me a job to assist Krishan Chopra, my first assignment was the film *Lal Batti*. During the making of this film, Balraj Sahni introduced me to Mala Sinha. And with time, I became a part of her family. The next film I worked on was the Balraj Sahni and Nirupa Roy starrer, *Heera Moti*, then followed *Char Deewari* with Shashi Kapoor and Nanda and with the fourth film, *Gaban*, starring Sunil Dutt and Sadhana, my fortunes had started turning – I was headed towards a better phase of my life. By the time the film was shot, I found myself a part of Sunil Dutt's family. The kids in the Dutt family started addressing me as "uncle". And we have been going strong for the past fifty years. Not only this, Nargis *bhabhi*'s love for my family can easily be compared to the love my mother had for us.

People like Balraj Sahni, Sunil Dutt, Nargis and Krishan Chopra may have been relegated to the past, but continue to live in my heart. They are the people who taught me how to live my life. I have the strength to keep their places in my heart intact forever.

During my struggle period, I also met a few other people who were in the same boat as me. They will always be a part of my identity. Some of them are no more. And from those who are still around, the first person I would like to talk about is Kaka, aka Gurpal Singh Gandhi. His love for me was such that during my difficult period, he made sure I always had money and food. The second person I want to mention is Manoj Kumar. He is the person who knows me inside out – my good qualities and my bad ones too. And let me tell you, in this regard, it is a two-way street between us. You already know Jitendra Billu, my childhood friend.

Among the departed people who made a difference in my life are Sunil Dutt, Rajendra Kumar, Vinod Khanna and Prakash Mehra. I still maintain relations with their families and will continue to do so until it's time for me to depart too. These were names that became popular in India and Pakistan in equal measure. But my closest friend will always remain Manoj Kumar. We have seen some really good and bad days together. We skip back to the good old days very often and we also talk about Jitendra Billu.

One valuable principle that both of us strongly believe in is that when you make friends with someone, you must first understand the person for who he is. It should never be about what he is worth materially. The only thing that is not common between us is the fact that while Manoj Kumar's name is taken in every house, mine is taken only in my house or my in-laws' house! I don't have any regrets about this at all.

While on the topic of in-laws, I have to mention my father-in-law, Acharya Jialal Vasant, who was a famous musician. He took in a young and talented disciple under his tutelage at his music institute, Vasant Sangeet Niketan in Bandra, Mumbai. The boy's dedication saw him become a music guru himself in times to come. My wife Shashi and I are proud that after Guru Jialal Vasant's passing away, his disciple himself took over the mantle of the guru. Not only that, he, along with my sister-in-law, Prem Vasant, created a trust and started the Ajivasan Institute. Today it has more than three hundred students learning music. My father-in-law may not be alive today, but he would have been proud of his student Suresh Wadkar's success, and for keeping his name still alive.

I have always considered love to be my religion. And for anyone who has taken two steps towards me with love, I have reciprocated with four. I feel the extra two steps is the interest. I can say the same about my love for the Vasant family. In this context, I recall this story. I had started a film, *Thikana*, with Mahesh Bhatt as the director and Anil Kapoor, Amrita Singh and Smita Patil as the cast. I had signed Bappi Lahiri as the music director but when I got to know that he would not record any song with Suresh Wadkar, I consulted my friend Prakash Mehra and replaced Bappi Lahiri with Kalyanji Anandji. It was decided that Prakash Mehra would write the songs and Suresh Wadkar would sing them.

Love, unhappiness and disappointments go hand in hand. Now because I am the senior-most member in the Grover and Vasant families, I have tried to keep everyone bound together with my love. My wife Shashi too plays an important role in this endeavour and I pray to God that I get her as my wife in my next birth too. I know everything is in God's hands and no one else can control things. I have just made an attempt to put in words my various experiences in life. Maybe you will be able to read between the lines and discover the real person in me.

Ackowledgements

I am thankful for the numerous people for taking immense care of my book *The Legends of Bollywood*. These people contributed greatly to this book and made sure it saw the light of the day and got printed. So thank you to Professor Ilyas Shauqui, Shadab Rashid, Deepak Malhotra, Tirlok Malik, Shahid Latif, Srividya Menon, Ketan Patel, Rajan Gangahar, Sandeep Malhotra, Jitendra Billu, Arvind Kumar, Pradeep Chandra, and above all, Suchitra Iyer.

Writing this book has been one of the biggest trials of my life. To relive the times gone by, reaching out to lost friends, penning down every memory with them was a bittersweet journey. But, if that wasn't tough, I faced the worst when I looked around for someone who could translate my Urdu and Hindi musings into English. It isn't that I couldn't do it, but the expertise required for a full-blown English version of a book so close to my heart needed someone extraordinary. I had peeped under every stone and rock, and none could match what I wanted. I was done making trips to Mumbai and yet couldn't seem to find one English translator who fit my sensibilities.

It was in on one of those trips that I sat in Suchitra's work cabin in the Magna office, narrating my woes when I saw a twinkle in her eye. "I can do it!" she exclaimed. I thought it was a joke. It took a moment for the feeling to sink in. The editor of a premier magazine was actually offering her expertise in translating my book, a life-long dream come true. I admit I have been very lucky with relationships, and some have stood the test of the most difficult times. Suchitra is one of them. Over the next six months, her sincerity, her single-minded focus, and commitment to this book have blown me away. She adapted the book in her own way and made it more elegant, more beautiful.

Suchitra's involvement in *The Legends of Bollywood* provided me a new sense of rejuvenation, and the refreshing take is evident in the pages. If I am the grandfather of *The Legends of Bollywood*, Suchitra is its mother. Her contribution cannot be measured. But, all I can do is to thank her from the bottom of my heart to have made this wonderful labour of love into what it is today. I couldn't have asked for more.

Testimonials

I have known respected Raaj Grover since the last ten years. Right from our first meeting, I realised that this man was the epitome of love. While in most cases, friendships are forged when the other person is like-minded, in the case of Raaj Grover, one needs to be like-hearted. For him, friendship is not bound by the barriers of age or religion. And what to say about his good-heartedness and simplicity! He is a saint when it comes to his lifestyle, is talented and his nature is friendly. He still feels proud of his Saraiki and Multani origins.

As far as his book is concerned, it is obvious that not everyone is aware of the importance of memories. Moreover, there won't be too many people who would take the initiative to make a collection of all the old memories and present it in the form of a book. This book includes stories of the personal lives of some very famous personalities of the film industry. For us, it has historical importance. It will be a bible on the topic of film personalities and will set an example of sorts. With this book, Raaj Grover has turned into a Bollywood writer and his work will keep him alive for centuries. The book is replete with such exciting and informative incidents that it will surely interest readers of all age groups. To top it all, the rare photographs printed in the book will create history. I want to congratulate respected Mr Raaj Grover on the publication of this book and pray that: *Allah kare zor-e-kalam aur zyada.* (Hope God gives you the strength to write more and more.)

— Professor Hammad Khan, New York

Ek Karvan ki chhoti si kahani
Jo dastanon se badhkar hai
(The story of a small journey which is bigger than any epic)

Heer-Ranjha, Laila-Majnu, Shiri-Farhad, Sohni-Mahiwal, Mirza-Sahiban, Romeo-Juliet, if these weren't couples, these names wouldn't be uttered together, always, but their love has kept even their names together, all these years later.

The man who has created *The Legends of Bollywood* has penned it with the pen of love in such a way that it will have its own unique place in the world of books. The author of this book is known as Raaj Grover. While Heer inhabits his soul, so does Ranjha, and Laila and Majnu both. Raaj Grover has written about all those film personalities he has been associated with in his characteristic style. And people are sure to enjoy reading about them and will also end up being better informed.

Meanwhile, *The Legends of Bollywood* is a tribute to Sunil Dutt and Nargis Dutt – a tribute that they may have never received before. As for our friendship, it will require several tomes to describe it. It has glimpses of Krishna and Sudama where Raaj is Krishna and Sudama both!

— Manoj Kumar

Raaj Grover and I have grown up as playmates. The friendship that is forged in one's childhood is filled with selfless love and deep feelings. There is no question of give and take, no tests to be passed – it is just affection that takes childhood friends to the threshold of youth. Then, after the completion of your degree, you take your path in search of livelihoods. The truth is that both Raaj and I proved to be the incapable children of very capable and successful parents. His father Lala Dinanath*ji* came to Delhi from Multan after the partition and ran an eponymous school. And in the premises of the same school, Raaj would roam around with his shirt buttons open. No one dared to say anything to him because his father was the headmaster of the school. However, I have also seen a punished Raaj standing on the last bench pulling his own ears. I too used to be in the same state at times. After we scraped through and earned a couple of degrees, we were desperate for jobs. My father sent me to Bombay to be with my brothers. Like me, even Raaj was the youngest amongst his siblings. One of his brothers was close to Bhisham Sahni, the younger brother of Balraj Sahni. When Bhisham was only eighteen, he wrote a short, touching story about a school bus driver. This story found a place in the very well-known Urdu magazine of that time – Beeswein Sadi. Bhisham was a very good friend of the magazine's editor, Khushtar Grami. A copy of the magazine containing Raaj Grover's story was sent to Balraj Sahni.

When Balraj*ji* got to know the state of joblessness that Raaj was in, he was sympathetic. Like a great benefactor, he called Raaj to Bombay. One fine day, coincidentally, I bumped into Raaj near Lido cinema on Juhu Tara Road. When I hugged him, I had these lines on separation echoing in my mind:

Muddattein guzreen teri yaad bhi aayi na humein
Aur hum bhool gaye tujhe aisa bhi nahin
(It has been ages since I thought of you
But it is not even as if I have forgotten you)

Once we got talking, I got to know that Balraj*ji* had put Raaj under the wings of film director Krishan Chopra soon after his arrival in Bombay. He was making the film *Heera Moti* those days. Balraj*ji* is said to have told Krishan Chopra:

"*Yeh jawan apna barkhurdar hai, samajhdar hai aur dimag ka bhi tez hai. Batein bhi mazey ki karta hai.*"
(This young man is known to me, he is intelligent and sharp. Besides, he is quite a conversationalist.)

In reality, Balraj*ji* had done the perfect analysis of Raaj's personality. Whenever he met new people being demonstrative and expressive, he would gauge his compatibility with them immediately. Once he gets positive vibes from them, they become his friends for life. His mellow, sweet voice, boisterous talks, entertaining style and interesting jokes are so effective that I am sure that even God, who has created the universe and its people, will realise that he didn't make enough people like Raaj Grover. While in conversation, they feel that not only is the ground slipping from under their feet and the sky is changing colours, but also that they are being abandoned by the seven colours of the spectrum and the seven musical notes. However, soon enough, their fortunes take a positive turn and their lives begin to change. Some become directors, some cameramen, some music directors and lyricists and some become top actors. Raaj Grover was one such person. He became a director. He was in tune with every department and every quirk of the film industry. He had also understood the vagaries of life. He made films in association with others in the hope that some day, he'd fly solo, but he was fated for something else. Of the films he produced, some did well, and the others didn't. He has been face to face with the brazen reality of failure and success. There were times when he lost his peace of mind. People normally don't have much control over themselves when situations turn bad. But Raaj wasn't the kind of person to give up easily. He kept trying to start new films with all his might, but in those days, the film industry only understood the language of money. As a result of this affliction, several filmmakers had to give up the profession.

Both Raaj Grover's children settled in the US after their marriages. He, along with his wife, stayed back in Bombay alone for some time, but eventually joined their kids abroad. After all, no amount of wealth can compare to the bond parents have with their children. Parents find their own reflection in their children's lives. This tradition is ancient.

When Raaj settled in the US, his sweet voice, his exciting views and his *filmy* perspective on life came in handy. Being a social person, he soon found himself as an active member of the Asian community there. And he didn't have any enemies there to bring down his popularity. I am sure when he found out that his childhood friend Jitendra Billu's autobiography, *Dekho Humne Kaise Basar Ki* has been published, he possibly thought why shouldn't he publish something too! So he soon set about putting his old and fading memories into words. I pray that his efforts will bear fruit. Amen!

— From Jitendra Billu

It is the miracle of life that you have created an identity for yourself through myriad ways, at times through jokes, sometimes through literature and at other times through poetry. I consider this an example of humanity.

Rajju! The common perception that there is a limit to the comings and goings of life is not true. If this imaginary definition were true, then the entire humanity would be slave to it and in this revolution of time, Ali Raza would be born as Raaj Grover.

Na jaane kyun tumhari yaad ke sath yeh sher zaroor yaad ata hai (Wonder why I think of this couplet when I think of you):

> *Badhte hain amvaje havadis jitna insaan darta hai*
> *'Raaj' ne ik bekhauf hansi mein gharkh kiya toofan ko*

(The wave of calamities rise as much as the man is scared Raaj, with his fearless laughter, has arrested the tempest)

—Ali Raza
(Former Chairman, Film Writers' Aassociation)

I had heard about Raaj Grover from my friend and Member of Parliament, Sunil Dutt, but our meeting happened after a phone call from my friend Manoj Kumar. When he told me that Raaj Grover has penned his memoir, titled *Yaadein Zara Zara*, I read some chapters from it and thoroughly enjoyed them.

After having read about Sunil Dutt, Nargis, Dilip Kumar and Mahesh Bhatt in the book, I would like to say that Raaj Grover's writing skills can easily be compared to the acting skills of Amitabh Bachchan and Nargis.

I hope that every reader will enjoy the book as much as I have.

Raaj Grover has dedicated all the earnings from this book to the Nargis Dutt Foundation, which I feel, is a very benevolent act. My best wishes are with him.

— Kuldip Nayyar
(Former High Commissioner for India in the UK)

Letter from Suchitra Iyer

I think I have a karmic connection with Raaj Grover. I got to know him about eight years ago when a colleague, Prashant Rane, also based in the US, introduced me to him. He told me about Raaj*ji*'s close associations with the Dutt family and that it would be nice if I could meet him when he was in India next. I agreed, mainly because in those days, we used to run a column called Nostalgia in *Society* magazine which dealt with the lives of yesteryear actors, and I thought his recollections about the legendary Dutt family would make for a great story. As agreed, on his next visit, he came over to the office. His demeanour was so friendly, warm and genuine that it felt like I had known him forever. There was never any sense of formality or newness between us. I called Srividya Menon, who was in my team then, to interview him and file the story. In any other situation, this would have been the end of my association with any contact. Someone else would take over from there, the interview would be done, the story would be published, thank yous would be exchanged, then nothing. You just move on to the next person.

But it is not so when you are dealing with Raaj Grover. He has expertise in keeping in touch. I was surprised when the telephone in my office rang one fine morning and I found Raaj Grover at the other end of the line, calling me from the USA! And no, there was no agenda. He simply wanted to talk to me. Isn't it sad that in this fast-paced life, we have actually forgotten to remember people for no reason? Raaj Grover reminded me that people like him still existed. He would chat about this and that, recite some verses (he is a poet at heart), crack some jokes (he knows millions of them) and enquire about my well-being, before saying good night. Srividya Menon is also a recipient of the same love and attention from the grand and gregarious old man.

This is not all. None of his trips to India would be complete without catching up with us. Like little girls, we would wait for him to arrive, like a Santa Claus, with bags full of goodies – chocolates, little, thoughtful presents that his wife, Shashi (aunty), would have selected for us. Then it would be the same fun conversation.

It was on one such visit that he talked about penning a memoir on his relationships and experiences with the people in the film industry. He was writing it in Urdu and I could immediately see his passion. He would narrate incidents from the rough manuscript that he carried everywhere. I found them fun and unheard of but never thought, even in my wildest imagination, that I would become a part of it.

One day, he came over to my office, looking weary and tired – he had just finalised the printing of the Urdu and Hindi versions of his labour of love. He was dejected that he wasn't finding anyone to translate his book into English. Looking at him, I don't know what came over me, but I just blurted, "I will do it." Not that I am an experienced translator. This, in fact, is my first such assignment. I can never forget the look of relief on his face. In an instant, he handed over the tome to me, as if worried that if he took some time, I might change my mind. It was a thick spiral-bound manuscript in Hindi. Then began the mammoth task of writing, correcting and re-writing. But the stories in the book are personal accounts and bursting with emotions, they immediately transport you into another world – the starry world of film stars, with their quirks, their generosity – everything.

Translating *The Legends of Bollywood* was quite a revelation and an amazing journey. I have seen Raaj Grover toil over the book over the years and pray that all his hard work is rewarded with as much love and goodwill as he spreads all around him.

About the Author

Raaj Grover was the production-in-charge of the prestigious Ajanta Arts in Mumbai, which was owned by Sunil Dutt. Grover was an integral part of the Dutt family. During his days in the film industry, he also dabbled in film-making. He counts several iconic film industry people amongst his friends. He is the producer of the iconic movie *Thikana*. A poet at heart, he is known for his witty take on life and his joie de vivre. He moved to the USA with his wife Shashi, to be closer to his children and grandchildren. Now in his 80s, Raaj Grover's enthusiasm for life remains as infectious as it was several years ago. In spirit, he is still 18 and promises to remain so!

JAICO PUBLISHING HOUSE
Elevate Your Life. Transform Your World.

ESTABLISHED IN 1946, Jaico Publishing House is home to world-transforming authors such as Sri Sri Paramahansa Yogananda, Osho, The Dalai Lama, Sri Sri Ravi Shankar, Sadhguru, Robin Sharma, Deepak Chopra, Jack Canfield, Eknath Easwaran, Devdutt Pattanaik, Khushwant Singh, John Maxwell, Brian Tracy and Stephen Hawking.

Our late founder Mr. Jaman Shah first established Jaico as a book distribution company. Sensing that independence was around the corner, he aptly named his company Jaico ('Jai' means victory in Hindi). In order to service the significant demand for affordable books in a developing nation, Mr. Shah initiated Jaico's own publications. Jaico was India's first publisher of paperback books in the English language.

While self-help, religion and philosophy, mind/body/spirit, and business titles form the cornerstone of our non-fiction list, we publish an exciting range of travel, current affairs, biography, and popular science books as well. Our renewed focus on popular fiction is evident in our new titles by a host of fresh young talent from India and abroad. Jaico's recently established Translations Division translates selected English content into nine regional languages.

In addition to being a publisher and distributor of its own titles, Jaico is a major national distributor of books of leading international and Indian publishers. With its headquarters in Mumbai, Jaico has branches and sales offices in Ahmedabad, Bangalore, Bhopal, Bhubaneswar, Chennai, Delhi, Hyderabad, Kolkata and Lucknow.

SINCE 1946

www.ingramcontent.com/pod-product-compliance
Lightning Source LLC
Chambersburg PA
CBHW032037150426
43194CB00006B/310